Social Traps and Social Trust

Institutional Transformations in an American City following a Natural Disaster

Social Traps and Social Trust

Institutional Transformations in an American City following a Natural Disaster

Spring 2020 Volume 32, Issue 1

New England Journal of Public Policy

Michael A. Cowan, Editor

SOCIAL TRAPS AND SOCIAL TRUST:
INSTITUTIONAL TRANSFORMATIONS IN AN AMERICAN
CITY FOLLOWING A NATURAL DISASTER

iUniverse books may be ordered through booksellers or by contacting:

iUniverse
1663 Liberty Drive
Bloomington, IN 47403
www.iuniverse.com
844-349-9409

ISBN: 978-1-6632-1445-4 (sc)
ISBN: 978-1-6632-1446-1 (e)

Print information available on the last page.

iUniverse rev. date: 01/07/2021

In memoriam

Maestro Al Bemiss
Founding Musical Director
Shades of Praise
New Orleans Interracial Gospel Choir
2002-2019

"It's tryin' to happen."

Contents

Editor's Note

Padraig O'Malley

Dr. Rieux resolved to compile [a] chronicle so that he should not be one of those who hold their peace but should bear witness in favor of those plague-stricken people; so that some memorial of the injustice and outrage done to them might endure; and to state quite simply what we learn in a time of pestilence: that there are more things to admire in men than to despise.

Nonetheless, he knew that the tale he had to tell could not be one of a final victory. It could be only the record of what had had to be done, and what assuredly would have to be done again in the never ending fight against terror and its relentless onslaught, despite their personal afflictions, by all who, while unable to be saints but refusing to bow down to pestilence, strive their utmost to be healers.
— Albert Camus, *The Plague*

We stand nakedly in front of a very serious pandemic, as mortal as any endemic there ever has been. I don't know of any greater killer than AIDS, not to speak of its psychological, social and economic maiming. Everything is getting worse and worse with AIDS and all of us have been underestimating it, and I in particular. We are running scared. I cannot imagine a worse health problem in this century.
—Halfdan Mahler, director-general of the World Health Organization, address to the United Nations, November 20, 1986

When asked to compare AIDS to other epidemics, such as smallpox, that have infected and killed over the course of history, Halfdan Mahler, director-general of the World Health Organization, said that he "could not think of anything else that matched the estimates that one hundred million people would be infected with AIDS within ten years of its discovery."[1]

Like the novel coronavirus, HIV/AIDS spread fear, othering, false narratives, and social upheavals, decimating populations across 160-plus countries, carrying infection and lonely, agonizing death to hundreds of thousands.

As with the novel coronavirus, there were ominous forewarnings of the AIDS epidemic, and as with the coronavirus, these warnings were ignored, the threat was played down, the institutional response was inadequate and dysfunctional, always lagging behind developments, and medical supplies were short. As with the coronavirus, the political response was muddled and defensive. President Donald Trump has mishandled the coronavirus pandemic much as President Ronald

Reagan botched the AIDS epidemic. And, as with the novel coronavirus, statistical models were used to try to track the path of HIV/AIDS.

In the United States, as of September 1988, when the special issue of the *New England Journal of Public Policy* on AIDS went to print, 74,500 cases had been reported, and approximately 42,000 of these persons had died. The Centers for Disease Control (CDC) estimated that the number of new cases alone in 1991 would exceed 52,000, and it projected a combined total of 270,000 cases by the end of 1991, with perhaps 180,009 deaths, 365,000 cases by 1992, and 453,000 by 1993.

At one point, the CDC estimated that one in every thirty males between the ages of twenty and fifty was infected with AIDS, that of the nation's then estimated 2.5 million gay men and 25 percent of the estimated intravenous drug users had the virus, and that overall between 845,000 and 1.4 million were possibly infected.

Once the fear took hold that the virus might seep into the general population through simple heterosexual intercourse, as happened in other parts of the world, such as South Africa in particular and other parts of Africa more generally, AIDS in the United States became a disease of the poor, of African Americans and Hispanics, and of women and children—communities with high concentrations of minorities. A disease of "them," with "us" as virtuous onlookers. Attitudes began to change only when intravenous drug use became a problem in their own communities and the white middle class took heed and demanded action from the government. The discovery of antiretrovirals meant that HIV/AIDS no longer carried a death sentence.

Overall, between 1981, the start of the epidemic, and 2018, 74.9 million people became infected and 32 million died from AIDS and related illnesses, 770,000 alone in 2018. By the end of 2018, 37.9 million people remained infected.[2]

In the early years, fear was pervasive among the public that the HIV virus could be spread by human touch. To police a demonstration in Washington, DC, during the Third International AIDS Conference in 1987, officers wore yellow gloves to prevent possible contamination. HIV/AIDS patients died in isolation from other hospital patients; stigmatization was rife. Othering and scapegoating were pervasive.

New York was the epicenter of the pandemic in the United States.

Sound familiar?

By the first of April this year, New Orleans had incurred one of the highest per head rates of infection and death from the coronavirus in the country—1,212 infections, 101 deaths. In one twenty-four-hour period, these figures spiked 30 percent. If Louisiana were a country, its death rate from Covid-19 would rank among the top fifteen globally. Within the state, the New Orleans metropolitan area, which includes Orleans and Jefferson Parishes, accounts for two-thirds of all cases.[3]

Like other cities, especially in the South, New Orleans was slow to impose a lockdown and social distancing. Mardi Gras proceeded with little concern for the virus that revelers might have carried hanging over it like the Sword of Damocles.

Are there lessons from Katrina that might let New Orleans better cope with the coronavirus?

The lessons of Katrina are the subject of this special issue.[4] The eighteen articles were assembled and overseen by Michael Cowan, the guest editor for this issue. Michael founded Common Good, a civil society action network, after Hurricane Katrina. He is Senior Fellow in the Centre for the Resolution of Intractable Conflict and Research Affiliate in the Centre for the Study of Social Cohesion, both in the University of Oxford. He is also a Visiting Research Associate in the Irish School of Ecumenics in Trinity College Dublin.

The Coronavirus is an exponential spiral of infections and death that is no respecter of class, color, creed, or culture. It is changing in profound and mundane ways how we live and work and socialize, collapsing the mightiest of economies within weeks, bringing hitherto unimaginable levels of unemployment and plunging incomes and spreading unbearable suffering, so overpowering the pervasiveness and constancy of cumulative losses that the time for grieving has been eviscerated.

Perhaps in the post-pandemic world that will emerge when this pestilence passes—and pass it will because there is nothing particularly new about plagues through human history—we will be more tolerant, so we can say, as Dr. Rieux observed, that "there are more things to admire in men than to despise," more empathetic, that social distancing will be understood as an act of connection, of pulling together while staying apart, and more humble in the knowledge that we are just a species, both fragile and resilient, but that there is nothing inevitable about us at all.

Notes

1   Halfdan Mahler, director-general of the World Health Organization, address to the United Nations, November 20, 1986.
2   Global HIV and AIDS statistics—2019 Fact Sheet, UNAIDS, unaids.org/en/resources/fact-sheet, accessed April 2, 2019.
3   Vann R. Newkirk II, "Watch New Orleans," *Atlantic*, March 27, 2020.
4   To enrich your experience, we suggest that after reading this issue you listen to the *Atlantic*'s eight-part podcast, Floodlines, on what happened in New Orleans after the levees broke. The podcast is available at https://www.theatlantic.com/press-releases/archive/2020/03/floodlines-story-unnatural-disaster/607858/.

Introduction

Michael A. Cowan
Special Issue Editor

At the threshold of this volume, I must acknowledge the agony that people of New Orleans endured in the wake of Hurricane Katrina in August, 2005. 1800 people dead. 80% of the city under water. Thousands suffering in the brutal heat and humidity of late summer in New Orleans. Failed city, state and federal responses. Bodies of deceased family members missing for tortuous months. The articles in this volume arise from that historic tragedy.

They do not simply reflect the thoughts of individuals. They emerge from the shared experience of a larger group in which the authors participated. Like a choir's songs, they arise, not from separate individuals, but rather from the actions of a group. My abiding respect for the choir of reflective actors whose words and deeds await you in these pages arose in the fearsome crucible into which we were all thrown on August 25, 2005 by the sheer power of nature coupled with the shameful failure of those responsible for constructing and maintaining the levees between New Orleans and the water all around her.

This tragic moment also opened the door to the most serious social change in New Orleans since the Civil Rights Movement. The authors of this volume, who for the most part had not known each other before the storm, responded to this devastating blow by building coalitions and coalitions of coalitions focused on particular issues. In the pages ahead you will catch glimpses of the complex, self-organizing, informal process of coalition-building for social change in the words of those who lived it.

I acknowledge with gratitude the unfailing encouragement I received in bringing this volume from imagination to fruition from Padraig O'Malley, General Editor of the *New England Journal of Public Policy* and my valued colleague in the Centre for the Resolution of Intractable Conflict in the University of Oxford. I can only hope that the completed work justifies his trust. Without the kind, patient professionalism of the journal's managing editor Nancy Riordan and copy editor Debby Smith, I fear that I would still be struggling with the grammar and syntax of eighteen articles. The final product also bears the mark of the editorial expertise and personal generosity of Jennifer Shimek of the Institute for Ministry of Loyola University New Orleans. Finally, this work was influenced by an ongoing dialogue about social network analysis with my brother, Dr. John Cowan of Northern Illinois University. A taste of the fruits of that conversation appears in the social network diagrams below. These not only organize a wealth of data, but also stand as powerful symbols of the complex process that transformed public relationships in New Orleans after Hurricane Katrina. They are the proverbial pictures worth 1000 words.

The contents of this issue are unusual for an academic journal for two reasons. First, most of authors are not scholars, but rather leaders in the areas in which I invited them to write. One built a neighborhood organization that became a living symbol of hope for those rebuilding devastated neighborhoods. Another directed the restructuring the city's notoriously dysfunctional administrative systems. Another founded an organization of women that led restructuring of levee-boards and property tax assessment. Another was the primary leader in the establishment of the city's first independent police monitor. Another brought indigent defense into the Twenty-First century. Another oversaw the process of dismantling waste and corruption in the operation of the city's airport. Another was a key leader of the business community's indispensable role in rebuilding the city. In theirs and the other stories, you will encounter seasoned, reflective actors building effective issue-focused coalitions amidst widespread uncertainty and despair.

The second, and to my knowledge unique, feature of this volume of an academic journal is that its authors were not individuals working separately on discrete issues, but rather partners in a fluid, informal, social action network operating in a moment of major crisis, with constantly shifting challenges and possibilities for change. Each person authored her or his own article, but also acted beyond the boundaries of their subject. More specifically, at critical moments, many of which are described in these pages, the author/actors collaborated strategically to deploy their organizations' collective power. They leveraged their social, political and financial capital to initiate change in collaboration and confrontation with national, state and local officials. As with all shrewdly invested capital, theirs grew.

The diagrams below show how the degree of connection or density within a social action network among a group of civic, business, and religious leaders, changed from before to after Hurricane Katrina.

Pre-Katrina Whole Network

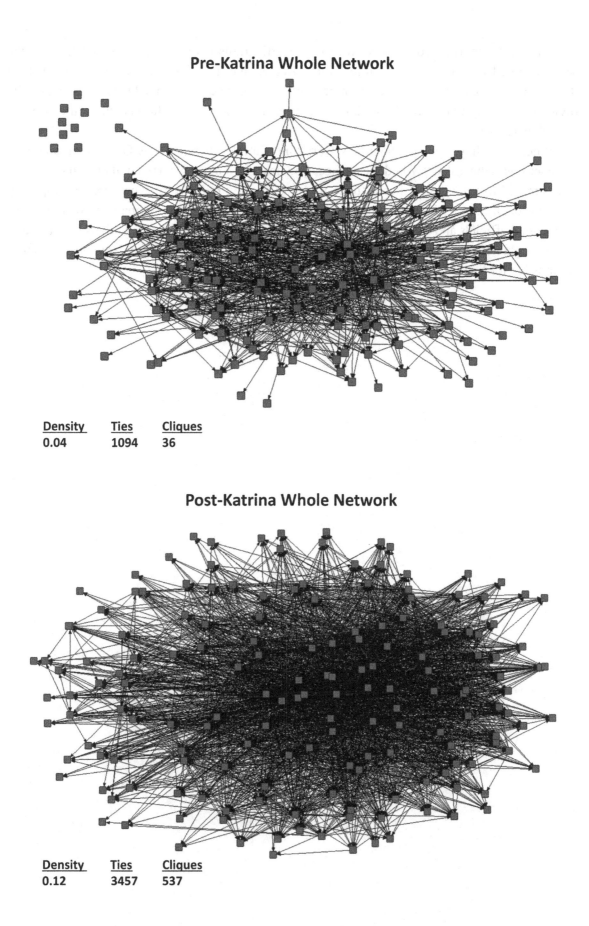

Density	Ties	Cliques
0.04	1094	36

Post-Katrina Whole Network

Density	Ties	Cliques
0.12	3457	537

The most important contrast between the two diagrams is that the relational density of the second (post-Katrina) network is three times greater than the first (pre-Katrina). This salient difference is a measure of how actors in networks like these created social trust in a historically divided city. They did so, not in addition to partnering in diverse coalitions, but in the very act of such partnering.

Whenever I have spoken about how Hurricane Katrina changed New Orleans, an audience member invariably asks: "Would the changes you described have occurred without a hurricane?" The simple answer is "no," but a fuller response is required: "Nature can create temporary vacuums but it cannot fill them." The coalition-driven public meetings, campaigns, collaborations with public officials and legislative actions recounted here, and the transformations they brought about, might not have happened in the wake of the great storm. But they did. Now meet the choir responsible for them.

Standing for the Whole:
Leaders Take the Initiative

Social Traps and Social Trust in a Devastated Urban Community

Michael A. Cowan

Michael A. Cowan founded Common Good, a civil society action network, after Hurricane Katrina. He is Senior Fellow in the Centre for the Resolution of Intractable Conflict and Research Affiliate in the Centre for the Study of Social Cohesion, both in the University of Oxford; a Visiting Research Associate in the Irish School of Ecumenics in Trinity College Dublin; and Professor Emeritus at Loyola University New Orleans.

A "social trap" is a situation where individuals, groups or organizations are unable to cooperate owing to mutual mistrust and lack of social capital, even where cooperation would benefit all. . . . People will cooperate only if they can trust that others will also cooperate.
—Bo Rothstein, *Social Traps and the Problem of Trust*

If people cannot trust that public officials will act according to norms such as impartiality, objectivity, incorruptibility, and non-discrimination they cannot trust "people in general" either. . . .
—Rothstein, *Social Traps*

The last national survey of adult literacy prior to Hurricane Katrina found 40 percent of New Orleans adults reading at or below the sixth-grade level and another 30 percent at or below the eighth-grade level. During the three years before the hurricane, New Orleanians watched as public meetings of its elected school board became models of incivility, where the politically connected struggled for control of contracts and patronage and self-appointed activists ridiculed school officials, board members, and fellow citizens who were attempting to raise the performance of the city's public schools out of the ranks of the nation's worst. During this same period, neither citizens nor public officials were able to address the deplorable condition of the city's once nationally acclaimed youth recreation department, even as homicidal youth violence escalated, putting New Orleans consistently at or near the top of national per capita murder rates. In short, the adults of the city proved unable to provide adequate public education and recreation for children and young adults. Their failure resulted in violence, economic despair, and deepening racial division.

Shortly after his election as a pro-business, reform candidate in 2002, Mayor C. Ray Nagin was denounced at a press conference of clergy by one of the city's most visible ministers as a "white man in black skin." What had the new mayor done to so offend this powerful, politically connected cleric and his colleagues? He had announced that under his administration, local congregations seeking federal grants distributed through the City of New Orleans for after-school programs for children and other social ministries would be required to secure that funding by responding to public requests for proposals and to give a formal accounting at the end of the grant period of how funds awarded were actually disbursed and with what results. This was hardly a radical policy. Rather it was and is the standard way of disbursing and accounting for public dollars. A member of the mayor's inner circle described this public denunciation, widely reported and replayed by local media, as having had a "chilling" impact on the new, reform-minded mayor, one from which he never fully recovered.

On the evening of December 31, 2004, eight months before the hurricane that would change the city forever, a young African American man visiting New Orleans to participate in a flag-football tournament was pinned on the ground by three white bouncers in a confrontation outside a French Quarter bar. He never arose. Levon Jones was suffocated on Bourbon Street that night. On a cold and rainy Thursday evening some weeks later, at Mayor Nagin's request, I chaired a public meeting of the Human Relations Commission of the City of New Orleans in a packed city council chambers. During the meeting, the commission listened for more than three hours to expressions of public outrage and grief sparked by the killing and by the New Orleans Police Department's treatment of African Americans over many years. Threats of racial riots to destroy "this plantation" once and for all were sprinkled throughout the public testimony.

In August of 2005, the atmospheric disturbance forming over West Africa that would shortly be christened "Katrina" was not the only storm on the New Orleans horizon.

Immediate Aftermath of Hurricane Katrina

On August 29, 2005, Hurricane Katrina grazed the mandatorily evacuated city of New Orleans, reserving its most devastating force for coastal Mississippi just to the east. During the next two days, the federal levees, the wall between New Orleans and the water all around her, failed in multiple places. Public officials warned residents and business owners that they might be unable to return for months. The scope of devastation in certain parts of the city made returning questionable indefinitely for many. Failures of coordination among local, state, and federal governments added to the collective misery, confusion, and uncertainty about the city's future.

In the hurricane's wake, new hopes and old grievances shifted in uncertain balance, as the sense of a historic opportunity to build a better city for all clashed with people's anxiety about losing whatever political and economic assets they held before the storm. The profound disruption of local politics, religion, and economics resulting from massive flooding temporarily created a less racially charged atmosphere that would provide an opening for and provoke a contest about enhancing the well-being of the whole city through its rebuilding. For a moment, local civic, religious, and business leaders organizing for change across formerly impenetrable barriers of race and class did not face the massive political inertia and resistance that had met all such efforts before the storm. With those forces reduced, leaders could work together across racial lines for the well-being of the city with a measure of hope. Organizing for change in the wake of Hurricane Katrina was like walking on the moon.

A Disaster Gives Birth to a Transformation

Among the important post-Katrina reforms was the establishment of an office to reduce waste, fraud, and abuse of power in city government. It was a play in five acts: a recommendation from the mayoral commission established to bring New Orleans back after the hurricane; passage by city council members of an ordinance establishing an inspector general's office; approval by citizens of a charter change to protect the independence of the new office; the hiring of the founding inspector general; and the beginning of the work of the Office of Inspector General. (The "prequel" to this story can be found in David Marcello's contribution to this issue.)

Act 1: Bring New Orleans Back Commission

In November 2005, Mayor Nagin established the Bring New Orleans Back Commission, charging it to present him with recommendations on a number of critical dimensions of the rebuilding of the city by the end of January 2006. The commission consisted of working committees made up of civic, business, religious, and higher education leaders addressing culture, land use, public safety, infrastructure, city government, public education, economic development, and health and social services.

Gary Solomon chaired the commission's Government Efficiency and Effectiveness Committee and, at his request, I organized it. The mission of the committee was to improve local government as one response to the challenges and opportunities of post-Katrina New Orleans, to foster city government that is effective, efficient, transparent, and adequately and fairly funded. The committee's plan was to pick priority targets for change, identify examples of such changes already implemented in other cities, specify the steps necessary to put such proven practices in place locally, and establish a timeline for taking those steps. The committee's agenda was to build trust in city government by achieving transparency: No more deals behind closed doors.

In the temporary reduction of racial inertia caused by extreme political and economic disorganization immediately following Katrina, the guiding idea of committee members was that New Orleanians now had an opportunity not simply to replace what had been lost or damaged in the flood but to recreate city government for the greater benefit of all by fundamentally reforming its structures, policies, and operations. Our intent was sharpened by the observation of the committee's expert adviser, former mayor Steven Goldsmith, that local government's principal function is to assure businesses and citizens that the city's future merits their investment. What makes businesses and residents feel that a city's future warrants their ongoing tax dollars? Simply put, local government providing its services lawfully, fairly, and with limited waste—a concern of businesses and citizens everywhere. Waste, fraud, and abuse have been destroying cities and nations forever. Read any report on nations facing social disaster, and the word "corruption" will quickly appear. It is the cancer that kills cities, states and nations.

The post-Katrina emphasis on reforming city government was further energized by the keen recognition that if local leaders were not able to begin moving swiftly against New Orleans's legendary and habitual practices of patronage, waste, and corruption, the massive public and philanthropic funding available and necessary for the renaissance of the city would be withheld or rigidly controlled.

A review of national best practices to prevent waste, fraud, and abuse in government provided to the committee by the research team of the Kennedy School of Government suggested that an independent office of inspector general was the most powerful mechanism available to promote government transparency and accountability. C. Daniel Karnes, the committee's legal researcher, quickly discovered that the New Orleans city charter had mandated the establishment of an office of inspector general (OIG) in 1995, but an independent office had never been established. The significance of this finding was that "all" it would take to establish this key refo was an ordinance passed by city council. By contrast, another important post-Katrina reform of local government, the consolidation of seven local tax assessors into one, required a statewide majority vote to change the Louisiana constitution. This reform was also successful, but it was a much more heavier lift involving, among other expenses, statewide television and radio ads. (The story of this effort is recounted by Ruthie Frierson in the article following this one.) Such a heavy lift would not be immediately required to establish an OIG. Partly because of its strategic significance for reform at this critical moment in the life of the city and partly because the city charter already required its establishment, the Government Efficiency and Effectiveness Committee prioritized establishing an OIG in its recommendations delivered to the mayor in a plenary public meeting of the Bring New Orleans Back Commission in January 2006.

Act 2: Establishing the Office of Inspector General

Campaigning for the first local elections for mayor and city council following Katrina began just as the Government Efficiency and Effectiveness Committee made public its priority recommendation to establish an OIG. The storm's displacement of people registered to vote in New Orleans would make this the most highly charged election in New Orleans since the civil rights era. Thousands returned by bus and car from what many hoped would be temporary locations to cast their votes. It was a time of despair, anger, and confusion about the future.

The campaign included a public conversation, framed most unfortunately by Mayor Nagin, about the importance of New Orleans' remaining a "chocolate city." Several reform-minded city council candidates, drawn to public service in the wake of Katrina, made establishment of the OIG a priority plank in their campaign platforms.

When the votes were counted, three newly elected members of the seven-member city council were fully in support of creating the OIG. A fourth was open in principle, if proper checks on the power of the office could be put in place. At a critical juncture in the city's history, New Orleanians had elected a majority reform-minded city council willing to embrace serious transformation of city government.

Making the establishment of the OIG a priority for post-Katrina reform became the basis for two significant social partnerships of government, business, and civic leaders—one to establish the OIG in an updated local ordinance, the other to offer it constitutional protection from politics by amending the city charter.

Encouraged and supported by civic leaders, newly elected city council member Shelley Midura took the initiative to prepare an ordinance establishing an OIG for council consideration. She and her staff sought technical assistance from the national Association of Inspectors General. In fall 2006, the city council deliberated publicly on an ordinance recommended by the Government

Affairs Committee to establish an OIG as required by city charter. During these deliberations in a public meeting of the council, the proposed OIG was first publicly labeled a "white power grab," that is, an attempt by whites to accomplish by ordinance what they could not get at the ballot box—control over black government officials. Following several hours of intense public testimony and council deliberation, the committee passed the establishing ordinance after adding an amendment providing for an oversight committee to review OIG performance annually against its annual work plan. This would not have happened without African-American support by council members James Carter and Oliver Thomas.

Act 3: Changing the City Charter to Protect the Independence of the Office of the Inspector General

The city council members and citizen advocates who had collaborated successfully to pass the OIG ordinance and secure funding for its first year of operation were aware that every year a mayor could recommend, and a city council approve, reducing funding for the office in the annual city budget. The OIG's effectiveness and sustainability depended not just on its capabilities and accomplishments but also on protecting it from continually shifting partisan political and patronage interests. This protection would require a funding mechanism not subject to annual approval or adjustment by the mayor or city council.

Toward that end, citizen leaders worked with reform-oriented city council members to formulate an amendment to the city charter that, if approved by a majority of voters, would set aside .075 percent of the city's annual operating budget to fund the OIG and an Ethics Review Board. At the time it was created, the formula would have amounted to an annual operating budget of $2,500,000. As the city's annual operating budget goes up or down, the OIG budget follows. At the time of this writing, that budget is nearly $4,000,000.

The charter change proposal also included a provision negotiated by council members for the establishment of an office of independent police monitor (IPM) within the OIG. The inclusion of the IPM in the OIG made it timely for the local justice activist Norris Henderson and me to convene an interracial alliance—a coalition of coalitions—of citizen groups to support the charter-change vote. The coalition brought together organizations willing to support the police monitor but passionately committed to the OIG; others willing to support the OIG primarily because it would include an independent police monitor; and some backing both. In community-based organizing, as in other social efforts, people can work for the same goal, here, a change to the city charter, with different motivations.

The coalition's intention was to deliver a strong vote for the OIG/IPM to organize a multiracial charter-change alliance that also crossed lines of class and city neighborhoods. When the votes were cast in October 2008, 77 percent of voters supported the proposed charter change, with positive margins in all demographic subgroups.

This result meant that adequate and predictable annual funding tied to the city's yearly operating budget was guaranteed for the OIG and the IPM. As an additional benefit, the OIG's hard-won independence could provide political cover for the IPM. Only another majority vote of local citizens for a charter change could undo the offices or change their funding. The office's citizen, business, and government advocates had provided the OIG with the maximum degree of independence possible in a local democracy, while simultaneously creating the city's first independent entity to oversee police misbehavior.

The process of establishing and protecting the independence of the OIG just described required three years of sustained public work by organized citizens and business leaders, engaging strongly with both sympathetic elected and appointed officials and vocal opponents.

Act 4: Hiring the Founding Inspector General

Passage of the OIG ordinance set in motion the appointment by the mayor of a seven-member Ethics Review Board (ERB), with six members nominated by local university presidents. The ERB is responsible for choosing the inspector general and overseeing the work of the office. It met for the first time in 2006 and initiated a search for the city's first inspector general. From a national applicant pool, the board chose Robert Cerasoli, the former founding inspector general of Massachusetts.

Inspector General Cerasoli swept into New Orleans like the proverbial whirlwind. He promptly informed local media, which was keenly interested in the advent of his office and not a little skeptical about the possibility of its success, that on refusing a city car and gas when he went to process his paperwork at City Hall, he was told, "But everybody gets a car and gas." He declined. Thus began the well-publicized adventures of New Orleans' founding inspector general. By patiently building positive relationships with city council members and making himself readily available to the media and the public, the inspector general became a public favorite and, with support from city council and civic leaders, was able, before the charter-required funding described above was assured, to obtain approval of an initial annual operating budget of over $3 million, up from an initially proposed $250,000. He did so by singlehandedly drafting and winning civil service and city council approval for the roster of jobs he felt necessary to staff a credible office. For reasons of both symbolism and security, Cerasoli established the OIG outside City Hall, in the New Orleans Federal Reserve Bank, by far the city's most secure building. With fully intended irony and a keen sense of local public interest, the OIG announced that the target of his first investigation would be the city's use of vehicles and fuel. To no one's surprise, the resulting report found widespread waste and abuse and made recommendations to bring the city's policies in line with recognized practices in the administration of a city motor pool. (They have been.)

Despite professing support periodically for the establishment of the OIG, Mayor Nagin's administration did little to facilitate setting up the newly approved office. In one memorable instance, the administration took several months to purchase the computers required to set up the office, even after the funds to do so had been fully approved. This failure to support the office at a critical juncture, whether from incompetence or intent, delayed the inspector general's attempts to begin the work of hiring a staff and developing an initial work plan. Subsequent investigations by the OIG contributed to felony convictions of the mayor and his cronies.

Believing that business as usual in New Orleans city government could and must be interrupted if the city was to be rebuilt for the benefit of all after the hurricane, citizens and public officials successfully established the OIG as a nationally recognized method for creating enforceable standards of transparency and accountability for those holding public office. From that day forward, the commitment to reform local public institutions has been grounded, symbolically and pragmatically, in the OIG. That office is the principal lever that many civic and business leaders and government officials now pull to continue reducing waste and corruption in the public institutions of our city.

Act 5: Accomplishments of the Office of Inspector General

Since its establishment after Katrina, primarily under the leadership of Cerasoli's successor Edouard Quatrevaux, the OIG of the City of New Orleans has investigated and issued reports on waste and corruption in numerous areas of city government. Its method is simple and powerful: Investigate and report. The report is made to the public unless criminal activities are found, in which case they are referred to legal authorities. Each public report includes an invited response from the investigated body. Finally, the investigated body is given notice that its response to the report's recommendations will be revisited on a specific date and the results made public. This process continues until the matter is resolved.

A partial sample of OIG investigations includes city purchasing, use of city vehicles, sanitation contracts, collection of hotel-motel taxes, accounts payable and fixed asset control, and private management of major post-Katrina infrastructure rebuilding projects. Also, it produced major reports on financial management, drinking water safety, theft by sewerage and water board workers, and deployment of police manpower and management of rape kits. A signal accomplishment of the OIG is the embedding for years of an investigator at the New Orleans airport, a place where graft and waste had long existed on steroids. In addition to publicly unraveling a problematic set of vendor contracts and overseeing the creation of new contracts and oversight, the OIG oversaw planning for and construction of a new airport. In recognition of that work, the airport commission received a lower interest rate on major bonds, saving the city millions of dollars.

The office has also produced numerous public letters calling the attention of the mayor, city council, chief administrative officer, and others to practices that have left the city vulnerable to waste and corruption in expense reimbursement, awarding of city contracts, procurement of goods and services, electronic monitoring of parolees, disadvantaged business enterprises, and proposed contracts for remodeling the city's municipal auditorium. The office conducted investigations of the New Orleans Public Belt Railroad, the French Market Corporation, and the city's crime surveillance cameras. It published a report detailing $2.5 million wasted annually by the city's traffic and municipal courts. These and other investigations led to increased public scrutiny, specific recommendations for change, and sometimes criminal indictments. The cumulative impact of the office was something new and transformative in the life of the city.

The range and quality of the OIG's work belies the attempt to delegitimize the office by portraying it as an instrument of whites to check black politicians. The OIG is the first effective force to interrupt the history of waste, fraud, and abuse of power in New Orleans. The OIG has created a mechanism for transparency that for the first time in the city's history allows city administrators, legal authorities, and citizens to hold elected and appointed officials accountable for their stewardship of public resources. The OIG has done what few could have imagined, and none had been able to accomplish before the storm: It has created a baseline public expectation that waste, fraud, and abuse of power by elected or appointed officials are much more likely to be exposed, with timely and serious consequences for those who risk misusing public office for personal gain. Waste and corruption can no longer be practiced with impunity. This is a new thing in three hundred years of New Orleans history.

For the first six months of Act 1, the responses I received even from progressive business and civic leaders when I raised the possibility of having an inspector general in New Orleans ranged from an amused shake of the head to "In New Orleans? You must be crazy!" to "Good and evil are in the soul of New Orleans. If you take away evil, you'll kill the city." One prominent local media figure opined that a functioning inspector general would be the "biggest change in New Orleans since the Civil War." Fifteen years after the Government Efficiency and Effectiveness Committee of the Bring New Orleans Back Commission first put the possibility of an inspector general on the public horizon, the local citizenry and public officials, the cynics and skeptics, have something new to consider and the media representative's words may yet prove to be prescient.

Social Traps and Social Trust: Public Institutions, Economic Opportunity, and Intergroup Conflict

There is a deep pattern underlying the workings of corruption in public institutions. It has been called a "social trap." It occurs when there is insufficient trust to allow members of different groups to cooperate, even when the interests of all groups would plainly be served if they could do so.[1] Such situations are the result of historical struggles among racial, ethnic, religious, or socioeconomic groups over freedom, dignity, power, and resources. Racial conflicts are a classic example of social traps.

Bo Rothstein explains that when a social trap drives intergroup relations, it is not possible to overcome it at scale by directly building or strengthening voluntary relationships based on shared interest among members of groups in conflict. No number of better face-to-face relationships will resolve an intergroup conflict over the basic things that matter. The antidote to social traps is social trust, which arises only as access to economic opportunity grows for all who are prepared to work and learn. And that opportunity, in turn, is the product of good public institutions.

A "good public institution" is one that operates lawfully, fairly, efficiently, and effectively. On the link between institutions and social trust, Rothstein writes: "The more trust people have in political and administrative institutions, the more they are inclined to feel social trust in their fellow human beings, or the reverse: the more people believe that other people can generally be trusted, the more they trust in social institutions."[2] He adds: "If people cannot trust that public officials will act according to norms such as impartiality, objectivity, incorruptibility, and non-discrimination, they cannot trust 'people in general' either."[3] Bad public institutions do not stop at wasting and stealing public money; they also destroy trust between, among and within human groups. They fuel social traps.

The level of social trust required to break through social traps by cooperative intergroup relations is created indirectly through maintaining good public institutions that make economic opportunity available fairly. How people in general view the integrity of public officials administering and enforcing institutional rules shapes how they view the general trustworthiness of their fellow citizens: "If it proves that I cannot trust the local police, judges, teachers, and doctors, then whom in this society can I trust?"[4] It is a question worth pondering, one that always has answers that always matter.

The story of the New Orleans OIG details the creation of a public entity constitutionally mandated to reduce the barriers to developing good public institutions. In the light of the antithetical forces of social traps and social trust, the OIG appears as a powerful instrument for two critical steps that must be taken for the well-being of any city.

First, community leaders committed to increasing economic opportunity for all who are willing to learn and work must see to it that local public institutions that are supported by tax dollars serve all who are entitled to their protection and services fairly, efficiently, and effectively through programs such as adult literacy, community policing, workforce preparation and placement, and re-entry services for former prisoners. Local governments doing such things competently and free of corruption make businesses and citizens believe that investing in their city's future makes sense. It is also true that those who face the biggest economic challenges are the ones who most need government services, because they cannot provide privately for education, health care, neighborhood security, and so on. Absent good public institutions, the politics and economics of any city will degrade into social-trap power struggles among actual and would-be insiders, while access to opportunity for outsiders continues to diminish. This has been the pattern in New Orleans. Whatever the particular issue of the moment, the underlying, unchanging purpose of the OIG is to produce good public institutions. The examples of OIG accomplishments described earlier illustrate this critical point.

Second, New Orleans leaders committed to creating institutional conditions that promote expanding economic opportunity for all by establishing the OIG have also and simultaneously put their city on a path to building social trust among groups caught in social traps. No form or amount of multiracial or interfaith dialogue or education will add significantly to a city's reservoir of intergroup trust as long as corrupt institutions cause some to be assisted and others to be limited in achieving economic success, not because of their capacities, but because they do or do not belong to particular groups. Insider dealing corrupts institutions, damages economic development and opportunity, and heightens racial tensions. Whatever its particular purpose, every good public institution moves the body politic from traps to trust.

In summary, good public institutions are a direct link to increasing economic opportunity for all and an indirect link to building social trust among historically divided groups. Public institutions, economic opportunity, and social trust go together, for better and for worse. The OIG is a powerful influence now available to strengthen those links in New Orleans. If successful, its three principal outcomes will be directly reducing waste and corruption and indirectly reducing racial tension and enhancing economic opportunity for all who are willing to work and learn.

Where to Start?

Social scientists have made a compelling case that economic opportunity, honest and efficient public institutions, and social trust go together, their findings suggest three differing recommendations about where to start in order to move the circular relationship among the three factors in the positive direction.

Starting with Trust

Those who start with social trust believe that if you want to build the public institutions that are necessary to support the creation of economic opportunity, you should bring together people who have been divided, by encouraging the formation of groups based on shared hobbies and other interests, social concerns, geographic proximity, and so on. A civil society rich in "voluntary associations" provides the social glue that makes it possible for governmental and business institutions to function properly.[5] This approach to building social trust is direct: Members of historically alienated groups must meet face-to-face in voluntary associations in order to create the social trust required for good government and economic growth.

Starting with Economic Opportunity

Those emphasizing economic opportunity believe that markets left free to function will reward competence, create a growing pool of economic opportunities, and generate a stronger tax base to support necessary government services.[6] They are convinced that government attempts to create economic equality by forced redistribution schemes involving taxation of businesses and individuals or social policies, such as affirmative action, that give advantages to members of some groups based on ethnicity or gender to make up for past discrimination interfere with and can destroy the market's job-creating power by distorting the dynamics of economic competition and chasing businesses into jurisdictions with transparent, consistent ground rules applied evenhandedly to all.[7] When local economies flourish, more households build assets, local governments have the resources to address public concerns, and social trust rises. But when business owners must "pay to play," that is, bribe local officials directly with envelopes or indirectly with campaign contributions in order to get contracts or permits, or when public decisions are "steered" by nepotism, ethnicity, or political affiliation, the economic base and the employment opportunities only it can generate, the tax revenues it produces and social trust spiral downward together.[8] From this perspective, public institutions play a limited but crucial role in economic development: They establish and enforce transparent rules and norms for all, starting with property rights and equal treatment under the law, without which businesses and individuals will not invest in local communities and underlying inequalities cannot be addressed.

Starting with the Integrity of Public Institutions

Those whose starting point is the integrity of public institutions believe that ensuring that institutions that are truly universal, that is, that serve all citizens efficiently and effectively (not wastefully), honestly (limiting corruption and cronyism), and fairly (without regard for ethnicity, wealth, or connections) is the single most powerful way to create social trust in a community.[9] First, a definition: "Institutions are the rules of the game in a society or, more formally, are the humanly devised constraints that shape human interaction."[10] They consist of formal and informal rules and mechanisms of enforcement. Institutions are the rules of the game and their enforcement; individuals and organizations are the players.

When public institutions reduce waste of public resources, diminish corruption, and treat all entitled to their services equally, they increase social trust indirectly by creating the ground rules necessary to generate economic opportunity for more people.[11] The likelihood that people in general will trust each other—especially in circumstances where there have been significant ethnic, religious, or class conflicts and divisions—goes up as members of all groups experience the reduction of waste, corruption, and discrimination by public institutions, such as planning commissions, school boards, and city halls. When those institutions functional universally, that is, efficiently, honestly, and fairly for all, additional belief in "the system" fuels economic opportunity for all and breeds trust of other people in the community. When and so far as public institutions fail to meet the standards of universality, legitimate government services and benefits are denied to taxpayers, economic opportunity is limited and mistrust blocks and fractures relationships among people, reinforcing histories of division. A community's public institutions make possible and limit its economic vitality and opportunity, which in turn affect levels of trust among its various groups. Public integrity, economic opportunity, and social trust spiral up and down together.

Contrary to popular local and national opinions, the fundamental problem facing American cities is not poverty. Nor is it racism.[12] Those are symptoms of a deeper social malady. What has many American cities in steady decline is an underlying deficit of social trust fueling social traps. New Orleanians struggle to negotiate with integrity across race and class lines to bring into being a city that works better and more equitably for all groups. Both locals and outsiders typically misattribute our social dilemma to racism, the indifference of the wealthy, or pathology in poor black families; but an intergroup impasse over goals and action is the underlying social trap in which New Orleans and other American cities continue to be caught.[13] This awareness becomes plainer and more painful as we look to the east and to the west where our sister cities of Atlanta, Houston, and San Antonio slowly but surely find ways out of this trap and flourish as a result. In the years since Katrina drew an indelible line in the history of one American city, media and the press have done us the painful service of keeping a bright public spotlight on our crippling social traps. And while the uniqueness of the Crescent City is rightly legendary, what plagues our body politic is by no means our challenge alone: The incapacity of elected, business, and civic leaders to compromise and act across race and class lines for the common good is the American dilemma.[14] The story of one American city is a variation of the story of all America's cities, the story of social traps and social trust.

Notes

1   See Bo Rothstein, *Social Traps, and the Problem of Trust* (New York: Cambridge University Press, 2005).
2   Ibid., 111.
3   Ibid., 120.
4   Ibid., 122.
5   Robert Putnam, *Making Democracy Work* (Princeton, NJ: Princeton University Press, 1993) 181–185; Robert Putnam, *Bowling Alone* (New York: Simon & Schuster, 2000), 134–137.
6   David Boaz, *The Libertarian Mind* (New York: Simon &Shuster, 2015), 193–197.
7   Ibid., 228–242.

8   Eric Uslaner, "The Bulging Pocket and the Rule of Law" (paper presented at "The Quality of Government" conference, Quality of Government Institute, Goteborg University, Sweden, November 17–19, 2005), 15–16; Bo Rothstein and Eric Auslaner, "All for All: Equality, Corruption, and Social Trust," *World Politics* 58 (October 2005): 47–48.

9   Bo Rothstein, *Just Institutions Matter* (New York: Cambridge University Press, 1998), 106–117.

10 Douglass North, *Institutions, Institutional Change, and Economic Performance* (Cambridge: Cambridge University Press, 1990, 3.

11 North, *Institutions,* 27–35; Rothstein, *Social Traps,* 108–109.

12 Alex Jung, "How Black Is New Orleans? New Census Figures Don't Tell the Whole Story," *Colorlines Magazine*, May 1, 2008, 8, https://www.colorlines.com/articles/how-black-new-orleans.

13 Rothstein, *Social Traps,* 4–5, 17–18.

14 Gunnar Myrdal, *An American Dilemma* (New York: McGraw-Hill, 1962), lxix–lxxi; Stephen Graubard, "An American Dilemma Revisited," in *An American Dilemma Revisited*, ed. Obie Clayton Jr. (New York: Russell Sage Foundation, 1996), 1–24.

Slaying Two Sacred Cows: One Group's Part in Helping New Orleans Reform, Rebuild, and Renew

Ruthie Frierson

Ruthie Frierson is the founder of Citizens for 1 Greater New Orleans, an all-female volunteer reform organization. For her leadership in a movement advancing citizen activism during Southeast Louisiana's darkest hour, she received the Times-Picayune Loving Cup for 2006.

Citizens for One Greater New Orleans was a volunteer group of women that exemplified the surge of citizen activism that flourished in New Orleans after Katrina. Alarmed by their realization that local government was too dysfunctional to direct a successful comeback, citizens mobilized and charged at two seemingly untouchable local institutions they deemed ripe for reform, the ineffectual levee board and the notoriously biased board of tax assessors. Using skills honed through years of volunteer work, they mobilized public opinion, lobbied reluctant state lawmakers, and finally achieved success through the passage of constitutional amendments in two separate statewide referendum elections. Reforming these two "sacred cows" was a signal accomplishment that instilled badly needed confidence in government, spurring locals to return and thereby clearing the path for a robust recovery in the Crescent City.

Many ingredients define New Orleans—certainly our music, our food, and our architecture, but most basic and defining of all is water and our relationship with it. Nestled between the Gulf of Mexico and an enormous body of brackish water, the fifty-by-thirty-mile Lake Pontchartrain, the city sits near the mouth of the Mississippi River, which drains water from 41 percent of the lower forty-eight states. We are pelted with an average sixty-five inches of rain a year; famously wet Seattle gets about half that amount. Much of our city is built on land a few feet below sea level, protected from the consequences of that location by a complex system of levees, floodwalls, pumps, and outfall canals. We all own multiple pairs of rain boots; we avoid certain intersections during thunderstorms because of the dangerously deep water that collects there. We New Orleanians know water. We also know corruption, another near-universal part of our city's image. The fatalistic shrug with which locals receive allegations of improper dealings says, essentially, "What yah gonna do?" We laugh that, far from being the worst-governed city in the United States, we are the best-governed in the Caribbean. Roguish officials seem to have a place in many hearts. Wet and crooked, that *was* us.

The aftermath of Hurricane Katrina was the most catastrophic man-made disaster in the nation's history. Katrina changed everything, and every one of us. It was a shock and a wake-up call. Having obeyed Mayor Ray Nagin's order for a mandatory evacuation of the city, our family watched from afar as New Orleans went under water. We saw images of the city's devastation, the horror of people trapped in their houses or on rooftops waiting for rescue, of people in need of water, food, and medical attention, of deaths, of plunder and the sounds of gunfire. Eighty percent of our city was under water for more than three weeks. Our infrastructure was almost completely destroyed—our public facilities, schools, homes, businesses. More than eighteen hundred of our citizens lost their lives and thousands of others were displaced. The challenges we faced to rebuild our city were daunting and unparalleled in our history—on so many levels, and all at the same time. Yet, out of this tragedy of Katrina's aftermath have come opportunities and a new wave of activism and involvement.

We returned on the first day that anyone was allowed into the deserted city to find that we were among the lucky ones. We lived in the 20 percent of the city that had not flooded, known as "the sliver by the river." Our house was mostly intact, though damaged by wind. Yet all around us, it looked like our impression of a war zone: deep silence, no birds, no children, just the occasional roaring of distant chain saws, full blackness at night until electricity could be restored to our nearly deserted city.

One day, as I drove to City Park, I became disoriented—no landmarks, just miles and miles of total devastation. I broke down crying. A workman knocked on my car window and said, "Lady, you need help." I told him I didn't need help, that I would be fine. He said, "Yes, you do, lady, you do need help," and with that he handed me a bottle of water and said, "Please take this—it's all I have to give you—I wish I could help you more." This was the story of Katrina—of a stranger reaching out to another to ease her pain. My hand was gripped around the bottle all the way home, and it sat on my dresser for years as a reminder of that special gesture of kindness and of the deep pain we all experienced with the loss of our city. I knew at that moment that I had to be involved in our city's recovery.

Tears came easily to most of us; everyone spoke of having "Katrina moments" in our eerie surroundings, triggered by thoughts of whom and what had been lost. With the flooding that covered most of our city, it would take months before cleanup began, before electricity and communications were restored, before neighborhoods were livable, and six months to a year before school openings allowing children and their parents to return to the city, before key government agencies were up and running; many police and other first responders who had lost their homes had to sleep in their cars. Everywhere we looked was gray and dark. Many who returned suffered from depression and other mental health issues, but treatment was in most instances unavailable. We experienced a period of profound mourning. But gradually, mourning gave way to rage as we realized, terrifyingly: There is no plan; our government will not act!

The eye of the storm actually by-passed the city. The flooding was brought on by breaches of the levees, which failed under the stress of rising water from the lakes that surround the city. Because of poor construction and design compounded by complacency and inattentiveness, the breaches were a catastrophe waiting to happen

Before Katrina, Southeast Louisiana had eight politically appointed levee boards, each with a separate jurisdiction. Though water knows no boundaries, there was no comprehensive review of the levee system. Each board was made up of political appointees, most of whom lacked any expertise in levees or flood control. The US Army Corps of Engineers and the local levee boards were required to do joint annual inspections of the more than one hundred miles of levees. The inspections typically lasted a cursory five hours and were followed by a leisurely lunch. In New Orleans, the board had focused on their non-flood-related assets, such as a casino, marinas, an airport, and land holdings, which distracted them from their primary responsibility of the levees and flood control. Years of corruption, cronyism, and political patronage had stifled the board's effectiveness, inspiring the local press to comment dryly that this body "had a dismal history of political intrigue."

I had been a residential realtor for more than eighteen years when Katrina hit the city. Almost immediately after the storm passed, my phone rang from morning to night, with callers in total despair. Was it safe to come back? Should they rebuild? Could they risk it, or should they relocate? It became clearer to me every day that people would not return to start over in our city if they did not feel safe from a future catastrophic flood. Yet in November 2005, in a special session of the state legislature, a committee in the House of Representatives defeated a bill that would have done much to allay fears and reduce the uncertainty then preventing our recovery.

This measure, sponsored by Senator Walter Boasso and Representative Karen Carter Peterson, would have created a unified, nonpolitical levee board whose members had scientific and technological expertise and a single focus on flood protection. Provision was also made for a non–politically appointed nominating committee to insure the board's autonomy. It was the necessary confidence booster, without which our renewal could not proceed. The New Orleans Business Council had backed the defeated reform bill but the lawmakers in Baton Rouge had killed it in committee, not even letting it get consideration by the full house. The bill did not have the backing of Governor Kathleen Blanco—she was silent on the issue.

This shocking legislative refusal to act was the catalyst that moved us from mourning to rage and from there to action. My thought was to harness that outrage and to organize a petition drive requesting that Governor Blanco call another special session of the state legislature that would focus on flood protection and levee-board reform. I met with Jay Lapeyre, chairman of the New Orleans Business Council, to review the failed levee bill. I asked him to speak to a group of women the Monday after Thanksgiving. In preparation for the meeting, we printed hundreds of packets that included a levee petition, a list of all the legislators who had not supported the levee reform legislation, a page for fifty people to sign the petition, our statement of support, and a very strong letter from the New Orleans Business Council to Governor Blanco, which became a part of our messaging to the public, legislators, and media around the city, state, and nation.

We also made many calls, asking people in turn to call anyone they knew or met. Our efforts paid off: 120 concerned women met at my house. When Lapeyre spoke, he explained to the group why this reform of the levee boards was the number-one priority for our city and region and why the old system needed to be reformed: "[OLD], the Orleans Parish Levee District, claimed to provide and failed to provide local oversight for design and construction of the levees, and design flaws and construction shortcuts by the Corps of Engineers caused the failures. The Corps and OLD were responsible for not providing local oversight. The Levee Board claimed to be on watch and had none of the expertise, independence, or commitment to mission needed for the job."

These concerned women were excited to see that there was a way to be engaged in reforming and rebuilding our city in a meaningful way. In an article on post-Katrina gender politics, Pamela Tyler observes, "When the *New York Times* reported a 'wave of citizen activism' in New Orleans after Hurricane Katrina, it failed to mention that much of the wave was wearing lipstick and carrying a purse. Mopping up is, and always has been women's work, so it comes as no surprise that large numbers of local women were active in post-Katrina recovery efforts."[1]

After much discussion, we named ourselves Citizens for 1 Greater New Orleans. "Citizens" represents everyone and "Greater" refers to the region where all were affected and belonged to "1" of the eight politically appointed levee boards. Citizens for 1 Greater New Orleans was organized as a voice for reform and renewal of a Greater New Orleans and a better Louisiana. We became a grassroots all-volunteer, nonpartisan organization demanding an end to politics as usual. Brash and ambitious, we wanted to rebuild New Orleans with good responsive government, high ethical standards, and accountability at all levels. Lapeyre and the New Orleans Business Council became Citizens for 1's first coalition partner. We created a website that proved crucial to our success by providing education and two-way communications for us and our website participants. Those who signed a petition gave only their e-mail address, since their homes were flooded and uninhabitable, and we updated our website daily with citizens' names and e-mail addresses.

Women left the meeting with petitions for levee-board reform and spread out, often in pairs of two across our city wherever people could be found. The drive mushroomed, and churches, civic groups, businesses, and individuals from around the city and around the region sent in petitions. In one afternoon, two thousand e-mails were sent by fax from Covington, Louisiana. We sent our petition to Boston to be translated into Vietnamese, and Father Vien Nguyen, leader of the New Orleans East Vietnamese community, distributed them to his congregation, and soon we had two thousand more signed petitions and supporters. As we branched out throughout the community, we built relationships with individuals, the media, members of the business community and of churches and civic organizations, and some elected and appointed officials at the local and state levels. Our efforts built a new collective voice and trust among citizens from across our city and gave much-needed hope to thousands of our citizens in Southeast Louisiana's darkest hour.

After the initial meeting in November 2005, eight women, all professional and civic leaders, sat at our dining room table to plan strategy, including how to coordinate for the future success of our efforts—and our executive committee was formed. We ranged in age from late forties to eighty. Through our post-Katrina work, we formed a lifelong bond of deep friendship and respect. Among us were the heads of successful businesses, chairs of numerous civic organizations, and members of school and college boards of directors. One member chairs a significant foundation, one is the top residential realtor in Metropolitan New Orleans, and one received the Civilian French Legion Medal of Honor for risking her life to help her countrymen fight the Nazis in World War II. As members of the New Orleans Junior League, a women's community service organization, the majority of us had honed invaluable leadership skills in planning agendas, building coalitions, setting goals and objectives, and chairing community boards and committees. In doing so, we had each created a toolbox we have carried with us the rest of our lives. None of us, however, had ever faced anything so daunting as the task now before us. The dining room was dubbed "the war room." Citizens for 1 Greater New Orleans began with women of like background and expanded quickly to become "metro-wide, diverse and irresistible."[2]

We branded ourselves with red jackets, because we were seeing red and we wanted the legislators to see red too. We designed pins and signs calling for one levee board with a big red "1" in the middle of our logo. We created a PR committee to contact TV, radio, and print media at the local and state levels. One member of the committee ordered signs and stored them at her house; another ordered pins and organized our distribution. One small group took charge of organizing volunteers to distribute thousands of signs throughout the city. Another group planned community meetings to educate the public at six sites across the city. As chairman, I became the voice of Citizens for 1 in the media, at meetings, and later in the legislature. But all of us became skilled at simple focused messaging, because every day we encountered media and citizens with questions

Jay Lapeyre and his company helped us set up a more comprehensive website, which became a powerful voice to express citizen opinions to our state legislators and local city council. We met every afternoon for the three and a half weeks of the petition drive to plan for future outreach. My doorbell seemed to ring steadily from morning to evening, with people dropping off petitions. Everyone had a story, and we listened with sadness and concern as they recounted their heartbreaking losses. In a breathless three and a half weeks, we had garnered fifty-three thousand signed petitions, representing a third of our city's returned population. After this surge of activism, Governor Blanco called another special session of the state legislature on flood protection and levee-board reform and consolidation in Southeast Louisiana.

In preparation for the special session, Randy Haynie, the New Orleans Business Council lobbyist, trained a hundred of us in how to be effective, successful citizen lobbyists with an understanding of the ins and outs of procedures and appropriate protocol. The challenge was to mobilize and train volunteers for this legislative session. It was a grassroots movement. The majority of volunteers had never been involved in political activity, much less advocacy. But they saw this as an opportunity for real change. These women were willing to make the sacrifice and take time away from family and jobs to make this reform a reality. Our approach was to stay focused on the issue, to have facts to back up our messaging, and to never attack individuals.

On February 6, 2006, we staged a rally on the steps of the State Capitol on the opening day of the session. From across the city we had bused more than twelve hundred citizens, wearing red jackets, scarfs, ties, and Citizens for 1 pins. The women got off the buses and, in a sea of red, walked to the Capitol steps, carrying signs that read, "One Levee Board Voice" and "United we stand, divided we flood." The one that caught the most media attention read, "Drove my Chevy to the levee, and it floated away." It was spectacular. After I spoke briefly to the crowd of supporters and restated our position, Governor Blanco addressed the crowd in support of levee-board reform. She was followed by speakers from the Vietnamese, Hispanic, black, and white communities who reinforced our position. Representative from the media were everywhere that day and throughout the legislative session, providing significant coverage of our activities on the local, state, and national levels.

For the two-and-a-half-week special session, large numbers of our volunteers were very visible at the Capitol every day. Citizens for 1 members, now known as "the Redcoats," attended and testified at all committee meetings and attended all general sessions in the House and Senate. We met with individual members of the committees that were hearing the bill before their committees met to take a vote. We met with the legislators who had voted against the bill in the November special session. It was a battle that required constant vigilance, which we maintained by making phone calls, posting e-mails on our website, and giving testimony and many interviews with local, state, and national media.

We practically lived at the Capitol. Many of us slept in sleeping bags on the floor of places rented by evacuees from New Orleans. Several representatives told us that the levee-board reform would never pass. Opponents worked to undermine and weaken the legislation or to kill the bill in committee. But as citizen volunteers we knew it was government of, by, and for the people and that it was our Capitol, and so we persisted. Longtime observers of the legislative scene said that we were a different breed of lobbyists: We were prepared with the facts and, as some legislators put it, we "never went away."

Throughout the session, Citizens for 1 sent our messages to our interactive website participants, who played a significant role by responding directly to legislators through e-mails and phone calls. Our volunteers contacted their state representatives, most for the first time, and in the process, became overnight advocates. Through knowledge, commitment, a laser focus, and passion for our cause, we built strong alliances with many reform-minded legislators, who proved invaluable to our case.

Though the Senate committee that heard the levee-board legislation and the Senate voted to pass the bill, the big challenge facing us was the vote by the House committee. They had defeated the bill in the November 2005 special session of the state legislature. On the day the key vote was called by the House committee hearing the levee bill, we noticed the posting of the 9:30 a.m. meeting had been changed to 4:30 that afternoon. Perhaps legislators hoped we would go back home to New Orleans before then. But, to their surprise, a large contingent of Red Coats attended. The meeting went on until 2:30 in the morning. The committee voted to defeat the bill. Our hearts sank—we thought it was over. As I left the meeting, Robert Travis Scott, Capitol Bureau chief of the *New Orleans Times-Picayune,* asked me how I felt. I said, "Was it worth all the effort?" He said, "Yes, it is not over yet."

That same morning, the conference committee met and a compromise was reached. The revised bill created two levee boards, one on the east bank of the Mississippi River to be known as the Southeast Louisiana Flood Protection Authority East (SLFPA-E) and one on the west bank to be known as the Southeast Louisiana Flood Protection Authority West (SLFPA-W). The bill provided for the appointment of one member from each parish within the territorial jurisdiction of the authorities. The SLFPA-E board would be required to have nine members, five of whom must be an engineer or a professional in a related field such as geotechnical, hydrological, or environmental science. Of those five, one would have to be a civil engineer. Two members would have to be professionals in disciplines other than engineering, geotechnical, hydrological, or environmental science and have at least ten years of professional experience in that discipline, and two members would be at-large. SLFPA-W would have seven members with similar requirements. The governor would select board members from a list of up to three nominees proposed in each category by the nominating committee for each board.

The bill also provided for a non–politically appointed nominating committee consisting of members designated by the Public Affairs Research Council, the Council for a Better Louisiana, the Association of State Floodplain Managers, the National Academy of Engineering, the National Society of Black Engineers, the American Institute of Hydrology, the school of Science and Engineering at Tulane University, the College of Engineering at Louisiana State University, the National Society of Professional Engineers, and the American Society of Civil Engineers.

On Valentine's Day 2006, Senator Boasso called me and said, "Bring up the Redcoats—we have reached an acceptable compromise in conference committee that Citizens for 1 Greater New

Orleans can support." Governor Blanco, dressed in Valentine's Day red, attended the meeting in Senate chambers, pleased with the outcome we all had supported. She turned to me and said, "This is the toughest session I can remember. There were no carrots!"

A member of the conference committee told me that members of Citizens for 1 Greater New Orleans had been instrumental in the conference committee's decision to find a compromise. The legislature finally passed the historic legislation that dissolved local levee commissioners and created the East bank and West bank Southeast Louisiana Flood Protection Authorities. The legislation now required passage of a statewide constitutional amendment by a vote that would be held September 30, 2006.

The Louisiana congressional delegation warned that it would be difficult to persuade Washington to allocate the billions that were needed to rebuild our city unless the legislature enacted the necessary reforms to city government. As New Orleans faced the challenge of a massive recovery, issues related to local property valuations came into focus. Since the 1930s, good-government reformers had assailed the property-tax collection system, which encompassed seven separate assessor offices, for being unfair and rife with political patronage. It became clear after Katrina that local property assessments were so flawed as to be worthless in valuing damages done by the storm and flood. The New Orleans Bureau of Governmental Research had published excellent reports over the years on the need for citizens to address this issue, but the reports sat on shelves and no action was taken. These reports would soon be put to good use. Just as Citizens for 1 Greater New Orleans had demanded change in the levee-board system to protect the city from catastrophic storms, Citizens for 1 took up the gauntlet demanding change and protection from the city's antiquated and unfair property-assessment system. Many citizens through our website and in personal calls asked us to take on this needed reform. Once again, we would be calling for professional standards and honest, transparent government.

Members of Citizens for 1 saw an opportunity to change the entrenched property-assessment system and voiced a public call for assessor reform legislation that would consolidate the seven assessor offices into a single office that would require a uniform method of assessment. We were the only parish in our state and the only large city, except Indianapolis, in our country with more than one assessor. The existing system was wasteful and unfair, and it required deal making and cozy relationships with the friendly neighborhood assessor—one whose family had held the position for more than a hundred years. Citizens for 1 Greater New Orleans and the New Orleans Business Council worked directly with lawmakers to get a bill introduced calling for the reform and consolidation of assessor offices in Orleans Parish. Representative Austin Badon and Senator Ann Duplessis authored the bill.

Members of Citizens for 1 again spent weeks at the State Capitol, attending and testifying at every legislative committee hearing on the bill while it was under debate. We were met with strong opposition, because two assessors' family members were on the House Ways and Means Committee hearing the bill and they refused to recuse themselves. Our response to the opposition's arguments was that a committee vote in support of the bill would give the citizens of Orleans Parish and the state of Louisiana the right to decide the outcome and allow for democratic principles to prevail through a referendum. It would not be a vote to abolish the offices of the seven assessors. After much acrimony and heated debate, the bill was passed out of committee and sent to the full house, where the House voted 98–2 approval. Only two New Orleans area legislators cast no votes, but the two representatives related to assessors who had argued against the measure were recorded as absent on the final vote.

The bill finally passed in both House and Senate. The legislation now required passage of a statewide constitutional amendment in a referendum to be held on November 7, 2006. This amendment needed to pass in both the state and Orleans Parish.

The passage of these two reform bills on levees and assessors by the state legislature was a significant and historic victory that signaled that positive change and reform had begun in Louisiana. In 2006, through our Citizens for 1 website, more than 1.75 million e-mails were sent to state legislators. Ashton Phelps, publisher of the *Times-Picayune*, in his remarks about Citizens for 1 Greater New Orleans on March 25, 2007, said, "These citizens want a safe city behind sound levees so that no generation would endure what we have endured, and more than that they want honest, efficient city government, one free of old habits of cronyism and patronage, that stifles progress and made us all unsafe."

In summer and early fall 2006 our focus was to plan our strategy and organize our base for the fall constitutional amendment votes across the state. With support from the New Orleans Business Council, our group raised $850,000 to fund public education efforts, and we mounted statewide print, radio, and television campaigns. We identified key message strategies and tested these messages through market research to determine what spoke to the people. On levees, the simple message was about safety and flood protection. For assessors, it was Why pay seven to do the job of one? We developed a disciplined and focused message strategy and carried the same message throughout in campaign literature, advertisements, and radio and television spots. Because timing was important, television and radio spots and advertising were timed to run just ten days before the two elections. We spoke to numerous civic and business organizations around the city and the state. Our volunteers and supporters across the city attended community meetings, informed and worked with other civic organizations, neighborhood associations, and churches, including African American, Hispanic, and Vietnamese communities, and organized neighborhood get-out-the vote campaigns. Citizens for 1 flooded the city with One Levee Board signs that read "Vote Amendment 3" and placed them near every polling station before the September 30 vote. Before the November 7 vote on assessors, we placed Citizens for 1 signs that read "Vote Amendment 7." Hundreds of community volunteers walked neighborhoods going door-to-door with our flyers. Huge signs were hung around the city in strategic locations. We used our website to garner support from more than twenty thousand website participants. We wrote opinion editorials and letters to the editor in papers around the state and were interviewed on radio and television stations.

A seventeen-page feature article by Charles Mann on the one-year anniversary of Katrina appeared in the August 2006 issue of *Fortune* magazine. Citizens for 1 Greater New Orleans was featured in the article. "Against all that," Mann writes, "the efforts of Ruthie Frierson and her accidental activists to save a city and its economy seem a slender reed to lean on. The scale of this rebuilding effort is a reminder of the limits of local self-reliance and the need for effective government. Yet New Orleans' best chance for recovery may lie in its reawakened sense of community, born of shared disaster—because government, it is now clear, will not act unless pushed hard."

On the days of the votes, September 30 and November 7, we were at major intersections waving our Get-out-the-vote signs for each reform measure. Some of us drove around the city in cars, using megaphones and asking everyone to get to the polls to vote. Some of us rode on a fire truck, which created quite a sensation!

The results were resounding victories—the amendments passed with wide majorities throughout the state—for levees with 94 percent in Orleans Parish and 81 percent statewide. The assessor amendment received 80 percent statewide and 70 percent approval in Orleans. These two successful reform efforts brought a new era of professionalism, accountability, and transparency to the Greater New Orleans area. The most powerful thing about the votes was that the yeas crossed over former neighborhood, racial, and economic divides. The independent weekly newspaper *Gambit* ranked the stunning consolidations of the levee boards and assessor system as the number-one story of 2006.

After the levee-board reforms, the East and West Authorities brought the talent, focus, and independence needed to provide oversight of the design and construction and ongoing maintenance for miles of levee and pumping systems that protect the three-parish area. Inspection policies were included in a host of reforms in levee-board management after Katrina. The new $14.5 billion storm protection system on the east bank of the river, overseen by the new SLFPA-E, now has eleven full-time trained staff doing full-time checks on the levees. A three- man team is assigned to check the 39 miles of flood walls and 117 miles of levees four times a year, each check taking six weeks. A team of eight employees open and close 204 floodgates and 102 flood valves in Orleans throughout the year. "Absolutely better inspections might have found signs of trouble," Paul Kemp, a Louisiana State University geologist, member of the local flood authority board, and co-author of the report clearing local levee boards of causing the engineering failures, said. "There's no question what we are doing today is night and day from the old system."[3]

The passage of the assessor reform and consolidation amendments made the property-assessment system more equitable, more transparent, and more efficient for property owners, and it made the city more attractive to business. Also, having one assessor office saved money for the city, allowing more funding for critical services for schools, police, and fire protection.

The passage of these two statewide levee board and assessor amendments was the beginning of a reform movement that gave Citizens for 1 the stature and courage to focus on big issues that have no finish line but instead call for slow, incremental progress: criminal justice, pre-K–12 public education, and ethics/good government reform. Among these needed reforms were the creation of a New Orleans Ethics Review Board, the permanent New Orleans Office of Inspector General, and the New Orleans Office of Independent Police Monitor; the establishment of a 501c3 Court Watch NOLA organization; and the successful passage of legislation that transformed all New Orleans public schools, pre-K–12, into public charter schools.

Our approach to advocacy and the process we use to achieve our goals is simple.

Our committees' research and educate ourselves and others and advocate and monitor the issues.

- We build and work in broad-based coalitions of civic and business organizations on issues important to the common good of our citizenry.
- We build and sustain relationships with elected and appointed officials at the state and local levels.
- We testify at state and local legislative committees.

- We focus on clear messaging, never attacking individuals.
- We use our website and media contacts to communicate our positions.

In 2010, the Brookings Institution and the Greater New Orleans Data Center reported, "Since 2005, New Orleanians have undertaken more major reforms simultaneously than any other modern city."[4]

We recognize that our city's bright future depends on all of our citizens continuing to stay informed, persistent, and engaged. Above all else, we must remain vigilant and never lose sight of the importance of an informed citizenry—for we get the government we demand.

Yes, Katrina did change everything and every one of us. Success came with broad-based support from diverse groups: churches, individuals, neighborhood associations, civic and business organizations, and city and statewide elected officials committed to reform. These successes demonstrated the power of the citizen voice and gave our citizens much-needed hope that together we can reform, renew, and rebuild our city and region, stronger and better than before Katrina. Wet and crooked? Not so much anymore, thanks to a roomful of women who were first enraged and then engaged.

Notes

1   Pamela Tyler, "The Post-Katrina Semiseparate World of Gender Politics," in "Through the Eye of Katrina: The Past as Prologue?," special issue, *Journal of American History* 94, no. 3 (December 2007): 780.

2   Clancy DuBos, "Da Winnas and Da Loozas," *Gambit Weekly*, November 14, 2006.

3   Bob Marshall, "Post-Katrina Reforms Make Levee, Floodwall Inspections a Daily Job," *The Lens*, August 6, 2015, https://thelensnola.org/2015/08/06/post-katrina-reforms-make-levee-floodwall-inspections-a-daily-job/.

4   Amy Liu and Allison Plyer, "The New Orleans Index at Five: An Overview of Greater New Orleans—From Recovery to Transformation," Brookings Metropolitan Policy Program and Greater New Orleans Community Data Center, August 2010, https://www.brookings.edu/wp-content/uploads/2016/06/08neworleansindex.pdf.

The New New Orleans: Business
Leaders Take the Initiative

Gregory Rusovich

Gregory Rusovich served as board chair of the Business Council of New Orleans and the River Region, the New Orleans Police and Justice Foundation, the New Orleans Crime Coalition, the Board of Commissioners of the Port of New Orleans, GNO, Inc., and New Orleans and Company. He created (with Michael Cowan) Forward New Orleans, a citizen-driven process of holding elected officials publicly accountable for keeping their campaign promises. He is now board chair of the Metropolitan Crime Commission.

Eighteen hundred people dead, flooded streets, destroyed homes, dangling power lines, downed trees, a green city turned to brown, inept and corrupt political leadership, a broken school system, higher crime, and pervasive institutional dysfunction permeated New Orleans in the post-Katrina landscape. This nightmare was exacerbated for business owners and leaders of local companies who faced the added challenge of stemming the tremendous financial loses to our businesses caused by the post-Katrina collapse, and our commitment, dedication, and desire to help our displaced employees and their families get reestablished and economically supported in their time of dire need. All quite a challenge for a wonderful, unique community and a business leadership ready to return and rebuild from the worst man-made disaster in modern history.

The Business Council of New Orleans and the River Region was formed in 1985 by the iconic chairman and CEO of Freeport McMoRan, Jim Bob Moffett. The core mission of the Business Council during its thirty-four years has been to improve the region's business climate, enhancing the quality of life for the community, working to effect principled reform, and simply striving to make New Orleans a safer and better place to live, work, and raise a family. It consists primarily of CEOs and owners of the largest businesses and employers in the city and has ranged in total membership from a low of about twenty leaders in the early days to about seventy currently.

Immediately following the Katrina devastation and upheaval, the Business Council emerged with new leadership who were able to quickly return to the city, willing and able to pour heart and soul into saving a beloved city and home. The post-Katrina chairman of the Business Council, Jay Lapeyre (CEO of Laitram, LLC), accepted the immense challenge and became the leader of the dramatic reform effort that would positively impact the region for decades to come. Jay, along with the new Business Council leadership team, focused on the city's core institutional failures, critical recovery issues, and, most important, he worked tirelessly to make the city a better place. The Business Council team, confronted with the need to handle at once the multiple urgent challenges

24

and critical issues facing the community, pursued each issue with vigor and tenacity. Key business leaders stepped up and led task forces that attacked each critical reform and recovery issue. Massive work was urgently needed to protect the city from further flooding and levee collapse as future hurricane seasons fast approached; major overhaul was needed to reform the inept and nonaccountable levee board system; the public education system was broken as graduation rates plummeted and poverty rose; the criminal justice system was incapable of providing adequate public safety or fairness; and city government was failing to meet a requirement to deliver basic city services.

The task forces went to work formulating a strategy, narrative, and action plan to address each major need. We recognized the importance of building community and coalition support across the city to ensure diversity and deeper support for our actions and to put pressure on the political leadership to act. We recognized the urgency of securing government support and recovery funding. Business delegations traveled to Washington, DC, to present our case to the National Press Club. Regular meetings were held with congressional leaders and the Bush and Obama administrations. Business delegations held regular meetings in the state capital at Baton Rouge with Governor Kathleen Blanco and state legislative leaders. In New Orleans, we met regularly with the editorial boards of key news outlets, and we maintained an ongoing engagement with Mayor Ray Nagin and city council leaders. As coalitions were built with civic and neighborhood organizations, rallies were held on the steps of Capitol Hill and in the State Capitol demanding action.

While our business leadership was actively engaging political and media leaders, the neighborhoods of the city went to work rebuilding (with or without government help) and began to speak out on a similar set of issues, with aligned interests and goals. Civic and neighborhood leaders picked up the mantle and led their critical part of the revolution. Our business leadership pounced, joining forces and the beautiful art of coalition building was launched.

One of the earliest partners to lead the revolution with the Business Council was Citizens for 1 Greater New Orleans. Citizens for 1, founded and led by Ruthie Frierson, had begun the work of organizing a major grassroots effort to reform the corrupt and ineffective levee board system. Ruthie and other women volunteers (known and feared as "the Red Coats") had pushed for reform in an urgently held state legislative session in November 2005, about two months after the storm. The usual political insiders won the initial battle and defeated the reform effort. The insider's initial victory was short lived as public outrage grew and additional organizing and coalition building took place. Subsequent levee board reform legislation was successfully passed and the reform movement was set ablaze. A convoluted, archaic "good old boy" levee board system was abolished, replacing ill-intentioned politicos on the multiple boards with a single east bank and west bank professional levee board. The legislation insured an apolitical nominating process that required expertise connected to the board's functions. The levee boards of today are professional, independent, and appropriately responsible for regional flood protection. As important, new business and community alliances were forged and the foundation for reform was laid.

Simultaneously, massive design, engineering, and construction work had to be done to protect, remodel, and rebuild the region's levees, flood walls, and pump systems. It had to be done with urgency, but it had to be done right. The original design by the federal government decades ago had proven to be badly flawed and not constructed as a cohesive system. Compounding the problem, those charged with operating and maintaining the flood protection system worked in silos and failed to do their mission-critical job. While Hurricane Katrina was a force of nature, the devastating flooding of New Orleans should be appropriately categorized as a man-made disaster. Merritt Lane, chairman and CEO of Canal Barge and a member of the Business Council executive committee, took the reins and provided a strong, steady, and knowledgeable business voice to the federal, state, and regional discussion of the system's redesign and rebuild. Merritt's task force held weekly meetings with the leadership of the US Army Corps of Engineers to review, assess, and track the best path forward. As momentum built around the newly opened dialogue with the Corps of Engineers, the levee board, the Sewerage and Water Board, and state stake holders were added to the regular meetings, fostering increased cooperation and collaboration. The Business Council task force convened the meetings and deployed classic executive skill sets to the effort. As goals and objectives were agreed on, timetables and performance metrics were put forth to ensure that everyone stayed on task. Additionally, the task force provided strong encouragement, effective venues, and additional resources to assist the Corps of Engineers in communicating their plans and progress clearly and consistently to local industry groups, business, and civic leaders, as well as the public at large, all of whom needed confidence in the effectiveness of the flood protection system in order to reinvest. The state created the Louisiana Coastal Protection and Restoration Authority (CPRA) to organize state and federal funding for wetlands and coastal protection. The CPRA became a vital partner to the task force and to the overall effort to protect the region. Our Business Council team also worked hand in hand with our US senators, Mary Landrieu and David Vitter, and the entire Louisiana delegation to secure major funding for the redesign and rebuild. Regular lobbying in Washington became a key component of the team's mission. Bush administration officials and congressional leaders visited New Orleans regularly. After witnessing first-hand the extraordinary effort, resilience, and integrity local business and civic leaders were putting forth, they became supportive of our cause to rebuild from Katrina's devastation.

Since 2005, about $14.6 billion have been spent on Corps of Engineers upgrades for hurricane defenses in the New Orleans area. The largest surge barrier and drainage pump station in the world has been constructed. Levees and flood walls have been strengthened, and gated structures and pump stations have been placed at strategic locations to protect from storm surge and flooding. Business leaders working with federal, state, and local partners have nourished a culture of collaboration, cooperation, and accountability.

While levee board and flood safety reform and initiatives were under way, extensive work also had to be undertaken to enhance public safety. Members of the Business Council's criminal justice task force (which I led) met with representatives of the multiracial civic organization Common Good (led by Mike Cowan) and subsequently organized a series of meetings, led by the Business Council, with Citizens for 1, Common Good, and the leading crime-fighting organizations in the city (Metropolitan Crime Commission, New Orleans Police and Justice Foundation, and Crimestoppers) to launch a vigorous strategy for city leadership to adopt in fighting crime and rebuilding the criminal justice system. Mike and Common Good helped to further build the coalition by recruiting key members, such as the Urban League and Puentes into the coalition. Nolan Rollins, then president and CEO of the Urban League of Louisiana, became an invaluable partner in countless major reform efforts. Through Nolan's steady hand and ongoing outreach, a rock-solid Business Council/Urban League partnership was forged and became a formidable team throughout the recovery efforts.

The New Orleans Crime Coalition was launched in 2007 and was made up of the leading crime-fighting, business, and civic organizations in New Orleans. When rising crime and a broken criminal justice system threatened our recovery, the Crime Coalition used its political leverage to insist on specific actions to reduce violent crime and implement criminal justice reform. Our twenty-member coalition announced our action agenda on the steps of the Criminal District Courthouse. We called for urgent federal funding to help rebuild the badly damaged criminal justice system infrastructure and to fill the gap of depleted resources. Post-Katrina manpower losses had reduced the ranks of the New Orleans Police Department (NOPD) and the district attorney (DA) prosecutorial staff. Infrastructure for crime-fighting technology had been destroyed. We undertook an extensive lobbying effort in Washington in collaboration with our congressional delegation. The Crime Coalition scored its first major victory by securing federal funds to backstop critical needs. We would later also secure funding for at-risk-youth services, substance-abuse treatment, additional violent crime prosecutors, additional public defender services, community policing programs, and electronic monitoring. We were able to ensure integrity and metrics in expenditures by designating the independent New Orleans Police and Justice Foundation to act as the fiduciary agent. While the federal effort was under way, the Metropolitan Crime Commission (MCC), led by Rafael Goyeneche, took action at the local level, identifying and reporting serious problems in NOPD arrest strategies and an abysmally low felony conviction rates by police and prosecutors. In 2007, the MCC reported that approximately half of all arrests made were for traffic and municipal offenses. The first half of 2008 saw 26,718 arrests by NOPD but only 104 violent felony convictions. Felony conviction rates were well below nation averages. Only 24 percent of felony suspects arrested in 2007 were convicted of a felony.

The Crime Coalition in coordination with the MCC persuaded the New Orleans City Council and state legislature to enact new ordinances and statutes that allowed officers to issue summons rather than arrest nonviolent misdemeanor offenders. Furthermore, the coalition convened several joint meetings between the DA and the NOPD to improve coordination, collaboration, and cooperation by providing improved police reports and organizing joint DA-NOPD investigative teams at crime scenes. In 2010, the MCC reported that the felony arrest to conviction rate had improved to 45 percent, doubling the previous rate. And by 2011, total arrests went down 45 percent in response to legislative reforms.

The coalition also undertook semi-annual public surveys of NOPD performance to track levels of community satisfaction with local policing. In August 2009, overall public satisfaction with NOPD performance was 33 percent. By March 2014, the satisfaction level had risen to 60 percent. In recent years, the level has remained consistently at 50 percent.

In response to a lack of proficiency and judiciousness in the criminal district court system and among several judges that was creating bottlenecks, the Crime Coalition and a reform-minded newly elected city councilman, James Carter (with strong advocacy from Citizens for 1 and Common Good), launched Courtwatch NOLA. The program recruited more than a hundred citizen volunteers to monitor court proceedings. Carrying bright yellow clipboards, the volunteers cast watchful eyes and reported their findings to Courtwatch NOLA. As a result of their efforts, judicial efficiency was greatly improved, and subsequently. a new slate of judges was elected. Once again, the citizens of New Orleans implemented transparency and accountability.

Related to the challenges presented by violent crime and an ineffective criminal justice system was endemic public corruption. Too many politicians were feeding at the public trough, and the citizenry was fed-up. An invigorated US Attorney's Office under the leadership of Jim Letten, collaborating with a resource-enhanced local FBI office, led the effort to root out corruption. Local anticorruption organizations, such as the MCC (with support from the Business Council), began receiving a historically high number of citizen tips on corrupt actions by political officials. Through a review of national best practices, the business and civic community identified the need for the city to establish a robust Inspector General's (IG's) office. With support from the Business Council, Common Good organized a multi-racial coalition to coordinate the effort to establish an IG's office. A city council ordinance was passed laying the foundation for a public vote. In October 2008, New Orleanians voted overwhelmingly to establish an IG's office, whose main purpose is to investigate corruption in New Orleans and identify cost savings by eliminating waste, fraud, and abuse. The post-Katrina assault on public corruption culminated in 2013 with the conviction of Mayor Ray Nagin on bribery charges. The IG's office continues to carry out its mission.

Also on the agenda for reform was the city's dysfunctional and poorly performing K–12 public education system. The nationally recognized education reformer Leslie Jacobs, a member of the Business Council's executive committee and chair of its education task force, took the helm in advocating for significant change. Before Katrina, Leslie and the Business Council had supported the creation of the Recovery School District (RSD) through legislation and a constitutional amendment that provided the foundation for the state and RSD to take over and improve New Orleans' schools after Katrina. Several members of the Business Council volunteered and served on charter school boards. We were strong supporters of Teach For America and actively engaged in the state legislature to kill bills that were aimed at disrupting the charter reform movement.

Because the New Orleans school facilities, buildings, and campuses were also devastated by Katrina, the Federal Emergency Management Agency provided two billion dollars for rebuild and reinvestment. The Business Council, under task force chair Paul Flower, working with Leslie and her team, led the effort to ensure accountability, transparency, and tight oversight of the expenditure of funds. To ensure ongoing political support, we once again collaborated with the Urban League to form Forward New Orleans for Public Schools. Mandates were established to hold elected officials accountable to support charters, choice, and accountability. The tenacious effort has resulted in a dramatic turnaround and improvement for students and parents. By the end of 2019, 100 percent of public school students in New Orleans were attending charter schools. In 2004 (pre-Katrina), the high school graduation rate was 54 percent; in 2018, the graduation rate was 78 percent. In 2004, the college entry rate was 37 percent; in 2017, the rate was 61 percent. In 2005, 62 percent of New Orleans students attended Louisiana's lowest-performing schools; by the end of 2019, the figure was now down to 8 percent. New Orleans has become a national model in the education reform movement and is positively impacting the lives of students and their families.

As more and more major areas in need of reform were being addressed, it became clear that citizens, not politicians, would need to lead us to recovery. Broad coalitions that encompassed all segments of the community were needed to hold political officials accountable for their commitments, actions, and results and ensure political success. As a representative of the Business

Council executive committee, I met regularly at PJ's Coffee Shop with the Common Good leader Mike Cowan to organize a citizen coalition to attack the lack of public safely, lack of usable playgrounds, blighted properties, corrupt city contracting, poorly performing public schools, lack of business growth, significant budgetary deficits, and ineffective and unresponsive local government. We reached out to Citizens for 1 and the Urban League, then to more than twenty other civic, neighborhood, and business organizations, and in 2010, we launched Forward New Orleans. Since its founding, Forward New Orleans (FNO) has framed the debate in municipal elections by creating issue-based platforms guided by the basic tenants of good government: accountability, transparency, efficiency, and fiduciary responsibility. The coalition identifies the priority issues facing our city and develops a plan of well-researched action items for each issue. We then present the platform to candidates for elected office and seek written pledges of support. Before each election, FNO widely publishes a score card that shows each candidate's willingness, or lack thereof, to align on each issue.

After the election, the newly elected officials' pledges become mandates for action, effectively setting an agenda for the term. To hold officials accountable, FNO then publishes detailed reports that assess both progress and shortcomings on achieving platform objectives. Along the way, FNO members stand ready to help our local leaders translate the platform into successful action.

This coalition effort has had a tremendous, positive impact on critical quality-of-life issues facing the city from public safety to city finance, from economic opportunity to education, from blight reduction to improved city infrastructure. FNO continues building its community coalition, holding public officials accountable and positively impacting the lives of New Orleanians.

As reform and recovery took hold, the city and region had to create conditions that attracted new businesses to the area and an economic-development delivery organization to spearhead the effort. FNO had mandated a local New Orleans economic delivery organization, the New Orleans Business Alliance, into its platform, which was later adopted by Mayor Mitch Landrieu as a public-private partnership. For region-wide focus, Greater New Orleans, Inc. (GNO, Inc.) had hired Michael Hecht in June 2008 as its CEO. Since his hiring, Michael has led the successful effort to bring the devastated post-Katrina business and economic-development environment into a new realm of excellence and success unimaginable even in the years preceding Katrina. Conditions to improve the business climate were put into place through more competitive corporate tax policies and incentives, effective workforce training initiatives, and modernization of key assets, which helped lead to an economic renaissance for the region. Emerging industries, such as high-tech and digital media, and successful entrepreneurial start-ups were recruited to enhance the traditional foundational industries, such as energy, shipping, hospitality, and advance manufacturing. Young people poured into the region. Business Council members joined the GNO, Inc. board and actively supported its efforts.

When the NBA New Orleans Hornets (now Pelicans) announced in the fall of 2010 that they were leaving New Orleans at the end of their lease because ticket sales were falling short of the contractual benchmark, GNO, Inc. and the Business Council quickly formed the Hornets Business Council (HBC). The HBC worked closely with longtime civic and business leader Bill Hines, who had led the effort to secure the NBA franchise for New Orleans, and we used the model of the Saint's Business Council launched by the business leader Tommy Coleman in 2005 to keep the Saints in the region. The HBC rallied the business community and citizens and gobbled up enough tickets to deter the loss of the team. The effort was so successful that the Hornets sold more tickets per person than any other team in the NBA, leading Commissioner David Stern to go to other markets in North America and ask, "Why can't you perform more like New Orleans?" The Hornets were later purchased by Tom Benson, the local owner of the New Orleans Saints. The Pelicans continue to flourish in New Orleans to this day.

Recognizing the need for the region to have better global outreach and connectivity, Stephen Perry (CEO of New Orleans and Company and the leader in the post-Katrina resurgence of the city's vital hospitality sector), Iftakhar Ahmad (director of aviation at Louis Armstrong New Orleans International Airport), and Michael Hecht and I deployed shuttle diplomacy and positive passenger data to nab a direct regular flight by British Air from London to New Orleans, the first nonstop roundtrip flight to Europe for the region since 1982. British Air continues its regular nonstop, roundtrip service, which has had a major economic and tourist impact on the region.

The Greater New Orleans area won several awards for the favorable and friendly business conditions that can be directly attributed to a combination of strong executive and volunteer leadership. The area became number one for the decade for economic development wins in the South (*Southern Business and Development* magazine), number one for export growth in the United States (US Chamber of Commerce), and the fastest growing tech cluster in the United States (*Area Development* magazine). GNO, Inc. continues its incredible success. It was recently named the number two economic development organization in the United States (*Business Facilities* magazine) and continues to recruit and secure major national and global firms' investments, headquarters, and operations into the region.

New Orleans is a very different place than it was before Katrina. Since Katrina, the city has seen significant improvements in education, in the criminal justice system, and in neighborhoods through blight reduction and the reduction of violent crime. It has also seen economic and job growth, a renewed anti–public corruption vigor, and a vastly improved flood safety infrastructure and levee system.

But most important, a reinvigorated business community joined with civic and neighborhood organizations to rebuild and reform a beautiful and historic city. Post-Katrina recovery and reform demonstrated that a cohesive local community can take charge, lead, and succeed. Local political leaders who understand that collaborative business-citizen coalitions can be formidable forces, join the efforts, and succeed, while politicians who believe that the people work for them, fail. While the Katrina disaster was certainly not our best moment, the robust and vigorous business-citizen-led reform and recovery was historic, powerful, notable, and unique. After all, only one moment in recent New Orleans history matched the recovery effort and spirit: the New Orleans Saints Super Bowl victory in 2010. So, to all New Orleanians who toiled and recovered—WHO DAT!

Beacons of Hope: How Neighborhood Organizing Led Disaster Recovery

Denise Thornton

Denise Thornton is the founder and president of Beacon of Hope Resource Center, a grassroots, nonprofit organization created in the aftermath of Hurricane Katrina. Beacon of Hope assisted homeowners and businesses in navigating the complex issues associated with the restoration of their homes and communities by providing a blueprint for reconstruction that aided in the renaissance of twenty-five New Orleans neighborhoods.

After spending five days in the Superdome during Hurricane Katrina as a volunteer evacuee under horrific conditions, I vowed to do something more meaningful with my life if I got out safely.

On February 14, 2006, just six months after the storm, I opened my partially rebuilt home as a respite for my weary neighbors who were also facing decisions without information or government guidance. I formed a grassroots nonprofit organization and called it the Beacon of Hope. My home became a hub of activity and the heartbeat of the neighborhood. It was a place where neighbors could reconnect and get vital information that they would need to make informed decisions about their return.

I had no history of civic involvement or social activism. I was the kind of person who just wrote the check and relied on others to make sure that the homeless got fed and researchers looked for cures to the deadly diseases that plague our world.

I was initially stunned by the scope of the devastation, and I quickly realized that the damage was too vast and the pace of government action would be slow.

I simply didn't want to sit around and wait for someone else to come along and make it better.

Whatever progress we made was made by ordinary citizens, and that is a direct reflection of the resilience of neighbors who took ownership of their circumstance and the generosity of visiting volunteers, united in one cause. That cause was to reclaim the lives we had enjoyed before our city became paralyzed by catastrophic flooding and make them even better than they were before.

The goal of this article is to broaden the scope of reader's knowledge about New Orleans neighborhoods by describing our revitalization strategies and our common goals, which may be of value to civil society, business, and government leaders in other cities facing social and economic decay. Many have studied us, many have tried to blend into the colorful fabric of our society, but most fall short in truly understanding our rich and diverse culture and our remarkable social structure. This lack of understanding was detrimental to our recovery and is explained in the coming paragraphs.

I began this journey by providing a visual and realistic environment and a road map for others to follow. I remediated my own house, gutted to the studs, cleared all construction debris from the yard, installed sod, planted beautiful flowers, and painted over the big red "X" on the front door placed there by rescue workers. The façade of my house looked exactly as it did before the flood, and yet it was surrounded by devastation and mounds of debris as far as the eye could see. This powerful image gave rise to hope among my neighbors and showed that recovery was possible. Many residents had never managed a construction project and were simply paralyzed by the daunting task before them. My father was a master carpenter, so I grew up around construction. But since I was having difficulty, I knew my neighborhood would be doomed unless we joined forces to help each other. My feeling at the time was that everyone had something to offer and we would have to pool all of our resources to get this job done.

On February 14, 2006, I held a press conference and invited our city councilman, district police commander, postmaster, and homeowners association president. Also present to address residents' concerns were representatives from our local power company and our local internet provider, from the New Orleans Sewerage & Water Board, and from the Federal Emergency Management Agency and the Corps of Engineers.

And so we began:

- Serving hot meals six days a week
- Towing away flooded vehicles
- Providing internet access, land line telephones, and fax and copier machines
- Referring high-quality licensed, bonded, and insured contractors
- Hosting seminars on issues such as mold remediation and power restoration
- Hosting group meetings with the corps of engineers
- Hosting monthly block parties
- Organizing thousands of visiting volunteers to help clean vacant properties and gut homes
- Providing a tool-lending library for homeowners and volunteers
- Collecting and disseminating information about residents' intentions to rebuild
- Forming a block captain system
- Mapping the condition of each parcel of land in the neighborhood
- Providing free weekly legal assistance
- Providing help with submitting insurance claims
- Housing the offices for state employees to assist homeowners in completing applications for federal aid through the Road Home program
- Providing first aid
- Providing case workers to help residents qualify for other types of social services and grants

Word soon spread to nearby neighborhoods that help was available through this resource center in my home. We identified leaders who could implement this program and transform their neighborhoods in the next level of recovery. By the end of 2006, eight Beacon of Hope Resource Centers were established in nearby neighborhoods. By mid-year 2008, four more had been opened in the Gentilly area, for a total of twelve, and by 2011, twenty-five Beacon centers were providing services throughout the City of New Orleans.

Affiliate Beacon centers were also established in Cedar Rapids, Iowa, after the flooding in June 2008, and in Bridge City, Texas, in response to Hurricane Ike and in Laplace after Hurricane Isaac. In 2012 we opened the Beacon of Hope New York after Superstorm Sandy.

Beacon of Hope MODEL (Mapping, Outreach, Development, Education, Leadership)

Beacon of Hope develops neighborhoods by educating and empowering leaders to fight blight and work with various government agencies by mapping the conditions of each parcel of land in the neighborhood using a block captain system. Our outreach programs are designed to determine the needs of homeowners and the community at large.

Beacon of Hope provides a central location for all neighbors to gather, receive information, and obtain basic support. Once we determine the geographic boundaries of the neighborhood and select residents who will take responsibility for implementing the MODEL, we:

- Maintain and post hours of operation, including on at least one day of the weekend
- Designate a volunteer coordinator to organize volunteers and volunteer groups focused on cleaning and maintaining yards and public areas
- Create an advisory committee of individuals willing to assist and support the neighborhood's endeavor
- Designate an area to secure, store, and maintain lawn equipment for property owners and volunteer groups
- Support and nurture the Beacon of Hope MODEL within the geographical boundaries until the neighborhood becomes self-sustaining

The Beacon of Hope MODEL has many strengths. It mobilizes the residents in a very personal and individual way, making full use of their pre-existing social capital, and it nourishes the embodiment of each individual and unique neighborhood. Many of these residents have never served on a board of directors or a volunteer committee before. The MODEL teams engage in a constructive dialogue with local, state, and federal authorities that results in smoother and more efficient practices and governance. The MODEL is transferable to any neighborhood regardless of its demographics with respect to race or income level because the only requirement to light a Beacon is a handful of thoughtful, concerned citizens who want to make a difference in their community.

The *Beacon of Hope administrator* has a central role in the neighborhood. He or she:

- Works with the Beacon of Hope parent for support
- Works with and shares information with homeowners association presidents
- Implements a block captain system and identifies team leaders
- Maintains a page on the Beacon of Hope website and keeps current neighborhood information

- Meets regularly with all committees
- Disseminates information to all residents as reported by various committees
- Insures the highest standard in providing services and resources to the neighborhood

The *block captain lieutenant* maintains contact information on all block captains, works with the Beacon of Hope administrator and homeowners association presidents, and recruits block captains and assigns them to one or more teams. The *block captain* works with volunteer supervisors, identifying infrastructure needs and homeowner needs and disseminating information. Block captains assist the Beacon of Hope administrator and the homeowners association president and coordinate all teams. Each neighborhood is organized into eight teams.

- The *Survey Team* collects data quarterly and delivers it to the data information manager.
- The *Infrastructure Team* works independently of other teams to identify sewer or water leaks, nonfunctioning streetlights, streets in need of repair, and illegal dumping. This committee reports these issues to the appropriate city department and works with them to resolve these issues.
- The *Outreach Team* works with Beacon of Hope to identify homeowners in need of volunteer services and maintains a record of all homeowner work requests.
- The *Blight Team* works with the Beacon of Hope administrator, the homeowners association presidents, and the Survey Team to eradicate blight using information provided by the data information manager. Beacon of Hope provides quarterly condition maps.
- The *Crime Team* works closely with the New Orleans Police Department or crime prevention unit, keeping the Beacon of Hope administrator and homeowners association presidents apprised of safety concerns. Members of this team attend New Orleans Neighborhood Police Anti-Crime Council meetings and receive weekly Comstat maps and e-mail blasts from the police department on current criminal activity. The Crime Team is the neighborhood liaison for all safety matters. Through the block captain system, the team reports all suspicious activity and keeps the neighborhood informed about all alerts and activity.
- The *Quality of Life Team* is responsible for the well-being of the neighborhood. Its duties include planning block parties, administering the welcome basket program, holding fundraisers or soliciting donations, and organizing other social gatherings such as National Night Out Against Crime.
- The *Greenspace Team* works with the Beacon of Hope director of volunteers, the volunteer coordinator, the volunteer supervisor, the Beacon of Hope administrator and homeowners association presidents, and city agencies to identify public property in need of revitalization.
- The *New Orleans Redevelopment Authority (NORA) Team* works with the Beacon of Hope administrator and the homeowners association presidents to identify properties that are eligible for federal grants through the Road Home program, to record the conditions of those properties, and to solicit perspective buyers for the Lot Next Door 3.0 Program. The NORA Team is responsible for corresponding with the New Orleans Office of Recovery to research the buying process of the Lot Next Door program.

The *volunteer coordinator* works with the volunteer supervisor, the Beacon of Hope administrator, homeowners association residents, the Beacon of Hope director of volunteers, and the Outreach Team to determine the number of volunteers and the supplies and equipment needed to complete projects identified by these groups. The volunteer coordinator also monitors opportunities and maintains a record of visiting volunteers, waivers, and release forms and submits them to the Beacon of Hope director of volunteers to include in company stats for the purpose of providing outcomes to funders and to satisfy insurance requirements.

The *volunteer supervisor* works with the volunteer coordinator, the Beacon of Hope director of volunteers, and the Outreach Team and is responsible for supervising the volunteers in service and creating a safe environment for the volunteers to serve. He or she assembles the equipment, sets up the project, trains the volunteers on safety and equipment use, and works with block captains to supervise volunteer projects provided by the Outreach Team.

The *data information manager* must have computer capabilities with an emphasis on Excel spreadsheets because he or she is responsible for updating the master list of properties. All data collected is merged with other Beacon of Hope data for monitoring neighborhood repopulation, encouraging economic development, and eradicating blight. The data information manager also collects the information provided by the Survey Team, the Outreach Team, and the block captains into a master database and passes it to the Blight Committee, the Beacon of Hope administrator, and the homeowners association presidents. The data is then submitted to the Beacon of Hope parent for input in the master database in order to provide Beacon of Hope administrator, the Blight Team, and the Nora Team with quarterly condition maps.

Mapping: The Community Survey and Data Collection

The Beacon of Hope Resource Center developed a property condition survey that has been collected by residents on the parcel level. Beacon of Hope standardized the survey so that the City of New Orleans and community members receive the same training and collect neighborhood conditions data in the same format. This data tracks the progress of the neighborhood since Hurricanes Katrina and Rita (2005). To extend access of this data to neighborhood groups, the Beacon of Hope Resource Center created a centralized data file and a web-enabled repository, Smart Tech. The data viewer allows residents to view prior survey results and, with a secure log-in, to update survey data from remote locations. Typically the frequency of the community survey is based on a three-month cycle.

Figure 1. Individual neighborhoods within the Gentilly area
of New Orleans included in the web-based GIS pilot program

Public Participation Geographic Information Systems and Mapping

Beacon of Hope ran a pilot program that used desktop geographic information systems (GIS) technology, then continued with a three-tier program. The Smart Tech web-based community interactive data and mapping system used an internet mapping service (IMS).

ArcGIS9.2 and NeoGeography were introduced to expand the existing mapping and analysis. Data from the IMS was exported into the ArcGIS9.2 system to create a base map and to update the original map series. This project was undertaken to organize, support, and document the creation of a Beacon of Hope GIS that allows flexibility in data collection, maintenance, mapping, and analysis. An important aspect of the project is the capability for residents and other community-based organizations to learn how to create and maintain the data with, or without, direct assistance from Beacon of Hope staff. Additional online documents are available to support the training and site maintenance.

Hurricane Katrina did not discriminate. It cut across all social and economic boundaries. For twenty-one days, 80 percent of our entire city remained under water, collapsing our infrastructure.

Fifteen years later, that destruction remains a problem. Katrina also displaced residents, some of whom were never able to return to their homes.

Many of the volunteers who came from all across the United States had never heard of our neighborhoods. But when the national media began reporting extensively about the devastation caused by Katrina, citing, in particular the 9th Ward, "9th Ward" became, according to the *Times-Picayune,* "an international buzzword," and volunteers expressed disappointment when they were not sent there. The "9th Ward" as it appears in national media, in scholarly works, and in public discourses does not encompass the actual geographic area that is administratively the 9th Ward of New Orleans. Neither does it correspond to a planning district or to a neighborhood. It has come to represent all New Orleans neighborhoods after the flood, a phenomenon that was detrimental to the people of New Orleans.

For example, Pontchartrain Park, in the Gentilly neighborhood, like the 9th Ward, was 97 percent African American before the flood. Before Katrina, less than 10 percent of the population of the 9th Ward was living under the poverty level, but the entire neighborhood flooded, and once the flood waters receded, more than 81 percent of the homes in this neighborhood were uninhabitable. Because of New Orleans' complex racial history, a large population of middle-class and upper middle-class African Americans lived in Gentilly, Broadmoor, and New Orleans East, well outside the geographic boundaries of the 9th Ward. This could be the one category of population that was the most affected by Hurricane Katrina.

Paradoxically, the disproportionate investment of public attention on the 9th Ward to the exclusion of all other neighborhood volunteers hindered our recovery. The truth is that approximately half of the neighborhoods that flooded were racially mixed and populated by middle-class and upper middle-class people. Many of those living in the suburbs of Gentilly and New Orleans East moved there after World War II and are now elderly and living on fixed incomes.

Widely Shared View

This selective but distorted representation of New Orleans in the country's collective consciousness bred frustration in the neighborhoods that received less national attention, aggravating the breaches that already existed within the city's diverse population and thus endangering the sustainability and recovery of the entire city as a whole. The neighborhood leaders of the diverse neighborhoods of the "9th Ward" I'm sure will agree that these depictions were often inaccurate and perhaps hindered their recovery as well.

As we rebuilt in these areas under the radar of some public awareness and often without the help of the many nonprofits that "flooded" New Orleans after the storm, we took our situation as an opportunity to develop new strategies to mobilize our best asset in the recovery: the citizens of our neighborhoods themselves.

The relief provided by the dozens of nonprofits that descended on New Orleans neighborhoods was temporary and therefore unsustainable. Many of the nonprofits seemed to be unaware of the civic organizations that existed before they arrived, and so their actions and strategies were rarely embedded in the civic structures of the neighborhoods where they worked. Also, the visions these nonprofits developed for the neighborhoods where they worked rarely coincided with the visions the neighborhood residents held. The result was often confusion and frustration. Furthermore, competition for funding and attention made collaboration between the dozens of nonprofits present in these neighborhoods almost impossible. The fading national attention on New Orleans and the economic crisis that followed Katrina rendered the fate of these resources even more uncertain. The nonprofits' "fix-it" approach unsupported by in-depth knowledge about how local leaders can organize and empower their own community was effective in treating the symptoms of our neighborhoods' decay, but it did not heal the community or promote sustainability. It created dependency rather than self-sufficiency in these neighborhoods. More important, it portrayed New Orleans's residents as victims and failed to acknowledge the formidable effort of its citizens to engage in and improve their community. In contrast, the Beacon of Hope MODEL worked, and it was sustainable.

The Beacon of Hope MODEL made us stronger as individuals and as community partners, and it united us in our common goals. One should never underestimate the power of the people, the tenacity of the human spirit for its survival.

Conclusion

The Beacon of Hope MODEL empowered residents all over the city, helping them learn new skills and develop strategies to tackle issues that had existed before the storm but were worsened by it. Many of these residents have become leaders and public servants in city government. One is on the city council and another is now our mayor.

As we shifted from a recovery mindset to one focused on addressing typical urban issues of neighborhood revitalization and sustainability, we insured our future by engaging people and empowering them to become self-sufficient and take ownership of their circumstances so that our neighborhoods will still be viable when national attention wanes, recovery funds are depleted, nonprofits lose interest, and our volunteer base ceases.

Since its inception, Beacon of Hope has hosted more than thirty-five thousand visiting volunteers, representing more $3.1 million in services rendered, completed more than twenty-three hundred homeowner projects, replanted twenty square miles of green space, restored eight parks and playgrounds, and created a monthly outdoor festival that continues to this day.

Wise words by Margaret Mead helped define our mission and inspired us every day: "Never doubt that a small group of thoughtful committed citizens can change the world; indeed it's the only thing that ever has." Beacon of Hope served a dual purpose. We created a symbiotic relationship between homeowners and volunteers to assist homeowners in their recovery and to provide a meaningful experience for the volunteers.

As neighborhoods became self-reliant, the Beacon of Hope teams formed new homeowners associations in the areas that had previously had none. The Beacon of Hope MODEL still exists but is now being implemented by the homeowners associations. Currently, we consult with neighborhood leaders and government officials who are in need of a proven model for recovery.

It is my hope that this article offers a blueprint for neighborhood organizations recovering from natural disasters.

Across Racial Lines: Three Accounts of Transforming a City after a Natural Disaster

James Carter[1]
Nolan Rollins[2]
Gregory Rusovich[3]

James[1] Carter was elected to the New Orleans City Council in 2006, following Hurricane Katrina. He served as chair of its criminal justice committee. He was later appointed by the mayor as criminal justice commissioner of the City of New Orleans. He is a managing partner of James Carter and Associates.

[2]Nolan Rollins is a former president and CEO of the Urban League of Greater New Orleans. He was appointed chair of the New Orleans Aviation Board.

[3]Gregory Rusovich served as board chair of the Business Council of New Orleans and the River Region, the New Orleans Police and Justice Foundation, the New Orleans Crime Coalition, the Board of Commissioners of the Port of New Orleans, GNO, Inc., and New Orleans and Company. He created (with Michael A. Cowan) Forward New Orleans, a citizen-driven process of holding elected officials publicly accountable for keeping their campaign promises. He is now board chair of the Metropolitan Crime Commission.

At 1:30 p.m. on August 29, 2005, Hurricane Katrina grazed the mostly evacuated city of New Orleans, reserving its most devastating force for coastal Mississippi, just to the east. During the next two days, the federal levees protecting the city failed in multiple places. Eighteen hundred people died in the metropolitan area. Residences and businesses in 80 percent of the city went underwater. Public officials warned residents and business owners that they might not be able to return for two to three months. The scope of devastation in certain parts of the city made ever returning questionable for many residents. Grievous failures of coordination among local, state, and federal governments exacerbated the collective misery, adding general confusion and uncertainty about the city's very future to deep personal anxieties about homes, jobs, schools, and neighborhoods.

What follows are accounts of the post-Katrina transformation of New Orleans by three of its leaders. None had met before these events but became trusted allies and later friends in the crucible of the events they describe. James Carter recounts the creation of an office of independent police monitor to address a longstanding history of racial bias and brutality. Nolan Rollins offers an account of how the governance of a major economic organization was transformed for the benefit of the whole city. And Gregory Rusovich explains the role of diverse, action-oriented coalitions in addressing a range of key issues, including criminal justice reforms and holding elected officials accountable for campaign promises.

A unique piece of the historical background to this article is that each of the authors was the key leader in the public work he describes but also active in supporting the work described and led by each of the other authors. Events brought these authors these events together; they met in the public arena. This is a story of collective leadership that built bridges across the racial divide in the rebuilding of an historic American city after a catastrophic event.

Transforming Policing
James Carter

Early in life I recognized the misery associated with inequities. As an African American male growing up in urban New Orleans, I was consciously and unconsciously aware of the adverse circumstances surrounding me. The African American neighborhood where I lived flooded whenever there was very heavy rainfall, while the predominantly white neighborhood a few blocks away did not. A trash incinerator in my neighborhood bellowed out unpleasant odors, and, while I was off in college, a train leaked toxic chemicals and burst into flames on railroad tracks close to my parents' home.

At the same time that I was experiencing challenges laced with issues of race and class, I was blessed with a strong and principled upbringing. My father, James Carter, Jr., instilled in me the virtues of hard work, discipline, determination, and dedication. I also observed him develop strong cross-racial relationships. My mother, Mildred Carter, brilliantly orchestrated my positive self-image, intellectualism, and resistance to oppression. Both of my parents exhibited kindness to the elderly, generosity to the less fortunate, and remarkable self-determination. Moreover, they fought against injustice in their own ways. Like Oprah Winfrey, I was taught "excellence is the best deterrent to racism." Because of my parents' profound influence, all three of my siblings, like me, are college graduates who have been a tremendous source of encouragement to me in my life's journey. Another monumental figure in my formative years was my grandfather, William Thomas Sr. This spiritual giant lived to be 103 years old and was the bedrock of our family.

Though I attended predominantly African American elementary, middle, and high schools, for half day every week throughout my high school years I also attended New Orleans Center for the Creative Arts, a racially diverse artistic environment that further opened my mind and expanded my worldview. In addition to the many extraordinary black educators who taught me, there were some white teachers who touched me in profound ways along my educational journey.

African American males in New Orleans have regularly experienced an adversarial relationship with law enforcement. I, however, did not develop apprehension toward law enforcement until I was in my teenage years. Before that time, I had a completely positive attitude toward the police. I attribute that attitude to two very distinct experiences in my life: the Officer Friendly Program and my dad's friend Officer Joe. The Officer Friendly program was designed to build positive community relations by having New Orleans Police Department officers visit schools and develop a rapport with the students. The officer who was sent to our predominately African American school was always a white man. More important, he was consistently kind and personable, and I looked forward to his visits. My dad's friend, Officer Joe, was an African American man who visited us when I was very young. He always wore a beautifully neat and clean police uniform. He was professional, well groomed, in good physical condition, and he wore a big smile. Later, however, in my formative years, I began to hear stories about negative experiences between the African American community and law enforcement that caused me to develop apprehensions that live in me to this day.

Filled with a desire to fight for humanitarian causes, I was blessed with the opportunity to graduate from Howard University as a philosophy and theater student and from the Howard University School of Law. During my time in law school, I was exposed to the thinking of some of the greatest legal minds in U.S. history, including Pauline Murray, A. P. Tureaud, Spotswood Robinson, Thurgood Marshall, J. Clay Smith, Jack Olender, and many others. I firmly embraced the words of the great former dean of Howard Law, Charles Hamilton Houston, who said a "lawyer is either a social engineer or a parasite on society." Moreover, while in law school, I received life-changing support from remarkable people such as Reginald Robinson, Annette Mixon-Burkeen, and Melissa Woods-Barthelemy. I left Howard University School of Law with an understanding of the importance of mastering the Constitution and applying its time-honored principles in the court system and returned to New Orleans filled with hope that I could change the world in which I had grown up. The timeless message that I had a responsibility to use my education to affect the world positively was simply another version of the teachings ingrained in me by my sage mentor Yolande Dillon.

Armed with a freshly minted juris doctor degree, I was given the opportunity to pursue community advocacy in 1997 when the city administration appointed me the first director of the New Orleans iteration of the nationally acclaimed United States Department of Justice "Weed and Seed" initiative. In 2001, I served as a staff trial counsel for the Orleans Indigent Defenders Program. That experience allowed me to see firsthand the very worst consequences of racial discrimination, economic deprivation, broken families, poor education, and the failure to take self-responsibility. I also developed my skills as a jury trial attorney.

After the devastation of Hurricane Katrina, with the blessings of my wife, Rene, and our three-year-old son, Brice, I chose to take an active part in the rebuilding of my beloved community and city. In 2006 I was elected to the first New Orleans City Council seated after the storm. The council district I served was the most diverse and eclectic in the city and included the world-famous French Quarter. From 2006 to 2010, I served as chair of the newly created Criminal Justice Committee by appointment of council president Oliver Thomas. Post-Katrina New Orleans was ripe for change, and there was a spirit of reform in the air. For the first time in the city's history, the city council enacted laws that created the Office of Inspector General (OIG). It was a historic moment in city council chambers when the ordinance passed, and it would not have passed without the support of the African American city council members.

Following the establishment of the OIG, in 2007–2008, I played the lead legislative role in establishing the first independent police monitor (IPM) to fight police brutality and misconduct. Though it was my desire to create a stand-alone IPM, the politics at that time would not permit me to do so. Seeing the mighty wave of support for the OIG, I strategically used it to establish the IPM as a division of the OIG. The original impetus for creating the IPM did not come from me.

In response to a history of police-brutality in New Orleans and many years prior to my efforts, great community leaders and fearlessly courageous activists worked tirelessly to create a credible layer of protection for citizens against police misconduct through an oversight body outside the police department.

I found myself entwined in what appeared to be an unwinnable dynamic. How could I get interracial support for a matter that seemed to be an exclusively African American problem? Unlike some in the black community, I had not been conditioned by my upbringing to have a total distrust for white people, though my upbringing did feed my apprehension. I was a realist, however, and initially not confident that I would get the support needed from my white colleagues on the city council to pass this important governmental safeguard into law. The city council was majority white at the time, and I was leading the legislative charge for the IPM. My predicament brought to mind the words of Atticus Finch, protagonist of the classic *To Kill a Mockingbird*: "Real courage is when you know you're licked before you begin, but you begin anyway and see it through no matter what." I did not know that I would be licked, but I felt it was a strong possibility. I began anyway, prepared to see it through.

I was ready to make an attempt to get the IPM legislation passed in the midst of personal uncertainty born, on one hand, of historically based racial assumptions and, on the other, of belief in the universal goodness of all human beings. What I found was amazing. As I did more research on the issues regarding police brutality and maltreatment to the citizens of New Orleans, I encountered some interesting and unexpected realities. Though not to the same degree as African Americans, a sizable segment of white citizens had experienced unprofessional and hostile treatment from the New Orleans Police Department. More important, a determined portion of the white community supported the IPM simply because it was the right thing to do. These were facts that many African Americans did not generally know because the African American community had good reason to believe it was targeted by rogue elements of the New Orleans Police Department. It was as if there were a conspiracy to keep that knowledge from one part of our great city to further divide our common experiences along fictional racial lines.

A lesson revealed during the development of the New Orleans IPM was so powerful that I believe it is instructive for a broader segment of humankind. It offers a modicum of hope for a world grappling with the albatross of sometimes imaginary but often real racial divisions. I found that when one is sincere and willing to put one's best self forward to work hard in pursuit of higher ideals, similarly motivated people from various racial, gender, class, and ethnic groups will on occasion provide robust support. This is not a wishful thought or regurgitated cliché. I saw it happen while an interracial partnership was creating the IPM. Comfort is truly the enemy of progress. I stepped out of my comfort zone and hit a jackpot of multi-racial support. I ultimately received solid support from the black as well as the white council members.

After the IPM and OIG were established by city ordinance, with the former as a division of the latter, a move was made to place the OIG into the city charter and grant it a dedicated annual budget of 0.75 percent of the city's annual general fund. This was a critical juncture, because those who had worked tirelessly for the establishment of the two offices understood that unless they were protected by the charter, a future mayor or council could simply slash their funding. The city charter is its constitution; its ordinances may not contradict the charter. Amending the city charter requires a majority vote, first by the city council and then by the citizenry. Placement of the IPM within the OIG meant that it would have charter protection as well. This proposal was also well received cross racially. A multi-racial campaign led by Michael Cowan of Common Good and Norris Henderson of VOTE (Voice of the Ex-Offender) played a key role in garnering multilevel support and a strong majority vote for the charter change. Other civil society leaders, including the New Orleans Business Council, also embraced the charter proposition.

The establishment of the IPM was visionary. It was done before the most recent onslaught of media coverage of all-too-frequent officer-involved shootings of African American men. It was created in an honorable manner that did not indiscriminately vilify all police officers. A commendation section placed in the IPM was designed to recognize the vast majority of police officers who daily uphold the law to the highest possible standards. New Orleans may be the only city in the United States to have a charter-mandated OIG and IPM, with budgets protected from political interference. The formation of the IPM is not a panacea for all problems of police brutality and misconduct in New Orleans or the sickening curse of racism. But it is a sign of progress and offers hope to all citizens who, under the US Constitution, are entitled to just treatment from law enforcement. It was done with tremendous multiracial support that I received after I stepped out in the faith that the moral forces of the universe would prevail.

Recovering a Vital Public Asset for the Benefit of All
Nolan Rollins

An intractable problem that limits and damages human development requires that change makers identify it as a problem for everyone to solve and to agree that regardless of station in life or personal impact on them, they are responsible for its resolution for humanity's sake. As a collective from New Orleans, the authors have been asked to shed light on how, after one of the most devastating man-made disasters in U.S. history, a group of individuals varying in age, race, life experience, and socioeconomics can come together to tackle the challenge of working across racial lines to rebuild a city?

While some would argue that the devastation wrought by Hurricane Katrina created the problems that existed when our collective began its journey, I would argue that the devastation exacerbated and brought to the surface the historically inequitable system that masked the differences between the haves and the have-nots, which generally followed racial lines. This division cut across the cultural traditions that seemingly connect the entire city in a tapestry of cultural equality. When closely observed, however, that tapestry revealed differences in quality based on resources that ran plentifully in socially and economically connected networks.

With the tapestry metaphor as a backdrop, the critical question is, How does one work in a city so highly divided by race and class to build a more inclusive environment, where the content of character, competence, and work ethic, not skin color, social network, political circles, and zip codes are the determinants for accessing the American Dream?

As a transplant to New Orleans from the similarly struggling city of Baltimore, I saw that the very basic protections for humanity during this time of tragedy must begin with those public institutions that are constitutionally required to provide equitable access to publicly controlled opportunity. Soon after I relocated to New Orleans to rebuild the Urban League of Greater New

Orleans, a historic civil rights organization in a post-Katrina environment, it became clear to me that the city's major economic industry was the public sector and that I needed to focus my efforts through a civil rights lens on public economic access and accommodations. That focus would be key to fighting for everyday New Orleanians to have access to the basic necessities of life. At the core of the city's rebuilding were a few principles that had to be worked on across all past lines of separation: education, criminal justice, economic opportunity, and public sector transparency.

To show what it takes to successfully rebuild a city after a modern-day disaster, the four authors of this article have been asked to focus on a subset of our key efforts to work across racial lines to change divisions of the past into allies for a brighter future. Again, as a transplant, I found myself fortunate to be included in some of the most critical rebuilding circles throughout the city, whether it was playing a significant role in the reimagining of the New Orleans educational system so that there was high quality and access for all regardless of zip code, tackling the crime problem in New Orleans to include serving as a co-chair for the search for the police chief, and membership in critical private sector institutions such as the New Orleans Business Council working on issues that impacted the whole city. I accepted an appointment by New Orleans mayor Mitch Landrieu as the chair of the New Orleans Airport Authority, which was perhaps my most challenging role. My primary responsibility was to regain the public's support and trust after a long period of self-dealing and corruption by appointed officials and staff, by demanding a more transparent way of doing business and delivering a high-quality public service. Highlighting our work at the airport allows me to drive home in a very specific way how working across racial lines can achieve outcomes never imagined before.

The New Orleans International Airport is not just a transportation mechanism but also a critically impactful economic development tool for the City of New Orleans and the surrounding counties. It provides thousands of jobs, directly and indirectly through such ancillary services as taxis, hotel, and ride-sharing. What we realized was that historically, regardless of whether those who held political power were white or black, political patronage had been used as a weapon to bolster the social and exclusive networks of those in power. Furthermore, in the highly charged and racially divided city of New Orleans, the skin color of the powerful had been used as a blunt object against others. In the post-Katrina environment, where the devastation affected all, if we were going to rebuild public institutions, it became critically important that all New Orleanians see themselves as having a voice in the solution process rather than feeling it was constructed for someone else's benefit. When the mayor asked me to chair the board of directors of the New Orleans International Airport, I made clear that, because of my other role as the president and CEO of a historic civil rights organization, I would want to ensure that economic opportunity for all would be the philosophical foundation for our rebuilding process and policy. With this agreement in hand, I determined that the primary purpose of my job was to identify all the issues and things wrong at the airport and to identify the allies I would need to make the necessary changes while also providing opportunity for all.

The New Orleans International Airport serves more than eleven million people a year. But at the time when I became chair it had more than a hundred contracts that had not been rebid and or updated in many years. It had wasted operational expenditures in a manner that had unnecessarily impacted its budget. It faced a public perception of being rife with fraud and corruption. Finally, there was no overall vision for the future of one of the most important public assets in the state of Louisiana. Against this backdrop, my job was to connect with people who looked like me and people who did not, in an effort to bring solutions after a time of great chaos and devastation. A catastrophe such as the one in New Orleans soon blurs the lines of race because almost all citizens suffer equally the pain of losing their house, their business, their school, and their roads. There is no more ideal time to work across racial lines than when disaster falls across all past lines of division. As I began to identify allies to work with me to change the reality and the perception of the airport, I insisted that those around the table acknowledge that we had a problem in New Orleans of race and class and that for New Orleans to be what it aspires to be there must be a common goal of equal access for all who are willing to work for it.

To achieve the goal of bringing along a group to which you do not belong, it is critical to find like-minded individuals who can carry a message in their communities in ways that you as a race or class outsider cannot. Thus, I sought to develop relationships with the largely white business class and the largely black political class in New Orleans and to make clear to each group how important it was for us all to work together to create a thriving airport with a mission focused on operational excellence and economic inclusion. I knew I had to make a clear argument to the white business class about the importance of economic inclusion as we began the work to rid ourselves of corruption and operational inefficiencies at the airport. White business leaders, among others, understood the imperative not only of talking about race and economics but of accepting the past with a forward-looking perspective on what a more inclusive New Orleans might look like. As we continued to develop our relationships, these leaders talked with their networks in the white community about the concept of a forward-looking perspective, and I talked with my networks in the African American community about the challenges identified by the white community. We ended up agreeing that blaming the actors of the past regardless of color was an exercise in futility but deciding how to rebuild in an inclusive manner was an imperative for the future of all. This operating protocol allowed me to make bold moves at the airport, including forging an agreement with the Inspector General's Office that provided them office space at the airport to monitor operations consistently and allowed me to advise them about how best to position the airport to be a responsive public entity. Thus we were able to develop an economic inclusion policy that insured minority business opportunity and overhauled the operations of the airport so that transparency and the elimination of deficiencies were focal points. In doing so, we restored the public's confidence in the airport's ability to represent New Orleans as its optical gateway and as a public entity that operates with integrity.

While these changes may seem only loosely connected to race, I believe that without our being honest about past exclusions based on social networks and political power, none of the transformations described here would have been possible. But for reasonable white folks and black folks in New Orleans joining together in owning the past and, more important, designing a collective future, we would never have seen the transition of a public entity well-known as a bastion of patronage politics into a place where all New Orleanians can see themselves in its success.

Holding Elected Officials Accountable for Campaign Promises
Gregory Rusovich

The devastating aftermath of Katrina left one of the world's unique cities in peril. The physical infrastructure was severely damaged, the city's capacity to deliver basic services to its people was badly flawed, and the primary political leadership stoked racial tensions and neglected basic responsibilities. This abysmal neglect by the city's political leaders sparked a robust response by civic, business, and community leaders, and some emerging reform-minded elected officials, who successfully organized a dynamic, citizen-led recovery. This group of leaders refused to accept failure and racial discord.

As the longstanding CEO of my family-owned shipping company based in New Orleans, I decided that a renewed focus on helping to save my beloved community was imperative. It was clear that success was attainable and sustainable only through the building of organized diverse coalitions. Building the coalitions was difficult but exhilarating. We were able to rally a strong multiracial group of leaders and develop a laser focus on practical solutions to urgent community needs. We had vibrant discussions about whether the coalitions needed to review, assess, and tackle the topic of racism and historic prejudices before coming together on the issue of critical community needs with a dedication to immediately improving the quality of life for the citizens of New Orleans. Rallying around a shared set of principles and solutions became a far more effective and satisfying path. I was honored to be appointed chair of the Business Council of New Orleans, which provided a major post-Katrina platform by which to bring together civic, business, and community leaders to make decisions that would positively and significantly affect the present and future of our community.

Because crime had become the most serious threat in the aftermath of Katrina, we also developed the New Orleans Crime Coalition, for which I served as founding chair. The coalition was made up of a diverse group of organizations established on a set of clear public safety requirements to demand that the streets of New Orleans become safer. The coalition, consisting of twenty leading crime-fighting business and civic organizations, focused on identifying and implementing best practices required across the entire local criminal justice system by consistently and respectfully engaging political and criminal justice officials in partnerships to address key improvements required to protect the citizenry.

The New Orleans Crime Coalition has greatly improved the collaboration among key components of the criminal justice system. For example, before and immediately after Katrina, there was very little cooperation between the New Orleans Police Department and the district attorney's office. But now, because of relentless civic efforts and the appointment of a new police chief and the election of a strong district attorney (DA), the relationship between these two key criminal justice agencies is described by their respective leaders as optimal. Before and after Katrina, by needlessly arresting thousands of minor offenders, we were taking police resources away from efforts to focus on violent criminals. We have made tremendous strides in changing our focus to making felony arrests, and the DA's acceptance and conviction rates are the highest in decades.

I also became chair of the Forward New Orleans coalition, which consists of twenty-five of the leading civic and business organizations in the city. The coalition compiled a set of principles that include integrity, transparency, effectiveness, accountability, and fiduciary responsibility. Guided by these principles, we looked at national best practices and performance metrics and developed a set of solutions and mandates for the city's political leadership to address and fix immediately. Our mandates were included in a platform that addressed urgent quality-of-life issues—crime, blight, education, city services, infrastructure, city contracting, and economic development. Through the coalition's platform, New Orleans citizens demanded safer streets, improved education, enhanced infrastructure, integrity in contracts, and an end to rampant public corruption. A set of mandated actions was compiled for each central issue and presented in individual meetings with all mayoral and city council candidates. Each candidate was asked to sign a document indicating support for all or some of the mandates, with a promise that the coalition would publish the commitments each council member made before the election and hold those elected accountable through regular reports to the public.

Now, almost ten years later, the Forward New Orleans coalition is stronger than ever—publicly presenting a set of issue-oriented mandates to those running for local political office, seeking their public pledge to our platform, and subsequently issuing ongoing reports that objectively track whether pledges are being honored. We have just entered our third four-year cycle of extracting promises from would-be office holders and holding them accountable for their actions. This citizen-led involvement in local elections is the most sustained such effort in the three-hundred-year history of New Orleans.

These vibrant, action-oriented, diverse coalitions brought dramatic change and helped lead to a better functioning city. Their success demonstrates that results can be achieved and trust gained when citizens act together on matters of common interest and agreement. The coalitions' strategic effectiveness also demonstrated that the chances of success are far greater when groups focus on issues that affect local quality of life, matters of shared concern, rather than debating and agonizing over old wounds, which is typically counterproductive and does not lead to tangible positive results.

Even more important for me than having been a part of building a better city has been the life lessons and wonderful friendships that nourished in these coalitions. Reaching across race and class lines to others with radically different life experiences has had a great impact on my ability to listen, learn, and better appreciate others. We built trust and friendships by working together as one team to achieve our shared goal of helping our beloved community and neighbors. These friendships will last forever.

Concluding Remarks

On the day before Katrina, no civic, business, or government leader in New Orleans was imagining possibilities such as an IPM, an inspector general, a reformed airport commission, or a diverse group of citizens holding candidates for public office accountable for campaign promises. The fuller answer, like the fabric of a city three hundred years old, is more complex. It has two parts. First, Hurricane Katrina upended the status quo abruptly and without warning, creating a vacuum that allowed possibilities for change to emerge that had not existed before the storm. The opportunities of that moment could have been used for good or ill or simply neglected. Second, that vacuum was filled mainly by civic, business, and government leaders who worked across racial lines not to replace the city that had been there but to transform it for the common good by enhancing community/police relations, challenging waste and corruption, creating a more inclusive and growing economy, and reducing racial tensions. We strove boldly for a new New Orleans, not a wishful cliché but a transformed city. Katrina made such changes possible; to realize those changes, the leaders whose accounts appear here, and many more with similar convictions, together built a bridge across racial lines in a time of profound disruption, dislocation, and suffering.

Transforming City Institutions

Legal Origins and Evolution of Local Ethics Reform in New Orleans

David A. Marcello

David A. Marcello crafted the original Home Rule Charter amendments that led to the establishment of the Ethics Review Board and the Office of Inspector General. He currently serves as executive director of The Public Law Center at Tulane Law School, which provides clinical legal instruction in legislative and administrative advocacy.

The Office of Inspector General came first, and like many another reform in city government, it was born as a campaign commitment. When I met with state senator Marc H. Morial in September 1993 to discuss the issues component of his campaign for mayor, ideas poured out of him for an hour and a half, and I took copious notes. "We need an Inspector General," he said, "and we need Charter Revision"—the two ideas linked from this first campaign convening. When he was elected mayor six months later and inaugurated in May 1994, charter reform became an early and important item of business in his new administration.[1]

This article focuses in Part 1 on the 1994–1995 charter revision process that was the initial vehicle for local ethics reform. Part 2 examines the stuttering, stop-and-go history of implementation after the successful charter revision process—a period during which enactment of formal legal instruments was followed by halting implementation steps, accompanied throughout by the need for further legal instruments to reform and restructure ethics entities. Part 3 draws some considered conclusions, taking a long perspective on the evolution of local ethics reforms.

Part 1. Home Rule Charter Revision: 1994–1995

Mayor Morial made charter revision a centerpiece of his August 1994 State of the City address: "In the second of our centerpieces, I will by executive order reinvigorate the city charter process. . . . Other efforts to revise the charter have failed. We will not fail this time."[2] A year after our September 1993 campaign meeting, I was back in a meeting with Marc Morial—this time, as the mayor—again taking notes as he shared his vision of needed Home Rule Charter reforms. He promptly followed through by naming a Charter Revision Advisory Committee in October 1994 and appointed me as its chair.[3]

History of Home Rule Charter Reform in New Orleans

The city's home rule authority derives from the Louisiana Constitution of 1921 as continued in force by the 1974 Constitution.[4] The city's first Home Rule Charter, written and adopted during the administration of Mayor de Lesseps S. "Chep" Morrison, took effect on January 1, 1954, and continued in operation with very few amendments for more than four decades after its adoption.

Each of Marc Morial's three predecessors as mayor attempted charter revision, and each attempt failed.[5] Mayor Moon Landrieu appointed a charter committee in 1975, but its proposed revisions never reached the ballot.[6] Mayor Ernest N. "Dutch" Morial (Marc Morial's father) attempted twice to amend the charter in order to extend the mayor's term in office beyond the two-term limit; his proposals were twice rejected by the voters.[7] Mayor Sidney Barthelemy appointed a charter committee in 1991; its report went to the voters on October 16, 1993 (within the last year of his term), as four separate ballot propositions, each of which the voters rejected.[8]

These earlier charter revision efforts failed for various reasons. All of the previous mayors who fell short left charter revision until late in their terms. Some of these charter revision efforts dragged out over several years. In addition, some charter initiatives acquired suspect "political" overtones. And in one instance, dividing the charter into multiple propositions likely contributed to voter confusion and dissatisfaction.

Marc Morial sought to avoid many of these problems in his charter revision effort. He appointed the Charter Revision Advisory Committee within six months after his inauguration as mayor and charged the committee to accomplish its work within a very tight timetable, setting a deadline of December 15 for the committee's draft of proposed charter revisions. He asked the committee to avoid some "hot button" issues that voters might perceive as politically controversial (e.g., advising the committee "not to tamper with the basic framework of the mayor-council form of government that was instituted in 1954 or with the two-term limits on the mayor or City Council members").[9] And significantly, the committee presented its recommendations as a single set of proposed revisions, not fragmented among several different subject areas.

The Morial charter revision process benefited from the work of civic and business organizations that had identified their own priorities for charter reform, including the League of Women Voters of New Orleans and the New Orleans Business Council.[10] These earlier charter revision proposals all sounded the same theme: a need for greater flexibility in government.[11] The problem resided in the 1954 Home Rule Charter's inflexible enumeration of executive branch offices, departments, boards, and commissions.[12] Any modification of this organizational structure could be accomplished only through voter approval in a citywide election.[13] Because the 1954 charter made it difficult to reorganize or consolidate existing city agencies or to establish any new city agencies, many functions that were not part of city government in the 1950s (e.g., transit administration, minority business development, environmental affairs) were created as "divisions" within the Mayor's Office—an inadequate patchwork of ad hoc responses to rapidly changing political circumstances during the 1960s, 1970s, and 1980s.

Overview of Charter Revision Advisory Committee Meetings

The Charter Revision Advisory Committee that convened at Gallier Hall in October 1994 was far different from the 1951 charter committee that produced the 1954 Home Rule Charter. The Morial committee was larger, consisting of thirty-eight members as contrasted with twelve on the 1951 committee. The Morial committee also exhibited greater gender and racial diversity[14]; the 1951 committee was all white and had only one female member.[15]

In his charge to the committee, Mayor Morial identified several aspects of the current Home Rule Charter that he thought should be left unchanged, including the basic mayor-council form of government, the two-term limit for mayor and council members, the prohibition on road-use or real-property service charges without a vote of the people, and the "one casino" provision. He also identified several innovations and charter reforms that he hoped the committee would consider, singling out the inspector general as one of his campaign pledges. Like earlier mayors and students of charter revision, he emphasized the need for greater flexibility in reorganizing city government. He called upon the committee to include a bill of rights in the Home Rule Charter.[16] Mayor Morial also directed the committee to conduct its business in compliance with the open meetings[17] and public records[18] laws.

Charter revision took place in three significant phases. In Phase I, the committee reviewed and suggested proposed revisions to the 1954 Home Rule Charter, beginning at meetings in October 1994 and concluding with its delivery of proposed revisions to the mayor and the members of the city council on December 15, 1994.[19] Phase II consisted of elected officials' review and revision of the proposed charter amendments, beginning with the December 15 delivery of "Committee Recommendations" to the mayor and city council and ending at the August 17, 1995 council meeting that approved an ordinance placing proposed charter amendments on the ballot for a citywide election. The Phase III public information campaign launched even before Phase II ended, and its effectiveness was demonstrated when voters overwhelmingly approved the charter revision by a 68 percent to 32 percent margin of victory on November 18, 1995.[20]

Public information and citizen participation characterized every phase of the charter revision process. The committee conducted its meetings and subcommittee meetings in public, pursuant to Louisiana's Open Meetings Act, and treated all charter revision documents as public documents in accordance with Louisiana's Public Records Act. In every phase of the process, we solicited public input and shared information with the public through forums, newspaper articles, and public television and radio broadcasts. Before delivering its December 15 "Committee Recommendations" to Mayor Morial, the committee advertised and conducted two public hearings in the City Council Chamber (one on the evening of December 13, the other in the afternoon on December 14).[21] Throughout Phase I of the process, we met with members of the New Orleans City Council to solicit their views and suggestions for revision. Consequently, council members, the press, the public, and numerous civic sector organizations were already familiar with the direction of charter reform before the "Committee Recommendations" were delivered to Mayor Morial.[22]

Charter Provisions Proposing an Office of Inspector General

The first substantial task was to divide this diverse group of committee members into appropriate subcommittees to review assigned portions of the charter and suggest revisions. Each member of the committee served on one of six subcommittees, with a designated chair and vice chair.

The Regulatory and Licensing Functions/Ethics Subcommittee was chaired by Gary Groesch.[23] His views were shaped by his daily working responsibilities as director of the Alliance for Affordable Energy, which monitored utility proceedings before the New Orleans City Council and championed the interests of consumers and ratepayers.[24] Gary Groesch was acutely aware of the potential for ethical conflicts within city government; as an outside observer and sometime critic of city government, he was also keenly protective of transparency and public participation. These attributes qualified him to chair the subcommittee that was charged with ethics and regulatory reform.

The subcommittee produced an entirely new chapter 4 in article IX ("General Provisions") of the Home Rule Charter entitled "Office of Inspector General; Ethics," which detailed the establishment of an "Office of Inspector General"; its "Purpose and Authority" and "Powers"; the "Selection, Term and Removal of the Inspector General"; a "Prohibition against Political Activities"; and a veto-proof "Budget" procedure.[25]

Embedded within these six new provisions were far-reaching powers of investigation[26] that the Office of Inspector General (OIG) could deploy at its own initiative or in response to complaints, including confidential complaints[27]; a guarantee of "complete access, to the fullest extent permitted by law, to all city records and public records and documents, including employee personnel records" (sec. 9-401[1]); the power to subpoena witnesses and compel the production of documents (sec. 9-403[2]); protection for investigations and documents to remain "confidential to the fullest extent permitted by law" (sec. 9-403[4]); authority to "recommend that appropriate corrective action be taken against the person who is the subject of the investigation or that departmental policy or procedure be modified to prevent subsequent acts of misconduct or mismanagement" (sec. 9-403[6]); and the discretion to refer possible violations of federal, state, or municipal law to the United States attorney, the district attorney, or the city attorney (sec. 9-403[7]). The "Committee Recommendations" sought to establish without delay a vigorous OIG that would minimize politics in appointing the inspector general (sec. 9-404), insulate the office from political involvement (sec. 9-405), and insure "adequate annual appropriations" for its proper operation (sec. 9-406). These same provisions to establish a vigorous and nonpolitical OIG remained intact in the "Mayor's Recommendations" released three months later.[28] On its way to the ballot, however, our powerful 747 of an ethics engine flew through a political time warp and emerged as the equivalent of a Piper Cub.

Councilmember-at-Large Jim Singleton led the council's negotiations with Mayor Morial, requesting and receiving numerous changes in the evolving text. One of the most consequential eliminated two and a half pages of detailed provisions establishing a powerful OIG in the charter and substituted a single discretionary sentence: "The Council may by ordinance create an Office of Inspector General and otherwise provide with respect thereto."[29] More than a decade elapsed before a different city council finally acted on this discretionary power, establishing the OIG by ordinance in 2006.[30] Two years more elapsed before the OIG and other local ethics bodies secured Home Rule Charter protection and a dedicated source of funding in a 2008 ballot proposition.[31] The six detailed sections that were deleted would have immediately established the OIG in the revised charter on its January 1, 1996 effective date.

Another city council suggestion delayed and complicated implementation of an important ethics reform—procurement of professional services.

Professional Services Procurement Reform

New Orleans' 1954 Home Rule Charter required public bidding of all procurements except for "unique or noncompetitive articles" and "professional services."[32] Exempting *unique* or *noncompetitive* articles from bidding is unavoidable; they are effectively "sole source" procurements for which no realistic prospect of competition exists. The rationale for exempting professional services, however, is different: Professional services can—and should—be "competitively selected" (rather than "bid"), so that contracts can be awarded based on considerations such as experience and competence, rather than who submitted the lowest price.

Public bids typically go to the "lowest responsible bidder"—the respondent who satisfies all bid requirements and submits the lowest price. Bids work well when purchasing standard goods—for example, Number 2 pencils: Simply open the envelopes submitted by all responsive bidders and award the contract to whichever one offered the lowest per-unit price.

But a bid process is poorly suited to awarding contracts for professional services. If a public body wants its building to stay up, they may not be well served by hiring an engineer who offers the lowest price for engineering services. "Competitive selection" preserves an incentive for respondents to lower their prices, but it also preserves the discretion for public officials to award contracts based on a subjective evaluation of each respondent's capabilities—not simply who submitted the lowest price.

The 1954 charter appropriately exempted professional services contracts from "bidding" but fell short by not requiring an alternative "competitive selection" process for professional services. Leaving this important decision to the unfettered discretion of public officials meant that professional services contracts could (and inevitably would) be used for patronage purposes. Public officials could exploit their discretion by awarding contracts to contributors, political supporters, and even to family members without fear of contradiction or complaint under the terms of the 1954 Home Rule Charter.

The "Committee Recommendations" proposed for the first time that, "Contracts for professional services shall be awarded on the basis of a *competitive selection process as established by ordinance*" (emphasis added).[33] During the first months of 1995, Councilmember Singleton and Mayor Morial discussed and ultimately agreed that the two branches of city government should set their own separate procurement processes—by council rule for the legislative branch and by mayoral executive order for the executive branch. Mayor Morial adopted this change in his proposed revision of Section 6-308(5):

> Contracts for professional services administered by the offices, departments, boards and other agencies of the *Executive Branch* shall be awarded on the basis

of *a competitive selection process which shall be established by executive order of the Mayor.* Contracts for professional services administered by the *Council* shall be awarded on the basis of *a competitive selection process which shall be established by rule of the Council.* Each such order or rule and any amendment thereto shall be published once in the official journal and shall be the subject of a public hearing at least seven days prior to its effective date. (Emphasis added)[34]

The city council made a few more changes before approving a ballot proposition at its August 17, 1995 meeting.[35]

Commission members hoped that Mayor Morial would set rigorous competitive selection procedures for the executive branch and that public scrutiny would exert pressure on the council to "ratchet up" its own procedures to meet this high standard. What ensued instead more resembled a race to the bottom—a story of implementation that we'll consider in Part 2.

Elected Officials' Consideration of Charter Revision

The mayor distributed the December 15 "Committee Recommendations" to all department heads and the chief administrative officer and to many boards and commissions, requesting their review and comments during January 1995. In February, Mayor Morial met with the Charter Revision Advisory Committee to discuss changes he would make to the "Committee Recommendations" based on their feedback; his changes were later embodied in a new March 15, 1995 draft of "Mayor's Recommendations," which was delivered to all members of the city council and placed in each branch of the New Orleans Public Library system.

Mayor Morial asked the city council to conclude its consideration of his proposed charter revisions by early April so that charter reform could be included on a July 1995 citywide election ballot. When some council members repeatedly expressed reservations about this timetable, Mayor Morial postponed the target date to allow more time for council review.[36] Running on a parallel track in Baton Rouge, the Morial administration continued its efforts to secure amendments in state law that would be needed to implement some proposed charter changes.[37]

We used this window of opportunity to address concerns raised by civic groups during the comment period. The Bureau of Governmental Research (BGR) identified thirteen areas of concern, which were discussed and resolved in multiple meetings with BGR executive director Jim Brandt and other representatives of the organization. The commission also benefited greatly from detailed review and comment by the only surviving member of the 1951 charter committee, Moise Dennery, who met several times with Jon Eckert, director of the Mayor's Office of Policy Planning. They suggested more than a hundred changes, ranging from typographical errors to substantive improvements. By the time charter revision returned to the city council's agenda in early August, we had an improved document and BGR's support for the package of proposed revisions.

Significant negotiations took place during early August between city council staff and charter committee representatives. We received from council members more than a hundred proposed amendments and agreed to present a package of seventy amendments at the crucial August 17 council meeting. The amendments divided into three categories: Morial administration amendments, council amendments acceptable to the Morial administration, and council amendments to which the Morial administration was opposed.

Some of Mayor Morial's separate negotiations with members of the city council led to modest changes but still preserved important reforms—creating new flexibility in the charter, for example, after altering the proposed council review process: Rather than requiring a supermajority vote (5 out of 7) to *reject* a mayor's proposed restructuring of city government, the council would vote to *approve* it by a simple majority.[38] The OIG, however, elicited far more contentious pushback from the council and its two at-large members: "Jim Singleton and Peggy Wilson are among the Council members who have said they oppose creating such a position."[39]

Significant changes arose out of last-minute negotiations between the mayor and members of the city council on August 16, 1996—the day before the council would decide whether to put charter revision on the ballot. Most significant was a proposed "amendment by Jim Singleton and Peggy Wilson to eliminate the Office of Inspector General, which would have broad power to investigate elected officials and city workers in an effort to root out corruption. Morial has strongly endorsed the concept."[40] The council prevailed: Their 7–0 vote replaced multiple pages of robust OIG powers with a single sentence that made creation of an OIG discretionary with the council and delayed implementation of this important ethics reform for more than a decade. It could have been worse: "Wilson proposed eliminating the inspector general and review board altogether but lost 6–1."[41]

Additional damaging changes were proposed—some successfully, some not, and others fell in between. A Singleton amendment "to drop language requiring the council to approve money for the review board passed 7–0," surely contributing to the ERB's moribund status during the next twelve years. Councilmember Suzanne Haik Terrell proposed an amendment "to leave to the Council the decision on whether to establish a Revenue Estimating Conference," which would likely have consigned this worthy fiscal reform to the same limbo that ultimately afflicted the OIG and ERB. Her amendment first passed 6–0, then failed 3–3 on a reconsideration vote. She did succeed in weakening the reform, when she and Singleton "offered an amendment to make the conference's revenue forecast only a recommendation for spending levels, not a binding limit. It passed 7–0." Wilson and Terrell struck another blow for the status quo when they proposed "to let members of the Board of Liquidation, City Debt, keep their current unlimited terms" rather than setting staggered twelve-year terms; they lost by a 5–2 vote.[42]

Ultimately, the council unanimously voted the proposed charter revisions onto a November 18, 1995 citywide election ballot. In the aftermath, reactions were mixed. Mayor Morial said, "It's better than not having (them) at all. It's not what we preferred." Jim Brandt said that the "overall document reflects most of the major proposals that BGR has supported." The charter committee breathed a sigh of relief that "voters will be asked to approve the hundreds of changes as one proposition."[43]

Securing Voter Approval of Charter Revision

The entire Charter Revision Advisory Committee reconvened on October 12, 1995, to receive copies of the "Proposed Amendments" as finally approved by the council. Thereafter, committee members made many presentations to civic and community organizations as part of the Phase III public information campaign. Broad civic sector support coalesced as the November 18 election date neared: "The Bureau of Governmental Research, the Metropolitan Area Committee, the New Orleans Council of the Chamber of Commerce, and Victims and Citizens Against Crime have all endorsed the package of revisions. The League of Women Voters, which has worked for many years to revise the charter, also supports the effort."[44]

Ethics played a leading role in soliciting public support for every version of the proposed charter changes. The December 15, 1994 "Committee Recommendations" and the March 15, 1995 "Mayor's Recommendations" both began with a "Highlights" page that put front and center two proposed new local ethics entities:

> For the first time, an **Office of the Inspector General** is created pursuant to Charter mandate (pp. 155–57) and charged with the responsibility for investigating misconduct and mismanagement as it impacts city government.

> Finally, an **Ethics Code** and **Ethics Review Board** are established by Charter mandate (pp. 157–158) to restore public confidence in the ethical conduct of city affairs. (Emphasis in original)

The August 18, 1995 "Proposed Amendments to the Charter" (widely distributed to press and public in the run-up to a November 18 charter election) placed "Ethics" first in its list of "Charter Amendment Highlights" and expanded the list of ethics-related reforms in the legislative and executive branches:

- prohibiting a person appointed to fill a vacant council seat from running for the seat at the next election, thereby preventing "insider" appointees from having an unfair advantage (sec. 3-105[2]);
- providing for removal from office of a council member (sec. 3-106) or mayor (sec. 4-205) convicted of a felony or recalled by the voters;
- extending the city council's power to conduct investigations to any entity funded in full or in part by city revenues (sec. 3-124[1]);
- preserving the right to vote for a council member serving as acting mayor (sec. 4-204[3]);
- requiring the functions of a city notary to be performed in-house by salaried personnel of the Law Department rather than by outside counsel, thereby ending a costly patronage practice (sec. 4-404);
- requiring for the first time that city contracts for professional services be awarded only after a competitive selection procedure (sec. 6-308[5]); and
- retaining the charter restriction that permitted only one land-based gambling casino (sec. 9-310).

The "Ethics" highlights concluded with two familiar paragraphs championing the OIG and ERB and directing the city council to strengthen the city's ethics code:

> Section 9-401 authorizes the City Council to establish by ordinance an Office of Inspector General.

Section 9-402 requires the City Council to establish by ordinance an Ethics Review Board, whose members will be nominated by the university presidents and appointed by the mayor subject to approval of the city council. Section 9-402 also requires the City Council to establish by ordinance a city code of ethics incorporating the ethical standards of the State Code of Ethics and whatever additional requirements the council may deem appropriate.

The charter highlights leave little doubt that city leaders and Charter Revision Advisory Committee members identified ethics reform as one of the strongest, most appealing themes for the public information campaign. These ethics reform initiatives helped ignite overwhelming support among voters for the entire array of charter amendments.

The Home Rule Charter revision process officially ended on November 18, 1995, when voters approved the proposed amendments. A January 1, 1996 effective date left less than two months to prepare for implementation of numerous new charter reforms.

Part 2. Implementation of Ethics Reforms

New Orleans might never have seen the implementation of local ethics reforms but for the devastating damage inflicted by Hurricane Katrina:

> Ten years after New Orleans' 1994–95 home rule charter revision process, the city still had no ethics review board, no office of inspector general, and no reform in procurement of professional services. Ten years of no progress—and no progress in sight—provides us with a good test case. We must credit Katrina as the catalyst that led to implementation of the ERB, OIG, and professional services procurement reform in post-Katrina New Orleans.[45]

This pattern of first approving charter reform legal instruments, then encountering long delays and shortfalls in implementation unfortunately characterized ethics reform throughout subsequent decades.

Complications in Implementing Competitive Selection Procedures

The original charter revision timetable contemplated that proposed revisions would be approved by public officials during the first quarter of 1995, followed by public hearings and widespread citizen review in the second quarter, then seeking voter approval in mid-July.[46] This original timetable allowed about six months for planning and implementation before the revised charter's January 1, 1996 effective date. An extended period of review by the city council, however, delayed the election to November and left less than two months to prepare for the newly revised charter's implementation.

Complicating matters, City Hall's attention was diverted (in fact, consumed) soon after voters approved the charter changes, when Harrah's Casino laid off twenty-five hundred casino employees and idled a thousand construction workers shortly before Thanksgiving.[47] Harrah's had just succeeded in cutting its $100 million annual payment to the state to $50 million, securing this 50 percent reduction with enthusiastic support from city officials and the local workforce, who all touted the casino's beneficial effects on employment in New Orleans.[48] City officials considered the casino's draconian dismissals of its employees an egregious breach of faith and directed every effort during the remainder of 1995 toward securing an enforceable commitment against Harrah's that would protect the workforce. Charter implementation fell off City Hall's radar screen.

During the second week of January 1996, implementation of the new charter provisions roared back onto City Hall's radar screen with a vengeance. When the city council attempted a "routine" renewal of its utility consultants' contracts, Gary Groesch and the Alliance for Affordable Energy pointed out that effective January 1, 1996, the council could no longer award utility consultant contracts with the same unfettered discretion as in the past.[49] The charter now required that such contracts be advertised and awarded through competitive selection procedures set by a council rule not yet promulgated.[50] When the city council persisted in efforts to renew the contracts, the Alliance sued to enjoin them until they complied with the new competitive selection requirements.[51]

It's often said, "Hard cases make bad law." When the Alliance launched its litigation, utility consultants had been working since the start of the new year without a current contract; by the time this lawsuit worked its way through the appellate courts, judges were unlikely to throw out the consultants unceremoniously with no compensation for their months of labor. The Louisiana Supreme Court upheld a "grandfathering" provision written into Council Rule 45 that included the power to approve "Any contracts in existence prior to January 1, 1996 for: a) Renewal or extension of the contract, when continuity of service is essential."[52]

Hard cases make bad rules, too. The city council—already badly burned by the new competitive selection requirements—was determined to avoid being hamstrung in the future. Council Rule 45 ("Competitive Selection Process for Professional Services Contracts") was adopted in the midst of this controversy and was drafted permissively to maintain council control over the awards process; more than twenty years later, press coverage of the council's utility regulatory contracts still identified problems that could be traced back to this early, troubled council implementation effort.[53]

The council's proposed procedure elicited a vehement denunciation from Gary Groesch, who called the plan "a stab in the back of the voters in this city" and said that the council's self-serving use of its own staff to rank candidates was "a weakening of an already pathetically weak process."[54] A *Times-Picayune* editorial called the council's action "a disappointing reversion to old politics as usual."[55] Still today, paragraph 8 in (now renumbered) Rule 42 establishes selection review committees consisting of the council chief of staff, council research officer, and either the council fiscal officer or the chief of staff of council utilities, depending upon the type of professional service solicited.[56] All three of these members are salaried employees of the council and likely to be responsive to the council's wishes.

After a BGR status report entitled "Implementation of Amendments to New Orleans City Charter" in September 1996 identified "competitive selection procedures for professional services contracts" as one of several substantive changes awaiting implementation,[57] Mayor Morial issued a September 5, 1996 executive order fixing competitive selection procedures for all executive branch entities.

MHM 96-020 displayed the same shortcomings as the council rule in terms of in-house control: Selection review rating groups were to "supervise the entire selection process" and would purportedly "conduct an independent, objective evaluation of applicants."[58] But the selection review rating groups[59] and the grants provider selection review rating groups[60] were drawn from the unclassified service; all members of these evaluation groups held their employment at the pleasure of the mayor, who could undermine their independence at any moment. Theoretically, the chief administrative officer or an executive assistant could appoint to the rating groups "other persons with specialized knowledge or expertise" from the community at large or the university community; but these "outsiders" would be chosen by mayoral representatives—if chosen at all, since the executive order also provided, "Nothing herein shall be construed to require these additional raters."[61]

When evaluation groups consist entirely of surrogates for the mayor or council, the professional services procurement process remains rich terrain for patronage politics: "Any contracting process in which elected officials or their appointees participate can be circumvented or manipulated for political purposes."[62] A better solution, as I have pointed out elsewhere, would be to "let independent entities with specialized expertise designate evaluation committee members, thereby promoting politically independent evaluations" and producing evaluation committees that are "technically competent, politically independent and demographically diverse." And I added, "We can accomplish all three of these objectives."[63]

Mayor Morial's successor demonstrated how the failure to implement procurement reforms not only harms the public but also exposes public officials to temptation and the risk of severe penalties.

As a candidate, C. Ray Nagin promised in his 2002 mayoral campaign to submit a ballot proposition to the city council within one hundred days after his inauguration, inviting voters to unite the separate legislative and executive branch procurement policies into a single procedure fixed by ordinance.[64] He committed to this proposition in one of our earliest meetings about campaign issues, and he reiterated the hundred-day promise publicly many times thereafter.[65] But Mayor Nagin reneged on this commitment, as he frankly acknowledged in October 2002: "Times-Picayune reporter Frank Donze caught up with the mayor and asked him about the busted 100-day deadline for a ballot proposition. Yep, the mayor agreed, he'd missed it, and he wasn't going to give a new deadline because he didn't want to disappoint everyone again."[66]

At a meeting in the Mayor's Office two months before his public acknowledgment, I witnessed how this about-face on policy began:

> I attended an executive staff meeting in August 2002, less than 100 days after Ray Nagin was inaugurated. I'd been invited there to present a proposal for reform in the procurement of professional services.
>
> After my presentation, around the table they went, complaining that these "burdensome new procedures" would be "inefficient," would "tie our hands," would prevent the mayor's brash and talented new staff from hiring "the best and the brightest."

And Ray Nagin bought those arguments. "Procurement reform" remained for the rest of his administration merely a matter of "spin," as illusory as those "cranes in the sky."[67]

The one-hundred-day commitment was still within Nagin's grasp during this August 2002 executive staff meeting, and he was still making hollow promises of progress to the public:

> Although he pledged during his campaign to offer a plan for reforming the way the city awards lucrative professional services contracts within 90 days, Nagin said it likely will be another 90 days before a proposal is ready. He said a draft ordinance is being reviewed by "key stakeholders" such as the Bureau of Governmental Research and a coalition of minority contractors.[68]

Not even ninety days later, this campaign commitment was gone for good, with unforeseen consequences yet to be felt within his administration.

Nagin's first executive order dealt with professional services procurement; it was not a promising start. CRN 02-01 added new jobs to the list of professional services, thereby enhancing mayoral discretion in awarding lucrative contracts.[69] Several of the new job listings were merely arbitrary (e.g., the change from "physicians" to "doctors" and from "attorneys" to "lawyers") or inconsequential (e.g., the addition of "landscape architects" and "veterinarians" to the a list that included "architects" and "doctors"). Others were legally questionable: Adding "claim adjusters and/or administrators" and "insurance agents and/or brokers" to the list of "professional services" conflicted with successful court challenges holding similar services nonprofessional.[70] And some appeared to invite corruption: Two new terms, "telecommunications" and "data processing," opened a door to discretionary abuses that later led to indictments for Nagin and his chief technology officer.[71]

Permissiveness continued two years later in CRN 04-02, which expanded "Exceptions" beyond "emergency situations" to authorize acquisition of "certain items and services" through federal supply schedules.[72] This change increased Nagin appointees' discretion to award information technology contracts and likely contributed to the Nagin administration's later difficulties with federal prosecutors.[73]

CRN 05-01 repealed MHM 96-020 and the two Nagin executive orders but retained their shortcomings and made the professional services procurement process even weaker:[74]

1. By empowering the city attorney to determine "whether a service constitutes a 'professional service,'" the Nagin executive order expanded the number of contracts that could be exempted from public bidding wholly at the discretion of a mayoral appointee.[75]

2. A meaningless "monitoring" process in subsection 8(H) designated the city attorney to serve as an "independent" monitor of all *non-legal* procurements and the CAO to serve as the "independent" monitor for all *legal* services procurements—a reciprocal relationship between mayoral appointees that drained any value or meaning from the concept of "monitoring."

3. Most egregiously, subsection 8(I) deemed Selection Review Panel "Deliberations Confidential" and prohibited panel members "from disclosing the contents of such

discussions and/or deliberations to any third parties,"[76] all of which violated the state's open meetings law.[77]

When the city council tried to legislate greater transparency by unanimously approving an ordinance to require that evaluation committees meet in public, Ray Nagin vetoed it.[78]

Mayor Nagin and his chief technology officer later faced federal charges arising out of their manipulation of the professional services contracting process. Nagin's technology chief entered a guilty plea and "signed a statement admitting he steered roughly $4 million in no-bid city work" to a contractor who gave him "more than $860,000 in bribes and kickbacks in return."[79] Nagin went to trial and was convicted on twenty out of twenty-one counts, including fraud and bribery involving the award of city contracts.[80]

Nagin's successor, Mitch Landrieu, got kudos for improving the city's contracting process. He was praised for having evaluation committees meet in public, even though public meetings are already legally required under Louisiana's Open Meetings Law: "Nagin's committees [by contrast] did not meet in public; when the City Council tried to force them to, Nagin simply stopped using them."[81]

Other persistent problems endured, even as the new administration took over at City Hall. As under Nagin, evaluation committees consisted wholly of mayoral surrogates: "The acknowledged weakness in this setup is that all of the committee members owe their jobs to the mayor to one degree or another."[82] Another problem was the ephemeral nature of procurement reforms: "Like Nagin's selection process, Landrieu's new system is the result of an executive order, and a successor could undo the reforms with a simple rewrite."[83] Landrieu later proposed and voters approved an amendment to put three-member selection committees into the charter, but those members were all still appointed by the mayor from within local government. Landrieu declined to entrust the selection process "to independent experts from outside City Hall, as was recommended more than a decade ago."[84]

The most disappointing missed opportunity was in failing to unite the bifurcated system that set separate legislative and executive branch policies for procurement of professional service contracts. The political moment was propitious: The League of Women Voters of New Orleans had asked mayor and council candidates during the 2014 campaign, "Will you support a City Charter proposition that allows citizens to vote on unifying the processes for awarding professional services contracts, establishing a single procedure that applies citywide to all legislative and executive branch agencies, boards, and commissions?" Questionnaire responses were publicized in a newspaper column two months before the newly elected officials took office: "A majority of council members who take office in May have already pledged to support this Charter reform, and Mayor Mitch Landrieu has promised a charter amendment soon."[85] Regrettably, the amendment he put before voters later that year left this important work unfinished.

The fight for reform in professional services procurement goes on. At the time of the Landrieu proposals, BGR president Janet Howard identified a further need for improvement: "She would rather have the new chief procurement officer placed under civil service protection."[86] In a 2014 op-ed column, I provided my own list of other professional services safeguards that should be embedded in the charter:

Here's a good start: Assure OIG scrutiny of procurements from start to finish; hold evaluation meetings in public; make evaluation forms public; require weighted evaluation criteria; provide independence in selecting the chief procurement officer; and put independent technical experts on evaluation committees.[87]

Still today, we need a Home Rule Charter amendment that unites separate mayor and council procurement policies in a single citywide process covering all professional services contracts; this reform is "important because procurement policies approved by both branches of government can't be changed thereafter without joint mayor-council approval."[88]

The fight for reform remains "a history with multiple chapters written over two decades by many authors. And the final chapter has not yet been written."[89]

Case Study in Procurement Reform

We conclude this analysis of professional services procurement reform with a case study illustrating the use of "inside" and "outside" legislative strategies.

In the first months of 2011, a city council selection review committee met privately to consider the award of a professional services contract, claiming an exemption under the Open Meetings Act for "discussion of the character, professional competence, or physical or mental health of a person."[90] This long-standing exemption makes sense; sensitive information about people's private lives ought not be disclosed without good reason. This same provision does away with secrecy, however, in requiring that "discussion of the appointment of a person to a public body"[91] be held in public, which makes sense, too: If you want to sit on the City Planning Commission, you should be prepared to answer probing questions about your fitness for appointment to such an important public body.

The law had no similar requirement that the award of a public contract must be discussed in public, and this made no sense at all. Serving on a board or commission entails only a modest expenditure of public funds for per diem, travel, conference fees—"chump change" compared to potentially hundreds of thousands of dollars expended on a professional services contract. The Public Law Center drafted legislation to fill this gap, and Rep. Neil Abramson introduced it.[92]

Students in legislative and administrative advocacy learn about an "inside" game and an "outside" game in the legislative process. The inside game relies on a capable legislator to manage a bill quietly through the process. The outside game energizes the public and relies on indirect, grassroots lobbying to marshal support for the bill among legislators. It is possible to play both the inside game and the outside game—but only if properly sequenced. The inside game comes first: You can't hold a press conference on the steps of the State Capitol on Monday, then ask your legislator to quietly noodle the bill forward during the remaining days of the week after having made it a high-profile issue.

Rep. Abramson set HB 449 for a committee hearing early in the session. When opposition appeared in the form of the Governor's Executive Counsel, an amendment solved the problem, adding some inelegant language that did no damage to the bill's overall objectives.[93] HB 449 came out of committee with a favorable report and passed the House floor unanimously.

The measure was now surely visible to public officials, and we feared some of them might view its transparency as inimical to one of their "perquisites" of public office. HB 449 could now be vulnerable to their inside games and behind-the-scenes machinations. An op-ed column deployed the outside game to draw public attention to the bill and make it harder for potential saboteurs to impede its progress:

> Open meeting laws prohibit private discussions about appointment to a board or commission. Does it make sense to permit private discussions about awarding public contracts?

> That's just wrong. HB 449 would make it right, by prohibiting executive sessions to discuss awarding a public contract.[94]

HB 449 passed the Senate on a vote of 37–1, returned to the House, and again passed unanimously, then was signed by the governor and became law on August 15, 2011.

When the city council's selection review committee next met in the fall of 2011 to consider the award of a professional services contract, they met in public.

Ordinances and Statutes Elaborating Powers of the Inspector General

Professional services procurement became the leading edge of charter implementation, because it could no longer be ignored when the city council moved to renew its consultants' contracts in January 1996. Other aspects of ethics reform proved easier to ignore, however, including the Ethics Review Board (ERB) and the OIG.

The revised charter called for the council to pass an ordinance establishing the ERB within six months; the council met this goal on June 20, 1996.[95] The charter also called for university presidents to nominate and the mayor to name ERB members within the next six months. The university presidents each sent three nominees to Mayor Morial, who in turn appointed six of seven ERB members from those names. Inexplicably, he never named the seventh ERB member, who was to be a free mayoral selection.[96] Consequently, the ERB remained moribund during the remaining six years of the Morial administration and throughout four years of the first Nagin term.

The winds of Katrina blew through New Orleans in August 2005. In their aftermath, the winds of political change blew fiercely as well, and ethics reform came back onto the agenda. The OIG proved a catalyst in precipitating ethics reform, and once again, the implementation of an important ethics innovation grew directly out of a campaign commitment.

When I met with Shelley Midura, a candidate for the District A city council seat in the 2006 citywide elections, I said, "If you get the Inspector General up and running, you can roll up the sidewalks and go home! Your legacy will be complete." She took my comment to heart and campaigned on a platform of ethics reform.[97] Then, when elected, she championed an ordinance with single-minded determination. On the evening the OIG ordinance was finally approved,[98] my wife and I were at dinner in an adjacent state when I got a call on my cell phone from Shelley. She said, "Can I roll up the sidewalks and go home now?" But that would have been too soon, because more important work remained to be done.

The following year, two additional ordinances expanded the OIG's powers and strengthened its investigative tools.[99] One such tool, subpoena power, needed state legislation to be legally enforceable in state courts. In February 2008, a coalition of civic groups (including Citizens for 1 Greater New Orleans[100] and The Public Law Center[101]) appeared before the Municipal, Parochial, and Cultural Affairs Committee in Baton Rouge to support HB 80[102] by Rep. J. P. Morrell. As later enacted, it granted the following important powers to local ethics entities: designation as a law enforcement agency with access to criminal justice databases[103]; power to apply for a protective order and enforcement of a subpoena[104]; confidentiality for investigative documents; and authority to meet in executive session when discussing confidential materials.[105] Additional laws passed during 2010–2012 also proved useful in the legal evolution of local ethics entities—not just in Orleans but in other Louisiana jurisdictions inspired by New Orleans' example.[106]

Troubled Relationship between the Office of Inspector General and the Office of Independent Police Monitor

In 2008 the city council created the Office of Independent Police Monitor (OIPM) as a division within the OIG,[107] and therein lay a contradiction: Could the police monitor live up to its titular identity as "independent" while functioning as a "division" of the OIG? Over the next several years, this structural deficit generated increasing tension between the inspector general and the police monitor, finally breaking into open warfare by 2015 and threatening to tarnish the public profile of all three local ethics entities.[108]

Years earlier, before the OIPM got up and running, an important ethics reform arose unexpectedly out of the abusive hiring process used for selecting the first short-lived police monitor. Interim Inspector General Len Odom first announced during July 2009 that he intended to hire Neely Moody as police monitor with no public input; then he backtracked in the face of withering public criticism, only to make the same decision to hire Neely Moody just one month later after purportedly conducting a national search.[109] A month after that, both Len Odom and Neely Moody were gone, after having resigned their positions.[110]

Six months after this debacle, the city council passed an ordinance to prevent such abuses in the future, establishing a search committee that consisted of members from the local ethics entities (the inspector general and the ERB chair); the legislative branch (chair of the council's Criminal Justice Committee); the executive branch (the police superintendent and a mayoral designee); and two city residents appointed by the council's Criminal Justice Committee. The ordinance required a nationwide search for the police monitor and called for three finalists to attend at least two community meetings, where they would answer questions from the public.[111] The inspector general retained authority to hire but only from among three finalists who had been vetted by both branches of city government, by the local ethics board, and by the public. This process yielded Susan Hutson, who was hired as the second police monitor in 2010 amid a chorus of approving comments by ERB chair Kevin Wildes ("She has the right skills for the job") and Inspector General Ed Quatrevaux ("She plays in the big leagues").[112]

The search procedures worked well, but the structural deficit was unchanged; the OIPM remained a division within the OIG, a tumor perpetually threatening to metastasize as personal and institutional frictions intensified among the three local ethics entities. Structural reform emerged as the best solution—but separating the OIPM and OIG would require a charter amendment, which in turn required voter approval.[113]

A Home Rule Charter proposition overwhelmingly approved by 71 percent of voters on November 8, 2016, authorized three important reforms that (1) separated the OIG and OIPM, (2) apportioned funding among all three local ethics entities, and (3) required independent external evaluation of all three local ethics entities.[114]

A subsequent city council ordinance (approved on a divided 5–2 vote) separated the two offices but fell considerably short of ideal in its implementation of the charter proposition:

- The previous participatory search process for police monitor fell by the wayside, replaced with "Appointment procedures" that eliminated any role for the public or for the legislative and executive branches of city government.
- Gone was the written assurance of two community meetings at which the public could ask questions of the three finalists.
- Gone as well was any assurance that the search process would even yield multiple finalists; the public might see only a single applicant left standing.
- Finally, the implementing ordinance made no provision for independent external evaluation of the third local ethics entity, the ERB.[115]

In the last month before her departure from the council, District A councilmember Susan Guidry took a partial step toward implementing this last requirement with an ordinance repeating terminology from the charter: "the ethics review board shall be subject to an independent, external peer review every three years."[116] With no details about how the evaluator was to be chosen, however, the measure fell far short of actual "implementation"; even so, it mustered only a bare 4–3 vote of approval.

Part 3. Conclusion

Seafarers embarking on a journey without benefit of a compass employ a strategy called "point-to-point navigation" to keep themselves on course: Pick out a target and make your way to it, then pick another landmark and keep leapfrogging forward, stringing together a succession of advances until the journey is complete.[117] The 1994–1995 charter revision process initially charted an ambitious and far-reaching course, but the actual ethics implementation process has consisted of incremental, point-to-point gains over an arduous period of years. When blown off course, ethics advocates have repeatedly had to navigate "course corrections" by setting specific targets and working to achieve them.

The forty-member Citizens' Advisory Group saw the ethics component of its "Committee Recommendations" diminished during an essential but frequently damaging dialogue with elected officials. First, the "Mayor's Recommendations" rejected a single, citywide professional services procurement policy in favor of two separate procedures, one for the executive and another for the legislative branch. Then, the city council eviscerated powerful provisions to establish an OIG and removed mandatory funding for the ERB before voting its own version of "Proposed Amendments" onto the ballot,

In the wake of these troubling changes, ethics advocates set specific targets that have steadily strengthened the local ethics bodies:

- Shelley Midura accepted a short-term goal ("Get the OIG up and running!"), and her work precipitated the ERB's first meeting—twelve years after the charter mandated its creation. (So much for mandates—or at least, mandates without money!)
- The city's first inspector general, Bob Cerasoli, saw a target—enhanced powers for the OIG—then worked with the legislative coordinator Seung Hong in Shelley Midura's council office to draft and secure ordinance improvements in 2007 that revitalized many of the original OIG provisions in the "Committee Recommendations."
- Half a year later, a coalition of civic groups went to Baton Rouge in successful pursuit of state legislation that imparted legal force to local ordinance provisions on subpoena power, confidentiality, and access to criminal justice databases.
- Civic reformers produced a good outcome by advocating for the OIPM that was created in 2008. But again, remedial work proved necessary—first, by moving the OIPM out of the OIG, then by directing assured funding annually to each of the three local ethics entities.
- The second occupant of the IG's office (an interim appointee, Len Odom) inadvertently improved selection procedures for the independent police monitor (IPM): The abusive hiring process by which he appointed (more accurately, "anointed") Neely Moody as the initial IPM motivated the city council to pass a remedial ordinance that guaranteed transparency and public participation in any future IPM search process. Regrettably, these safeguards were lost in a later ordinance revision.

Thus, ethics advocates have a new target in this point-to-point navigation process: Pass an ordinance restoring two opportunities for members of the public to query multiple candidates in selecting a new inspector general or IPM.

As this newest target illustrates, not all ethics reforms require a frontal assault on corruption. Some reforms work simply by creating a healthier environment, such as the 2010 ordinance that insured public participation in hiring the police monitor or HB 449 in 2011, which enhanced public participation and transparency by bringing public scrutiny to bear on evaluating and awarding professional services contracts. Transparency is the key to accountability in government. We cannot hold public officials accountable for conduct we cannot see. Transparency laws lay the essential groundwork for accountability.

Complicating progress in this point-to-point navigation process are the diverse crew members who share the journey with us. Some pull one way, some in another direction, but all are acting in accordance with their own perspectives on the rule of law. How can we better understand the sources of their very different motivations? What follows is my attempt at a typology, first describing the four different perspectives (A–D) held by *disciples* and *subversives* and by *legalistic* and *personalized* interpreters of the rule of law, then ranking them (E) from best to worst on a rule-of-law spectrum.

(A) At the top of the heap (and a rara avis indeed) is the committed adherent to rule of law— the *disciple*, who values rule-of-law principles unconditionally. Rule-of-law disciples accept the discipline that rule of law imposes—constraints imposed not only on the conduct of others but also on their own conduct. Many people profess their commitment to rule-of-law principles as a matter of belief, but they suffer diminished enthusiasm when rule of law imposes limitations on their own conduct.[118]

(B) For example, a *legalistic* interpreter of rule of law could choose not to read the law liberally to accomplish the purposes for which the law was enacted—or could instead choose to apply a narrow reading, maximizing personal discretion while maintaining a plausible legal defense of compliance. Lawyers frequently adopt this posture in the service of their clients' interests, and who can deny the legitimacy of this approach when lawyers are acting in a representative capacity? We should view matters differently, however, when a lawyer is acting not in the service of clients but in the lawyer's own interest. This legal, analytical frame is seldom applied to broaden and strengthen the rule of law. It's more often deployed to curb and undermine the robust expression of rule-of-law principles.

This legalistic attitude is certainly not restricted exclusively to lawyers. It's a common mindset embraced by many a common man or woman: "Let me get as close to the line as I can get without going over—or at least not too far over." With this sentiment, we've left behind the domain of the rule-of-law disciple; we've entered a realm of rule-of-law constriction—or worse, rule-of-law subversion.

(C) Rule of law *subversives* need not be engaged in corruption or outright criminality. Subtler and more insidious is their subversive assault on safeguards that protect the rule of law—safeguards such as the transparency in open meetings and public records acts; the distribution of power in a checks-and-balances political system; the accountability and conflict avoidance served by financial disclosure and campaign finance laws; and a preference for independent expertise over political influence in a well-crafted system for awarding professional services contracts.

We often refer to rule-of-law systems. The concept of a system is inextricably linked with rule-of-law principles. I once wrote in a similar context, "Ethics reform does not mean that people start behaving better. Ethics reform means that systems are put in place to deal with people who are behaving badly."[119]

Respect for the rule of law requires respect for systems that protect the rule of law. The 1980s mantra about nuclear disarmament is pertinent: "Trust but verify." We might trust a *person* while nonetheless championing *systems* to document that person's compliance with the law—that person, and everyone else who holds public office.

Systems both verify good conduct and encourage it. Erode the system, and erosion of the law follows closely behind. Some public officials govern as if no one will ever follow them in office. They seek relentlessly to dismantle or undermine systems that limit their ability to maximize discretion; they single-mindedly accrete power unto themselves during their brief term in office. They give no thought to how dismantling systemic safeguards might enable their successors in office to use these enhanced prerogatives abusively, adversely impacting the public interest. These dismantlers of systemic protections are accurately and aptly described as rule of law subversives.

So rarely does a dismantled system get put back together again that Lt. Governor Billy Nungesser made headlines in 2019 when he announced his intention to reverse legislative changes muscled through by his predecessor, Mitch Landrieu. Before Landrieu's legislation, "the state's No. 2 official could appoint only three members" of the Louisiana State Museum Board; the 2008 law "transformed a 21-member board . . . into a group chosen solely by Landrieu, with some input from the various groups that support the museum's mission." The new law had a predictably disastrous effect on stable administration of the museum: "in the 11 years the law has been on the books, the museum system has had seven different directors, sparking criticism that politicizing the job has made it difficult to find and retain qualified candidates." Nungesser's decision to reverse this policy "heartened members of the Louisiana Museum Foundation, who 'erupted in applause.'" Foundation president Melissa Steiner said, "It is a rare day indeed that we hear of an elected official giving up this kind of control, and we could not be more pleased."[120]

(D) Systems exist to punish bad behavior, and here, perhaps, the appropriate image is Lady Justice, blindfolded. Rule of law in this context means a willingness to administer rules and dispense outcomes without regard to personal considerations. We put the blindfold on Lady Justice because we don't want her to see and be influenced by whoever stands before her. Some people find it hard to resist a *personalized* rule-of-law perspective, surrendering an impartial commitment to rule-of-law principles for what they may think are the most benevolent of reasons: "We know this person!"

To give this rule-of-law principle of impartiality its most appropriate and broadest application, we need to lift it out of the adjudicatory context that may be implied by the Lady Justice metaphor. Judges are *expected* to be impartial arbiters of legal disputes, but the same expectation of impartial judgment should apply to government officials who administer their duties in an executive or legislative office rather than in a courtroom. A public official's use of discretion to fix a traffic ticket—or to "fix" the procurement process in favor of a preferred contractor—would be judged an abuse of public office in some jurisdictions, even if neither action quite involved an exchange of money or constituted a criminal quid-pro-quo bribe.

This principle of blindness toward the parties should also guide civic sector advocates and members of the press, who might otherwise rely on their personal preferences and apply a double standard when evaluating procedures that govern people in public office. In evaluating policies for the procurement of professional services, for example, it's not in the public interest to say, "Oh, we know this person is trustworthy and will administer these new procedures fairly." In today's fractured and fractious society, we needn't travel far to find someone else who would say of the same person, "Oh, that untrustworthy excuse for a public servant! Those new procedures better be foolproof!"

People are not policies and procedures. People change; policies and procedures endure—at least until they change through democratic, transparent procedures. We might trust certain people, but we should be blind to people when evaluating procedures: "Trust but verify." Systems and procedures supply the essential, verifying half of this mantra.

Do we go too far in suggesting that this duty of blind impartiality should also govern the conduct of private parties, such as civic sector advocates and members of the press? No, because these "private" players exercise important "public" influence. The BGR speaks with authority to its members and to the civic community. A newspaper columnist enjoys a privileged platform from which to tell a credible story to readers. Where and when these influencers of public opinion choose to invest their beliefs, so too do many others. These private parties should not "play favorites" when dispensing their wisdom. Comments on a policy for procurement of professional services should be based on an assessment of the policy, not the policy maker who promulgated it. Take that favored person out of the chair and drop in your worst nightmare of a public official: Does the policy withstand this test?

(E) How should we rank this diverse spectrum of actors who intersect with ethics and the rule of law? *Disciples* occupy one end of the spectrum. *Subversives* anchor the other end; their lack of respect for the systems that sustain rule of law constitutes an existential threat. Others, who *personalize* the rule of law or who subject it to a *legalistic* frame, inhabit the middle; their actions have a compromising but not a cataclysmic effect on the integrity and strength of rule of law.

Which is more important: good people or good laws? Truthfully, we shouldn't have to choose one over the other, and in fact, the two tend to go together. Good people in public office often produce good laws and should be expected to administer these laws fairly. When the occasional bad actor enters the room, however, we need to have done all we can to impose rigor and transparency under the rule of law. Ethics rules, transparency laws, procedural safeguards—all are compatible with the administration of government by good people. But when the need arises, they also serve as indispensable checks on abuse by bad actors.[121]

"Rule of law" means that everyone—the government and governmental officials included—obeys the law. Good people in government, bad people in government, all people in government must be equally bound to and judged by their compliance with the rule of law. Until this principle is uniformly embraced, ethics reform work must continue.

Notes

1   A front-page article on the day of his inauguration identified as one of the new administration's priorities "placing a revision of the 40-year-old City Charter before voters." See Frank Donze, "Morial's Flashy Rehearsal to Give Way to Reality," *Times-Picayune*, May 2, 1994.

2   See Marc H. Morial First State of the City Address, August 11, 1994, http://www.gnocommunications. com/marchmorial/speeches/firststateofthecityaddress.htm.

3   See Frank Donze, "Morial Makes Good on Charter Change," *Times-Picayune*, October 15, 1996.

4   La. Const. of 1921 Art. XIV, §22, as amended by Act 551 of 1950; La. Const. of 1974 Art. VI, §§4 and 6.

5   "Every mayor since Moon Landrieu promised to update the City Charter, but Morial was the first to deliver—and he did it just a year into his first term." Clancy DuBos, "Marc's Marks," Gambit, May 6, 2002, https://www.theadvocate.com/gambit/new_orleans/news/article_2ed3b5e6-4ba7-5dd7-a224-fd6dce2a1581. html.

6   See James H. Gillis, "Power, Politics, and the People," *Times-Picayune,* August 7, 1975.

7   The first attempt launched early in 1983 with a petition drive to secure ten thousand voter signatures calling a charter election to repeal the two-term limit and authorize unlimited terms. See James H. Gillis, "Unlimited Terms for Mayor?," *Times-Picayune*, March 1, 1983. The second attempt in 1985 sought approval for "Just One" more term, but this third-term drive also failed to win voter approval. See Susan Finch, "Vote Set on Allowing Third Term for Mayors," *Times-Picayune*, June 21, 1985.

8   The Bureau of Governmental Research supported proposition A (reinforcing home rule authority in New Orleans) and proposition D (making improvements to the city's operating and capital budget process), opposed proposition B (changing the election process for at-large council members), and took no position on proposition C (restructuring city government by creating the Civilian Review Board and adding contradictory language about the Sewerage and Water Board and the Public Belt Rail Road). See Dawn Ruth, "Bureau Urges Rejecting Pair of Charter Issues," *Times-Picayune*, September 30, 1993.

9   See Donze, "Morial Makes Good."

10 "The League of Women Voters of New Orleans in 1986 and the New Orleans Business Council in 1989 actively sought to secure key changes in the city's home rule charter. Both groups urged that the charter be amended to make it possible for the Mayor and City Council to save money by eliminating or combining

existing municipal agencies." "New Orleans Incorporated: 200 Years of the City Charter" in the Louisiana Division of the New Orleans Public Library (hereinafter, NOPL Charter Archives), 148, http://nutrias. org/~nopl/exhibits/charter/chartercontents.htm.

11 Item #3 in the League of Women Voters of New Orleans' "Charter Change Consensus" (1986) provided that except for "the Board of Liquidation, City Debt which should be mandated in the Charter, the Mayor may create, change, or abolish offices, departments, agencies, boards and commissions, by submitting an ordinance to the Council which provides a plan of city structure." "New Orleans Charter Revision Business Council Presentation," dated March 1, 1989, identified "Lack of flexibility" as the principal "Need for Charter Revision (slide #3) and recommended "Provide flexibility in organizing functions of city government" as one of the "Objectives of Charter Revision" (slide #4). See materials for the League of Women Voters of New Orleans and the Business Council in NOPL Charter Archives (http://nutrias. org/~nopl/exhibits/charter/businesscouncil.htm).

12 See §4-102 of the 1954 Home Rule Charter.

13 See article IX, chapter 2 (§§ 9-201 through 203) of the 1954 Home Rule Charter.

14 See listing in the frontispiece of the Home Rule Charter for members of the 1994 Charter Revision Committee: David A. Marcello, chair; Charlotte G. Bordenave, vice-chair; Philip M. Baptiste; Cora Basile; Jane Booth; Bill Bowers; Ellenese Brooks-Simms; Wilbert E. Brown Sr.; Gilbert Buras; Dana Combes; Joseph DeRose; Henry A. Dillon III; C. B. Forgotston Jr.; Ronald J. French; Antoine Garibaldi; Moses Gordon II; Harold Green; Gary Groesch; Bobby M. Harges; Gladstone Jones III; Henry P. Julien Jr.; Diana Lewis; Lee Madere; Carla Major; Ronald Mason Jr.; Louis F. Miron; Geneva Morris; Joel Myers; T. F. Rinard; Dolores O. Robertson; Elsie Rose; Marty Rowland; Deborah Rhea Slattery; Fritz Wagner; Christian Washington; Charles D. Williams; Betty Wisdom; Warren G. Woodfork Sr. (https://library. municode.com/la/new orleans/codes/code of ordinances?nodeId=HORUCHNEOR).

15 See listing in the frontispiece of the Home Rule Charter for members of the 1951 Charter Revision Committee: Harry McCall, chairman; Lester J. Lautenschlaeger, vice-chairman; Moise W. Dennery, secretary; Denis A. Barry, treasurer; Robert A. Ainsworth Jr.; Clifton L. Ganus; A. P. Harvey; Eugene A. Nabors; Ralph P. Nolan; Mrs. Martha G. Robinson; Robert W. Starnes; and Edgar B. Stern Sr. (https:// library.municode.com/la/new orleans/codes/code of ordinances?nodeId=HORUCHNEOR).

16 See Donze, "Morial Makes Good."

17 La. R.S. 42:11, et seq.

18 La. R.S. 44:1, et seq.

19 See Mayor's Charter Revision Advisory Committee, "Committee Recommendations," December 15, 1994 (hereinafter, "Committee Recommendations"), posted at The Public Law Center's website: https://law. tulane.edu/the-public-law-center.

20 "Orleans Charter," *Times-Picayune*, November 19, 1995.

21 See "Notice of Public Hearing" (published December 9, 12, 13, and 14) in the *Times-Picayune*, December 9, 1994.

22 See, for example, Alfred Charles, "Panel Discusses Host of Changes to City Charter," *Times-Picayune*, November 17, 1994.

23 The following comprised the committee's Scope of Responsibilities: §§4-1601, et seq. - Utilities; §§5-1001, et seq. - N.O. Alcoholic Beverage Control Board; §§3-124, et seq. - Investigations; §3-125 - Removal of Unclassified Employees; §§ 9-309 & 309.1 - Prohibited Activities; Just One Casino; Franchises & Permits; Ethics; Environment; Office of Municipal Investigations, Office of Inspector General, Human Relations Commission.

24 See Alliance for Affordable Energy website: https://www.all4energy.org/.

25 "Committee Recommendations, sections 9-401 through 9-406 at 155–157. Section 9-406 reads: "The Council shall make adequate annual appropriations to the Office of Inspector General to enable it to implement this Chapter efficiently and effectively. The amount so appropriated shall not be subject to veto by the Mayor."

26 The proposed new section 9-402 in ibid. authorized the OIG "to investigate *to the fullest extent allowed by law* any allegations of misconduct and mismanagement involving *any city officer or employee, including the Mayor and the City Council and their respective appointees, all boards and commissions* established, recognized or continued under this Charter, *all other municipal elected officials and their appointees*, and *all officers and employees of any person or entity receiving or expending City funds*" (emphasis added).

27 "Such investigations may be initiated upon reasonable suspicion by the Inspector General or in response to an inquiry or complaint by a city officer or employee or a member of the general public, including confidential inquiries or complaints." Ibid.

28 See sections 9-401 through 9-406 at 160–162 in Mayor's Charter Revision Advisory Committee, "Mayor's Recommendations," March 15, 1995 (hereinafter, "Mayor's Recommendations"). A copy of "Mayor's Recommendations" is posted at The Public Law Center's website: https://law.tulane.edu/the-public-law-center.

29 See section 9-401 in the Home Rule Charter, which was adopted without change from the version at 144 in "Proposed Amendments to the Charter," August 18, 1995 (hereinafter, "Proposed Amendments"). A copy of "Proposed Amendments" posted at The Public Law Center's website: https://law.tulane.edu/the-public-law-center.

30 Bruce Eggler, "Inspector General Plan Passed," *Times-Picayune*, November 3, 2006.

31 "Voters overwhelmingly approved an amendment to the City Charter to make the recently established inspector general's office permanent and guarantee it a sizable budget." "Election Returns—Orleans," *Times-Picayune*, October 5, 2008.

32 See section 6-307(5) of the 1954 Home Rule Charter of the City of New Orleans: "Except in the purchase of *unique or noncompetitive articles*, competitive bids shall be secured before any purchase, by contract or otherwise, is made or before any contract is awarded for construction, alteration, repair or maintenance or for the rendering of any services to the City, *other than professional services*, and the purchase shall be made from or the contract shall be awarded to the lowest responsible bidder after advertisement prescribed by ordinance or by applicable State law" (emphasis added).

33 "Committee Recommendations," section 6-308(5) at 128. The committee renumbered section 6-307 ("Contracts") as section 6-308, so that a later addition to the 1954 charter ("Section 6-306.1. New Orleans Municipal Trust Fund") could be renumbered in sequence in the revised charter. The newly renumbered section 6-308(5) mostly retained the earlier language of section 6-307(5) (with one minor modification not relevant for our purposes) but lettered the prior language subparagraph (a) and added the competitive selection requirement in a new subparagraph (b).

34 "Mayor's Recommendations."

35 As finally submitted to the voters, the relevant portions of section 6-308(5) in "Proposed Amendments" read as follows:

(b) Contracts for professional services administered by the offices, departments, boards and other agencies of the Executive Branch shall be awarded on the basis of a competitive selection process which shall be established by executive order of the Mayor.

(c)   Contracts for professional services administered by the Council, pursuant to its Charter functions, legislative authority and responsibilities, and regulatory authority and responsibilities, shall be awarded on the basis of a competitive selection process which shall be established by rule of the Council. Such contracts shall be signed by the Council president upon authorization by Motion adopted by a majority of the entire membership of the Council, except that pursuant to Section 4-403(2), contracts to employ special counsel shall require a two-thirds vote of the Council's entire membership. The Council rule may except contracts executed solely to assist the office of an individual councilmember.

(d) Each such order or rule and any amendment thereto shall be published once in the official journal and shall be the subject of a public hearing at least seven days prior to its effective date. The Executive Branch or Council competitive selection processes may include a threshold amount below which the competitive selection process shall not be required. The amount of the threshold shall be established by ordinance.

36 See Frank Donze, "Charter Revision Critics Question Timing, Merger," *Times-Picayune*, April 6, 1995; and Christopher Cooper, "New Orleans Charter Vote Is Delayed for Deeper Look," *Times-Picayune*, April 11, 1995.

37 See Ed Anderson, "N.O. Charter Changes Get Panel's Nod," "*Times-Picayune*, April 6, 1995, reporting on Municipal, Parochial, and Cultural Affairs Committee approval for HB 1021 (changing the appointment of Vieux Carre Commission members) and HB 1097 (broadening the nomination process and limiting the lifetime terms of members on the Board of Liquidation, City Debt).

38 See Bruce Eggler, "Morial Pulls Charter Ideas," *Times-Picayune*, July 21, 1995.

39 See Alfred Charles, "Morial Holds Fast on Inspector Post Issue," *Times-Picayune*, July 28, 1995.

40 See Alfred Charles, "Charter Revision Faces Hurdles," in *Times-Picayune,* August 17, 1995, B-1.

41 See Alfred Charles, "Morial Gets Most Wishes for Charter" *Times-Picayune*, August 18, 1995.

42 Ibid.

43 Ibid.

44 See Alfred Charles, "N.O. Charter Revisions on Ballot," *Times-Picayune*, November 15, 1995.

45 See David A. Marcello, "Systemic Ethics Reform in Katrina's Aftermath," in *Resilience and Opportunity: Lessons from the U.S. Gulf Coast after Katrina and Rita*, ed. Amy Liu, Roland V. Anglin, Richard M. Mizelle Jr., and Allison Plyer, 82, 91–92 (The Brookings Institution: Washington, D.C., 2011).

46 Louisiana law provided for a proposition election on July 15, 1995. See Louisiana Secretary of State, Elections Division, "Schedule of Regular Elections for 1995–1999," https://www.sos.la.gov/ElectionsAndVoting/ PublishedDocuments/ElectionsCalendar1995-99.pdf.

47 See Kevin Sack, "New Orleans Casino Project Is Halted in a Bankruptcy Filing," *New York Times*, November 23, 1995, https://www.nytimes.com/1995/11/23/us/new-orleans-casino-project-is-halted-in-a-bankruptcy-filing.html. See also Tyler Bridges and Mike Hughlett, "Casino Shuts Doors, Files for Bankruptcy," *Times-Picayune*, November 22, 1995.

48 In his Second State of the City Address delivered on June 6, 1995, Mayor Morial praised Harrah's for its employment record: "Let me give credit where it's due. Harrah's has hired 3,000 workers to date and will hire 2,000 more next year." Those hopes were dashed by Harrah's pre-Thanksgiving dismissal of thousands of workers, http://www.gnocommunications.com/marchmorial/speeches/secondstateofthecityaddress.htm.

49 See Alfred Charles, "Hiring Utility Consultants May Violate New Charter," *Times-Picayune*, January 13, 1996.

50 See Home Rule Charter sec. 6-308(5)(c).

51 *Alliance for Affordable Energy and Gary L. Groesch v. Council of the City of New Orleans, et al.*, 677 So.2d 424 (La. 1996).

52 Ibid. at 426.

53 Michael Isaac Stein, "Political Connections, Contributions Helped Utility Consultants Keep Lucrative Contracts for Decades, Former Council Members Say," *The Lens*, March 28, 2019, https://thelensnola. org/2019/03/28/political-connections-contributions-helped-utility-consultants-keep-lucrative-contracts-for-decades-former-council-members-say/.

54 See Alfred Charles, "Council Contract Selection Process Criticized," *Times-Picayune*, February 15, 1996.

55 See "Council Politics as Usual," editorial, *Times-Picayune*, February 19, 1996.

56 See New Orleans City Council, "Rules and Regulations of the Council of the City of New Orleans," as amended through May 9, 2019, https://council.nola.gov/rules/#rule42.

57 See "Implementation of Amendments to New Orleans City Charter, *BGR Report*, September 1996, in NOPL Charter Archives, 50, http://nutrias.org/~nopl/exhibits/charter/bgr1996.htm.

58 For a detailed explanation of procurement procedures, see city of New Orleans, Chief Administrative Office, Policy Memorandum no. 8 (R), September 24, 2014, https://www.nola.gov/chief-administrative-office/policies/ policies/no-8-(r)-professional-services-contracts/no-8-(r)-professional-services-contracts-attachmen/.

59 Ibid. Subsection 8(c) named as members of the selection review rating groups the chief administrative officer (CAO); deputy chief administrative officer, departmental director, or agency head requesting the contract; and city attorney.

60   Ibid. Subsection 8(d) named as members of the grants provider selection review rating groups the executive assistant to the mayor; deputy chief administrative officer; departmental director, mayor's office division head, or other agency head requesting the professional services contract; and city attorney.

61   Ibid.

62   See Bureau of Governmental Research, "Contracting with Confidence: Professional Services Contracting Reform in New Orleans," March 2010 (hereinafter, BGR Contracting Report), 3, https://www.bgr.org/wp-content/uploads/2017/07/Contracting_w_Confidence.pdf.

63   See David Marcello, "A Way to Depoliticize Contracts," *Times-Picayune*, November 29, 2013, https://www.nola.com/opinions/article_411aba7b-6983-5f34-ba4e-c61956cd67e0.html.

64   See David Marcello, "Seeking Real Reform in City Procurement," *Times-Picayune*, February 28, 2009: "In his Dec. 11, 2001, announcement speech, candidate Nagin promised to present a ballot proposition within the first 100 days of his administration, eliminating separate mayor-council selection procedures in favor of a single process fixed by ordinance."

65   "In January 2002, candidate Nagin signed a written pledge to issue an executive order creating selection committees within 90 days after taking office. He again promised a ballot proposition within his first hundred days to unite mayor-council selection procedures." Ibid.

66   Ibid.

67   See "Contracts Should Be Done in the Open: A Guest Column by David Marcello," *Times-Picayune*, May 15, 2011, https://www.nola.com/opinions/article_ca5b1b03-d159-58d2-bcd4-749f304203e5.html.

68   See Frank Donze, "Mayor's Happy with His First 100 Days—City Hall Investigation Continues, Nagin Says," *Times-Picayune*, August 14, 2002.

69   Executive Order CRN 02-01 (June 2002), section 4, "Definition."

70   Ibid. See *Council of City of New Orleans v. Morial*, 390 So.2d 1361 (La. App. 1980).

71   Two new terms, "telecommunications" and "data processing," may have laid the groundwork for corrupt contracting practices that led to indictments of Nagin administration personnel. Executive Order CRN 02-01 (June 2002), section 4, "Definition."

72   Executive Order CRN 04-02 (June 23, 2004), section 14.

73   See David Hammer, "Public, Private Lines Blur at City Hall," *Times-Picayune*, April 5, 2009.

74   See BGR Contracting Report, note 11 (https://www.bgr.org/wp-content/uploads/2017/07/Contracting_w_Confidence.pdf).

75   See "Definition."

76   The last sentence of subsection 8(I) declares: "the completed evaluation forms shall be a public record and, as such, shall be made available for review and/or copying upon request," and section 9 (C) similarly provides: "Each completed evaluation form shall bear the signature of the reviewer and it shall be maintained by the Chief Administrative Officer for review as a public record." Ibid. These two concessions to transparency and the Louisiana Public Records Act must have been an unintended oversight, because later versions of the Nagin procurement procedure eliminated any requirement that individual evaluation forms be released as a public record.

77   La. R.S. 42.11, et seq.

78   See Frank Donze, "Nagin Vetoes Bill on Hiring of Firms," *Times-Picayune,* February 17, 2009.

79   See David Hammer, "Greg Meffert, Former City Tech Chief, Pleads Guilty in Kickback Scheme," *Times-Picayune*, November 2, 2010, https://www.nola.com/news/politics/article_d1589801-6a53-5f12-a142-7ceaeabbb975.html.

80   See Ginny LaRoe, "Ray Nagin, Former New Orleans Mayor, Convicted of Federal Corruption Charges," *Times-Picayune*, February 12, 2014, https://www.nola.com/news/crime_police/article_cfc47a26-db20-5bcc-8f8c-4302e4eb1692.html.

81   See Andrew Vanacore, "City Contract Process Improved," *New Orleans Advocate*, February 23, 2014.

82   Ibid.

83   Ibid.

84   Ibid.

85 See David Marcello, "N.O. Contract Reform Has Long History," *Advocate,* March 5, 2014.

86 See Vanacore, "City Contract Process."

87 Marcello, "N.O. Contract Reform." See similar reforms called for in BGR Contracting Report, 6: "an objective proposal evaluation system that includes the use of detailed criteria, weights and grading"; "all documents should be considered public records and made readily available for public inspection"; and "maintain written evaluations."

88 Marcello, "N.O. Contract Reform."

89 Ibid.

90 La. R.S. 42:17(A)(1).

91 Ibid.

92 See HB 449 in the 2011 Regular Session (which later became Act 188): http://www.legis.la.gov/Legis/BillInfo.aspx?s=11RS&b=HB449&sbi=y.

93 The amendment inserted into La. R.S. 42:17(A)(1) the following language: "except as provided in R.S. 39:1593(C)(2)(c)." The cited provision no longer exists.

94 See David Marcello, "Contracts Should Be Done in the Open," nola.com, May 15, 2011, https://www.nola.com/news/crime_police/article_cfc47a26-db20-5bcc-8f8c-4302e4eb1692.html.

95 M.C.S., Ord. No. 17,612, enacting City Code section 2-719.

96 In an article published just days after he left office, Mayor Morial shed some light on what may have motivated his failure to launch the ERB and OIG: "He says the need for an Ethics Commission all but evaporated when the state Ethics Commission was strengthened in 1996 by getting authority to launch its own investigations instead of having to wait for a formal complaint. Moreover, he says, it will cost millions to establish and staff an office of Inspector General and an Ethics Commission—money the city does not have" (DuBos, "Marc's Marks"). The lack of money is always a compelling reason—or an excuse—for not doing something in city government. But the first of these two reasons overlooked dual state-local jurisdiction to enforce the separate state and city ethics codes. See David A. Marcello, "Ethics Reform in New Orleans: Progress—and Problems Ten Years Post-Katrina," *Loyola Law Review* 63 (2016): 435, 450–452.

97 See James Varney, "Batt Battles 7 for Council Seat," *Times-Picayune*, March 30, 2006): "Midura calls for the creation of a local inspector general and board of ethics. The two watchdogs would improve the stewardship of the public purse and help detach politics from planning decisions, she says."

98 M.C.S., Ord. No. 22,444 (November 2, 2006).

99 M.C.S., Ord. No. 22,553 (March 1, 2007) and M.C.S., Ord. No. 22,888 (November 11, 2007). The 1994 "Committee Recommendations" provided a useful template for drafting these 2007 ordinances, which revived many of the powerful provisions that were extinguished by the city council in its "Proposed Amendments."

100 For a description of Citizens for 1 Greater New Orleans, visit their website at http://www.citizensfor1.com.

101 For a description of The Public Law Center, visit their website at https://law.tulane.edu/the-public-law-center.

102 HB 80 became Act 18 of the 1st Ex. Sess. 2008, now codified as La. R.S. 33:9611, *et seq.*

103 La. R.S. 33:9612.

104 La. R.S. 33:9613.

105 La. R.S. 33:9614.

106 See, *e.g.,* Acts 2010, No. 98 (expanding coverage beyond New Orleans to include parishes of a certain size); Acts 2011, 1st Ex. Sess., No. 20 (explicitly encompassing the city of New Orleans and the parishes of East Baton Rouge Parish and Jefferson); Acts 2012, No. 838 (detailing procedures for the issuance and enforcement of a subpoena or subpoena duces tecum).

107 M.C.S., Ord. No. 23,146 (July 18, 2008).

108 See Jim Mustian and Matt Sledge, "New Orleans Inspector General Moves to Fire Independent Police Monitor as They Wage Political Warfare," *New Orleans Advocate*, September 28, 2015, https://www.nola.com/news/politics/article_774723dc-0481-5837-888e-1e6675e42724.html.

109 See Brendan McCarthy, "Independent Police Monitor Named in New Orleans," *Times-Picayune*, August 11, 2009, https://www.nola.com/news/article_cdeb7170-4e9f-57de-8a06-f476eacefb74.html.

110 See "A Year of Crisis: A Timeline of Upheaval at New Orleans' Ethics Review Board and Office of Inspector General," Louisiana Justice Institute (blog), October 29, 2009, http://louisianajusticeinstitute.blogspot.com/2009/10/year-of-crisis-timeline-of-upheaval-at.html.

111 See M.C.S., Ord. No. 23,886 (Feb. 25, 2010).

112 See Brendan McCarthy, "New Orleans Independent Police Monitor Is a California Lawyer," *Times-Picayune*, April 24, 2010.

113 See Matt Sledge, "Relationship between New Orleans Watchdog Agencies Fragile, 'Divorce' of Departments Would Need Voter Approval," *Advocate*, May 9, 2015, https://www.nola.com/news/politics/article_a90e957b-7202-591f-a790-7e13f6f693a2.html.

114 The referendum text identified three purposes: "(1) to apportion funding among the three local ethics entities; (2) to establish each such local ethics entity as financially and operationally independent; and (3) to provide for annual independent external evaluation procedures for each such entity." Ibid.

115 M.C.S., Ord. No. 27,308 (March 9, 2017).

116 M.C.S., Ord. No. 27,746 (August 19, 2018).

117 I owe my acquaintance with this terminology to Gore Vidal and the second volume of his memoirs, *Point to Point Navigation: A Memoir* (New York: Doubleday/Random House, 2006).

118 "Discipline" comes from *discipulus*, the Latin word for "pupil," which also provided the source of the word "disciple." See "The Root and Meanings of *Discipline*," in Merriam Webster Dictionary, https://www.merriam-webster.com/dictionary/discipline, accessed February 29, 2020.

119 Marcello, "Systemic Ethics Reform," 82–83.

120 Jessica Williams, "Lt. Gov. Billy Nungesser Supports Loosening His Authority over State Museum," nola.com, July 2, 2019, https://www.nola.com/news/article_73031636-9c1a-11e9-b8b3-dfaf74bd5163.html.

121 I address the implications of "Municipal Ethics Reform" in an international context in *The International Legislative Drafting Handbook: A 25th Anniversary Celebration* (Durham, NC: Carolina Academic Press, forthcoming 2020).

Preventing Bankruptcy and Transforming
City Finances after Hurricane Katrina

Andy Kopplin

Andy Kopplin was the chief administrative officer of the City of New Orleans from 2010 to 2016. He is now president and CEO of the Greater New Orleans Foundation.

In 2010, when the Landrieu administration took office in New Orleans, we inherited a financial situation that the mayor compared to the massive oil spill occurring at that very time in the Gulf of Mexico, the worst in US history. The city was nearly bankrupt. Much of what we faced was the result of factors—Hurricanes Katrina and Rita, the subsequent failure of the federal levees, the great recession—that were far from the control of the prior administration of Mayor Ray Nagin. Much was the result of a culture of ineffectiveness and inefficiency that predated his administration. But much was the result of gross mismanagement and corruption during his time in office, too.

When the public sector management expert David Osborne visited New Orleans in 2010 at our request to assess the situation, he said: "I just haven't run into this level of dysfunction before, and I've been doing this work for almost 25 years." He noted it was the most corrupt city government he had ever seen.[1]

So we faced both natural and man-made disasters—ones that wiped out our resources and nearly washed our city away. We knew that New Orleans could come back stronger than ever before, but it was hardly obvious that she would. This would be incredibly hard work, but Mayor Mitch Landrieu was an inspiring leader and, as a team, we were committed to doing whatever was required. I remember the moment Mayor Landrieu invited me to join him and his team as the first deputy mayor and chief administrative officer. I was living in Baton Rouge at the time, and he sent a text message that said simply, "Come help me rebuild a great American city." With that, he basically reached into my chest and pulled out my heart. I had previously served Governor Kathleen Blanco as the executive director of her Louisiana Recovery Authority, in charge of rebuilding the state after Hurricanes Katrina and Rita. And I knew Mitch from our work together in Baton Rouge when he was a legislator and later when he was lieutenant governor. This was unfinished business for both of us.

I had been one of many who had urged Mitch to run for mayor in 2006. He ran but lost a close election that year. So when he won in 2010, I could not say no. I was probably one of very few people even more excited by his victory than by the New Orleans Saints' winning their first Super Bowl the day after his election.

Our entire team was moved and motivated. We knew that for New Orleans to thrive again, our city finances had to turn around. Much of the joy of our city—the music, the arts, the food, the culture, the sports—could not be sustained without the unglamorous work of preventing bankruptcy and getting the city back on its feet. More important, though, lives depended on city government working, and working well. Without a rebuilding of the city's finances, critical public safety and infrastructure needs would go unmet.

We were driven by the depth of the problems at hand. Two months into office, Mayor Landrieu gave a State of the City speech titled "Eyes Wide Open." In it, he made that oil spill comparison and he charted the reality we faced. Our city was beautiful. Our city was resilient. Our city was also in grave financial trouble. When we came into office, he explained, we had been told of a $35 million budget gap. As we had looked at the books in detail by then, we determined it was really $67 million.[2]

"Like the spill," Mayor Landrieu said, "it's worse than we thought, and there are no quick fixes."

It only got worse after that. We found more bills to pay that former Mayor Nagin's administration had left behind. By the end of the year, we thought we had nailed down all of what was knowable to a budget gap of about $80 million—more than double what we were initially told. Unfortunately, there was still more to uncover. The team in charge of payroll projections for the city made their projections in terms of when cash was required, rather than when expenses were accrued. They were not accountants and did not recognize that payroll costs would accrue to the period when employees worked in 2010, rather than when they got paid for those hours in 2011.

These costs expanded our gap to $97 million for the year 2010,[3] most of which we closed through cuts, applying an undesignated insurance payment and increasing collections in key areas. But this last mistake we found too late to solve in 2010, which put us in a deficit posture to end the fiscal year.

Since Hurricane Katrina, the city had often submitted audits late; three out of the five comprehensive annual financial reports between 2005 and 2009 were not prepared on time.[4] The city's 2009 audit was still unfinished when we came on board.[5] Thus, we did not know right away that the city was already in negative territory in its fund balance. And because we had overdrawn our reserves, we were using next month's revenues to pay bills from months earlier. The 2010 deficit just added to the challenges. But without our determined actions, the city would have found itself insolvent and may not have had advance warning to even know the end was near.

That we had reached a negative fund balance was painful to imagine. When Katrina hit, the city had nearly $70 million in reserve and then received $240 million in FEMA loans that were forwarded to us by the state.[6] Mayor Nagin's administration had spent all of this money and then some. Though those funds were essential to begin to recover and repair our city, it was irresponsible not to track those expenditures, recognize when the money would run out, and make a plan for replacing it in the budget.

To make matters worse, we had to pay $170 million to JP Morgan Chase for bonds that had been called because of the financial crisis in 2008 and a poor financial decision the city had made to do an unnecessarily risky bond transaction eight years earlier. We needed to pay them all back by 2013, along with a substantial termination payment.[7] The city was again looking squarely in the eyes of bankruptcy. We had overspent our reserves. Our recurring revenues were still smaller than our recurring expenses. Who was going to lend us money? We had to fix it—and fix it quickly.

We continued to uncover problems; they were numerous and serious. Some departments were overspending personnel budgets by 20 percent.[8] Our general ledger system was out of date and operated on a mainframe computer system.[9] The payroll system was decades old and no longer supported by the vendor. The only person who knew how to fix it had returned home to India; we contracted with him to maintain and fix it when it broke, which was often. Every week, when payroll hit, we were on the verge of a catastrophe; there was always the chance that more than four thousand employees would go without a paycheck. Our new city attorney arrived to a backlog of two hundred contracts to approve, all of which contained some sort of error. The Police Department was scheduled to run out of money in October.[10] Their approved 2010 budget, like the city's at large, was not paid for. Estimates for what payroll and overtime would cost were inaccurate. Additionally, the Nagin administration and city council had passed a budget that included a cut of nearly one-third in the more than $50 million health insurance program for city employees without announcing it publicly or even telling even the staff running the program.[11]

The city was also facing an incredible $200 million legal judgment for back pay and interest to firefighters dating from the 1970s.[12] Simultaneously, we were facing dramatic increases in firefighter pension because of an equally incredible set of state legislative and firefighter pension fund management decisions. The fund itself was terribly managed, leaving it just 12 percent funded in 2014.[13] It was also irresponsibly invested. Significant investments had been made in speculative local real estate deals, including a failing golf course. Individual contributions were too small, and no contributions were required at all from firefighters with twenty years of service or more—the ones whose benefits were growing the most.[14]

We also faced potentially catastrophically expensive civil litigation from the United States Department of Justice regarding unconstitutional practices at the New Orleans Police Department (NOPD) and the Orleans Parish Prison. Our community had been calling for reforms here, and they were right to do so. In 2010, Mayor Landrieu had invited the Department of Justice to investigate NOPD practices and civil rights violations, and in 2011, the Department of Justice issued a written report about their concerns, and alleging unconstitutional practices.[15] Fixing these problems would require money we would be hard pressed to find, but we knew that doing so would make our city safer, more fair, and more just.

In addition to the investigation into the NOPD, a complaint had been filed against the Orleans Parish Sheriff's Office.[16] The Department of Justice followed up with an investigation and report finding grave injustice and mistreatment in the Orleans Parish Prison.[17] The Sheriff's Office filed a complaint against the City of New Orleans, calling it responsible for providing the funding they would need in order to make changes. Then, the Sheriff's Office moved for a proposed consent judgment with the plaintiffs and the United States Government.[18] Without dramatic changes in the overall size of the jail—including the sheriff's practice of holding thousands of state prisoners— this consent decree would require extraordinary amounts from the city; we had already budgeted around $20 million for the jail,[19] but the Sheriff's Office was requesting more than $60 million to comply.[20] We needed a seat at the decision-making table. As with the firefighter pension fund, the city had no control over management of the jail, but we were expected to pay for the overwhelming majority of additional financial requirements of the proposed consent judgment. For these consent decrees, we also had federal judges who could seize our bank accounts to extract payments.

For the consent decree for the NOPD, we estimated that we would need to pay $55 million over five years.[21] The Orleans Parish Prison Consent Decree could have cost at least another $40 million annually beyond the funding we already provided for the prison.[22] This was money we did not have.

Even as we became aware of these issues, we did not truly know how bad it was, because the city had not been reconciling its books every thirty days as it should have been. The finance department was almost a year behind. There was no system for forecasting expenditures, and the City's Revenue Estimating Conference had neither been meeting regularly nor scrutinizing the revenue projections with any rigor. What revenues they had budgeted were often speculative. For example, they included an anticipated $1.6 million from a proposed new program to ticket brake-tag violators,[23] but the Department of Public Works never implemented an enforcement program. It would have been impossible. Ticket writers did not have the capacity to write brake-tag tickets on the machines they had at the time. Even if they had had it, their efforts would not have generated much revenue, because there were too few ticket writers to complete the work at hand, and they were using nearly all of their available capacity on the more lucrative task of writing parking tickets.

Money was also being wasted in striking ways. The city had paid more than $50,000 to store $70,000 of furniture that was never used. They were set to pay $11,000 for an educational program for someone who was no longer a City Hall employee. Contractors were hired who failed time and time again. In Armstrong Park, simple tasks like pouring concrete had to be redone multiple times. Contractors not only did poor work but harmed the park they were fixing, damaging trees and curbs and even a statue of Louis Armstrong himself.[24]

The Osborne report had noted the need to reform civil service rules; our system was fifty years out of date. Government job classifications were muddled, and that meant it was difficult for managers to promote or give raises when appropriate. It was also difficult to fire people for poor performance, so employees stayed for years in jobs they did not do well. Hiring was also too slow, and recruitment was inefficient. The city practiced "bumping," through which someone whose job is eliminated can then take a job from someone with less tenure.[25]

The citizens of New Orleans knew things were bad; after all, they were paying almost a third of their property taxes for interest on city debt alone. In 2009, the year before we took office, 72 percent of residents felt their "city government was worse than others," and 61 percent felt there was "a lot of corruption in city government."[26]

The city's struggles were easy for them to see; basic functions of government infrastructure had failed. In May 2010, when we stepped into office, nearly a third of streetlights in New Orleans were out.[27] Pavement was riddled with potholes. Fifty-five thousand properties were blighted and 27 percent of homes were still unoccupied. City Hall itself had been without hot water for two years. Less than half of the city's crime cameras were working and there was no maintenance budget to repair them.[28] Poor finances meant poor infrastructure; New Orleans was in disrepair.

Action: Careful, Strategic, Data-Driven Change

That was the world we walked into. We knew we had to make drastic changes to get out of the hole we were in. We needed to fill a budget gap that represented 25 percent of the approved budget in just six months.[29] We did so thoughtfully, strategically, and with conviction. First, we froze hiring and nonessential spending. We conducted assessments, internally and with external support, to identify our next steps. Then, we set out guiding principles to anchor our work. We used time-tested best practices of fiscal responsibility and accountability. We used data to determine and track what would have the biggest impact. We made significant cuts in spending, and we found ways to increase short-term and long-term revenue through the work of a dedicated group of internal consultants we called the Innovation Team, led by our chief information and innovation officer, Allen Square, who put his background in business consulting to work finding efficiencies and opportunities to generate new revenues. Throughout it all, we committed to the idea that we owed it to our city to make hard decisions. That was our duty as a government—to make the smartest, most strategic choices with the sorely limited time and resources we had.

Taking Stock and Looking Forward

When we stepped into City Hall in May 2010, we knew part of our work was fully assessing the depth of the problems we faced. We would learn to our dismay that the $35 million deficit we had been told about was closer to $100 million. Beyond that, though, we had to understand the reasons behind the deficit, and the other results of mismanagement we stepped into. We needed to unearth the many granular failures behind the larger, more visible ones.

This undertaking took expertise and honesty. Norman Foster, our chief financial officer, who had held senior financial leadership positions in the Iowa and Minnesota state governments, did the necessary, thankless work of asking tough questions of teams across City Hall and demanding proof in answers. We also requested the advice of outside experts such as David Osborne of the Public Strategy Group and his team. We raised the money to pay these experts from generous local groups determined to help New Orleans get back on its feet, including Baptist Community Ministries, the Business Council of New Orleans and the River Region, Loyola University, the RosaMary Foundation, Tulane University, and the Urban League of Greater New Orleans.[30] This collaboration spoke to the urgency with which citizens and local institutions sought change; Osborne's team took their charge seriously. They interviewed city employees, residents, customers, and local civic and business leaders. They met with government leaders and analyzed background readings.

The report they produced was thorough and sobering; we used it as a guide. Osborne's team pinpointed where things had gone wrong and analyzed where and how we should start making change. The report set out a plan for improvement that included ways to cut costs, take in revenue, track performance, reform contracting, and track blight. These ideas would serve as a blueprint as we planned the ways we would turn city government around.

To do this hard work, we came together around our shared dreams. We anchored ourselves with a city vision, mission, and set of values, as well as six concrete priorities. Our vision was "With resilience, we transform challenges into instruments of progress with the belief and assurance that change is possible." Our mission was "The City of New Orleans delivers excellent services to its citizens with courage, competence and compassion." Our values declared, "We are committed to serving the citizens of New Orleans, not ourselves. We are honest and trustworthy." The need for this organizational value would later be made more obvious following the convictions of Mayor Nagin and one of his top deputies for corrupt actions they took while serving in positions of public trust. Our six priority areas were public safety, enhanced well-being of children and families, economic development, sustainable communities, open and effective government, and innovation. Within each priority area, we set outcome measures. When it came to finances, these measures included the city's bond ratings and the level of funding in our reserve accounts. We knew that if we were going to make change, we had to be grounded in the same guiding purpose and held accountable to the same results.

Making Budget Cuts and Hard Choices

Right away, much of our work involved budget cuts. We held fast to Mayor Landrieu's refrain that we "had to do the hard thing for the sake of doing what is right." It was impossible to avoid making cuts that hurt. So we stayed clear-eyed and focused, choosing the cuts that hurt the least and helped the most. We had no real choice; our only alternative was bankruptcy.

This choice meant, for example, furloughing city employees for eleven days in 2010.[31] That meant everyone from police officers to firefighters to the health department to the mayor himself would lose almost half a month's pay before the end of the year. Classified employees got those days off. Those of us in unclassified leadership positions worked through the furlough days trying to put the city back together again. These furloughs were the most difficult cuts we had to make, because the city employees being harmed were, with few exceptions, not the cause of the problems. But they prevented us from having to make massive layoffs instead. In addition, we cut overtime dramatically and virtually eliminated travel costs across government.

We also made the necessary, but deeply unpopular choice, to freeze hiring across the city except for revenue-producing positions. This hiring freeze included the police department, which represented nearly a quarter of the city's expenditures each year.[32] By June 2010, a month into our time in office, the police department had spent almost four times what they had been allocated for the entire year's overtime pay.[33] Even so, in all eight years of the Landrieu administration, we never cut police funding. Instead, we increased funding for the NOPD every year we were in office. We managed this combination of increased funding alongside the two-year hiring freeze with care. The NOPD was budgeted for only ten months of 2010, so we added money to get through our first year and budgeted increased funding every year after. That funding included massive increases in retirement spending, new vehicles, new technology, body-worn cameras, pay raises, new recruit classes, and another $55 million over five years to pay for the costs of the department's federal consent decree.[34]

We dramatically pared down and renegotiated our vendor contracts. If it was not "on fire or bleeding," we did not fund it. We ended contracts that were not about life or safety. We renegotiated every one of the city's three trash pick-up contracts and cut a better deal with the landfill for our dumping fees. We cut contracts for lawn-mowing on the city's medians, which we call neutral grounds in New Orleans.

Though it was controversial, we also started pushing back on the firefighters' backpay case and pension funds; we wanted responsible changes in their investment practices, contributions, and benefits. Because the rules for the fund were set by the state, all we had to negotiate with was our wallet. We made the decision to stop paying into the firefighter pension fund until the legislature changed the board's structure and investment practices and adjusted the firefighters' retirement contributions and benefits levels to ones more comparable with other jurisdictions. In response to this action, a New Orleans judge ordered the city to pay, but Mayor Landrieu held firm—even in the face of potential jail time over a contempt judgment from one local court.[35] We created a working group to review the problem at hand, which included members of city government, business leaders, pension fund experts, and firefighters' representatives.

We pushed aggressively to have a major role in creating change at the jail, because its size and management practices influenced not only how much New Orleans taxpayers would have to pay but the level of justice in our community. First, we knew we needed to reduce the number of nonviolent pretrial detainees in the jail and get out of the practice of housing state inmates, so we suggested reforms to move toward those outcomes. We also knew that to improve conditions it was important to invest more into the jail, even as the population was declining. Amid all this, we were well aware that any new funds could go to waste without real reforms in management and efficiency.[36]

Enacting Sound Fiscal Wisdom

Coming into a situation so out of control meant returning to basic principles of fiscal wisdom. The city would now use recurring revenues for recurring expenses, and one-time revenues for one-time expenses. These steps would lead us to create structural balance in our budget. We budgeted for outcomes rather than simply funding what had been funded before. We audited the utility and necessity of our government programs and funded the ones that worked. We maintained hiring freezes where we needed to and carefully managed choices around personnel. With over a dozen separate departments and many more boards and commissions, we needed to impose executive control. No department could make a hire or promotion or give a raise without my signature in blue ink on the civil service form. No purchase could be made without my approval.

We went through our budgets methodically, stretching where we could and analyzing constantly. We went painstakingly through payroll. We made sure we were managing overtime and avoiding the previous administration's mistake of doing their projections in cash rather than accrual. If a program was failing to perform, or if revenue was dropping, we knew we had to cut it. We consolidated government agencies, boards, and commissions where we could, eliminating overlap, saving money, and increasing effectiveness. We carefully triaged how we released checks. Every week, Norman Foster and I would sit down and plan the order in which we would pay our bills that week. If we had a sixty-day grace period on paying a vendor, we waited all sixty days.

We also reworked the systems that managed all these processes. The city's basic operations had languished; we sought order and efficiency to get city finances back on track and able to fund the important work of government. We updated systems that relied on paper records. After a request for proposals and a review, we outsourced payroll services to a leading company in the field.

As we made these cuts, we engaged our community. This effort generated valuable input and helped expand public understanding for the decisions we made. Mayor Landrieu held public budget meetings in each council district every year to get our citizens' views on how New Orleans spends money, runs city operations, and takes care of its people. These meetings included city council members, the police and fire superintendents, and all other department leaders.[37]

We enacted civil service reforms that made our city more efficient and allowed for talented city employees to make an even greater impact on New Orleans. We created sixteen commander positions at the NOPD, enabling Chief Ronal Serpas to pull high-performing officers from across the department and put them into leadership roles, such as running districts or divisions, on a temporary, at-will basis. This opportunity to get new talent to the top meant that officers could rise to leadership on the basis of their skills and exceptional past performance rather than their rank and the number of years they had served.[38]

Later on, our Innovation Team led the effort to pass the Great Place to Work initiative, which implemented reforms such as merit-based raises, flexibility on hiring and promotions, and delegation of hiring authority to departments.[39] These shifts had been recommended to us by the Bureau of Governmental Research and the Business Council of New Orleans and the River Region, among others; now, we finally put them into place.

Using Data to Track Problems and Progress

We did not have room for error. We knew that city governments and police departments nationwide were using performance measurement systems and data tracking to improve outcomes. The flagship program was the New York City Police Department's Compstat program, through which the department tracked crime statistics and met frequently to track patterns and determine plans of actions. The program was launched in 1994. Between 1993 and 1998, burglaries and robberies dropped more than 50 percent, and homicides were down 67 percent.[40] In 2000, Baltimore followed with a similar program, CitiStat, that tracked not just police but other civic concerns, eventually healthcare and education.[41]

It was clear New Orleans needed such programs, too. We created the Office of Performance and Accountability, our version of CitiStat, which we dubbed NOLAStat, and the ResultsNOLA report, which would track our progress (or lack thereof) and make it public. Oliver Wise, our relentless director of performance and accountability, focused on "what's working, what's not, and how to fix it." On an internal level, we began carefully tracking fiscal performance data, particularly revenue collections and expenditures. We called this BottomLineStat. To monitor our citywide work of responding to reports of blight and to performance manage our efforts to remediate it, we launched BlightStat. We also created QualityofLifeStat, which measured the responsiveness of departments such as Sanitation, Safety and Permits, and Public Works. QualityofLifeStat also notably included the NOPD's Quality of Life officers in the conversation, since they were often the first point of contact for citizens. When they could help solve a quality-of-life issue in their district, it bolstered trust in the NOPD and the credibility of city government. ReqtoCheck tracked the processes of contracting, from requisition to payment.

These programs would streamline processes, eliminate backlogs, unstick what had gotten stuck in bureaucracy, solve problems, fix systems that were not working, and make us more efficient. They would also help create the conditions for economic growth and increased tax revenue.[42]

Finding New Sources of Revenue

In addition to our cuts and analyses, we sought new ways to generate money for the city, inspiring Mayor Landrieu to call our strategy "cutting smart, reorganizing, and investing for growth." For example, we hired more tax auditors and collectors. Notably, in our first summer in office, we seized and auctioned a Bentley from the owner of a local bar who was not paying his sales taxes.[43] Businesses learned there were consequences when they didn't pay their sales taxes; taxpayer compliance, and in turn, revenues, increased. We also hired more parking ticket writers. We realized parking violators had not been consistently fined for illegal parking. Sometimes their cars caused a safety hazard, but often they were simply not paying for parking in metered spots—it had become citywide knowledge that people rarely faced consequences for unpaid traffic tickets. Even those tickets that had been issued previously were not being effectively collected, so we took action. We began booting vehicles that had unpaid parking or traffic camera tickets; we found that nearly half of those boots went to violators from out of town or state. We noticed that fleet companies, like FedEx and UPS, had tens of thousands dollars of unpaid tickets. Now, we followed up with them to get the money the city was owed.

We set the stage for future revenue, too. We took action to make the city more welcoming to business, trade, and tourism. We knew that by making New Orleans a better place to live, displaced residents would return, homeownership and home values would rise, and good conditions for additional investment would result. The fact that nearly a third of streetlights were out was unacceptable and would discourage people from moving to those neighborhoods and to streets that were not lit up at night. So we doubled the number of work crews on the project and assigned those crews thirteen-hour days, six days a week. We also found $8 million in federal recovery dollars to help fund the work.[44]

We invested in repairing roads, pipes, potholes, libraries, and school buildings. We reintroduced the city's 311 call center, with a new software system that would track requests and monitor customer service. We set up the "One Stop Shop" for all city permitting on the seventh floor of City Hall. Performance data from the "One Stop Shop" and 311 was monitored in QualityofLifeStat. Our close accounting enabled us to find and manage the money to do these things, and we knew it would result in more money for the city down the line.

In 2013, we set out ProsperityNOLA, a plan for building more revenue through economic growth. We focused on industries and opportunities, such as advanced manufacturing and information technology, as well as logistics around transportation and trade. We landed a major IT job expansion from GE Capital. Projects like building a brand new billion-dollar terminal for the Armstrong International Airport and leasing the World Trade Center for a Four Seasons hotel downtown would bring about new revenue later on and spur new retail development.

Hard-Won, Steady Success: A City Gets Back On Its Feet

As we took action, we saw progress. It was not overnight. For my first few years, it seemed that every time I stepped into the mayor's office, I had to announce bad news. But we were making shifts and reforms, and as we went, we saw results. By 2013, we had balanced the budget and successfully refinanced the JP Morgan bonds. It was one of the best fiscal turnarounds in the country. That year, we finished in the black for the first time since 2008, with a positive fund balance of $8.3 million. By 2015, we had gone from that $97 million budget gap and a negative fund balance of around $20 million to having nearly $70 million in reserves—meeting the best-practice standard of having 10 percent of the city's operating budget in reserves. By the time I left city government, our budget was structurally balanced and had grown by $72 million in four years, largely because of new sales and property tax revenues.[45]

Our credit rating improved to the highest in the history of the city.[46] This rating was the result of many factors, such as the expansion of commercial retail and the increased tax revenue it allowed us to collect, our city's strong financial management, and budgetary flexibility. This credit rating, in turn, allowed us more funding for city projects.

The city still had work to do by the time we left office, even with our newfound financial stability. Because of the mayor's commitment to grow the NOPD as quickly as we could, alongside the costs of the consent decrees and firefighter and police pension funds, much of our city's new revenue was spent on public safety. This left city infrastructure as the highest remaining urgent funding challenge for our successors.

Wise Choices Pay Off

We stuck to our guns and held firm, and after more than a year of mediation and lots of help from the Business Council of New Orleans and the River Region, we reached a settlement with the firefighters. It established a payment plan from the City of New Orleans to settle the firefighters' backpay issue. It also provided a structural fix for the pension fund by increasing contributions from the city, increasing contributions from the firefighters, decreasing retirement benefits, changing the board's membership, and putting a number of restrictions on the way the board managed their investments. The firefighters' pension fund and backpay litigation had been long-standing impediments to creating fiscal stability for the city; now, we could move forward. In addition to ending both legal conflicts, we estimated the settlement would save us $275 million over the next three decades.[47]

Our civil service reforms also garnered success. The two police chiefs that followed Chief Serpas—Chief Michael Harrison and Chief Shaun Ferguson—gained the experience they needed for that role through the opportunities our reforms provided. The reforms gave them the chance to serve as commanders, gaining operations management experience as well as exposure to the most significant leadership, management and policing issues facing the NOPD. This experience helped prepare them for the leadership opportunity that followed.

When it came to our disagreements with the Sheriff's Office, we finally reached solid ground. Through the mediation of magistrate judge Michael North, we succeeded in securing a settlement that dramatically reduced the size of the jail and reserved it for local pretrial detainees, while excluding most state prisoners. This action significantly limited the worst-case scenarios of our cost projections, because they were proportional to the jail's population. The costs to taxpayers of these reforms were still significant—nearly $30 million more annually in recent years[48]—but they were kept from being much higher because of our efforts. Importantly, these shifts brought down the number of people that were held in our jail unnecessarily; we had more than six thousand people in jail in 2000, and by 2017, there were fewer than fifteen hundred.[49]

Growth in Infrastructure

Transforming finances and building efficiencies allowed for growth in infrastructure and civic satisfaction. The data tracking structures we had in place worked quickly to promote change. Our data programs, such as BlightStat, all had open, public meetings with department heads monthly. In BottomLineStat meetings, for example, we looked into how many photo citation cameras were working in school zones—these were most fundamentally a matter of safety but also an important source of city revenue. It turned out that many of these cameras were taking photos, but the lights set to blink during school entry and exit hours were broken, so we could not issue a ticket. Over a series of meetings, we figured out why and set clear plans to fix those lights.

With the city financially stable again, we could invest in critical projects that we had had to set to the side earlier. By the time Mayor Landrieu left office, we had filled more than two hundred thousand potholes, expanded bike paths to 110 miles, built a new hospital in Eastern New Orleans, built new or repaired police and fire stations in every neighborhood across the city, opened five new regional libraries, secured a federal grant to build a new Loyola Avenue streetcar line,[50] and spent more than $160 million in rebuilding our parks and playgrounds.[51] We expanded public transportation and began rebuilding our ferry terminal.[52]

These conditions for investments all paid off. Costco came to the city, creating jobs and, most important, new sales tax revenue, as did the Mid City Market, the Magnolia Marketplace in Central City, and the completely renovated Riverwalk downtown. New and renovated hotels and apartment buildings were opening one after the next in the Central Business District. New Orleans was much more sought after as a place to work, live, and visit, and we had a $6 billion building boom.[53] The shifts required to spur such investment had been paid for by responsible governmental practices, and they set the stage for even more revenue to come.

Stronger Systems Brought Strong Results

BottomLineStat had helped fix our traffic cameras, and other such programs were working, too. Our community became very involved in this process of data, input, and change; BlightStat meetings were the most popular. Citizens held us to account, letting us know about gaps in our systems and where our data did not match their experiences. When our staff reported that each new case of blight was investigated within thirty days, citizens attending the meeting interrupted us, declaring that we were wrong. We looked into the matter, and they were correct; it was taking an average of thirty days, meaning some addresses were still languishing in the queue waiting for an inspection. We responded by changing the way we tracked blight cases and doing what we had said we would do in the first place. By measuring performance, we changed behavior. Blight inspectors increased their productivity nearly fivefold,[54] and we reduced blight by over fifteen thousand units by 2017, going from the most blighted city in the United States when we took office to the city reducing blight the fastest.[55]

By using data and outcomes to drive decisions, we made better choices about how to use our money, and how we could make more. By tracking contracts, we cut the time of procurement from six months to just over one month. Our city services were more efficient, too; our 311 hold time went from roughly a minute in the fall of 2012 to four seconds in January 2015.[56] Our government became more efficient and effective while managing and making the most of our money.

Lessons Learned: Preserving Our City Required Hard Choices in Hard Times

The financial transformation we facilitated in New Orleans was not an act of magic. It was the result of clear-eyed assessment, careful planning, hard choices, and focused action. In the work I did alongside my team at City Hall, I relied on five principles, which I present here in the hope that they will be helpful to other cities and regions looking to turn their finances around.

1. When finances are out of control, a government has to exert more internal authority and control and return to basic fiscal discipline. It is important to act quickly. When something is uncomfortable but necessary, delay does not make that discomfort go away—it simply extends and amplifies it. I had to wield that blue pen, even though it meant giving my teams less agency than I may have hoped for. We also had to make clear, prudent financial choices, such as not spending nonrecurring money on recurring expenses.
2. Data and performance management matter, and they go together. City Stat programs work because they provide the clarity required for precise, effective planning, and the accountability to see those plans through. When New Orleans used data to plan for targeted, outcomes-oriented action, we made better use of our resources and set the conditions for investment, revenue, and better quality of life.
3. In times of crisis, fund only what is "on fire or bleeding." We can allow the grass to go uncut if it means our Emergency Medical Services can keep running.
4. Nobody tries to make a city go nearly bankrupt, but it happens. Well-meaning, smart people in government can be engaged in a system of dysfunctional habits that are truly corrosive to a city. They lose sight of fiscal discipline and spend money their city does not have. In government, we cannot make everyone happy; we have to say no, make cuts, live within our means, and enact change. We never spoke publicly about the threat of bankruptcy until long after it had passed. It would have spooked the bond markets and undermined our recovery. But the fear of it gave me many sleepless nights, all of which responsible management would have avoided.
5. If one follows Mayor Landrieu's advice to "do what is hard for the sake of doing what is right," change is possible. Even dire situations like the one we came into can be turned around. A set of guiding principles, like our mission, vision, and values, can help city

employees stay aligned, focused, and inspired as they work together through even the toughest moments.

I am proud to be a New Orleanian. Our city is stronger each day than it was the day before. It helps that our government finances are back in order, and I am honored to share what I learned in that process—but I am also reminded of what I learned from my colleagues and former teammates at City Hall. The government employees I worked with showed me the best of their courage, dedication, drive, innovation, and public spirit. They were there for the right reasons and, inspired by Mayor Landrieu's leadership, they demonstrated the true potential of city government.

Mayor Landrieu taught me about leadership, governing without fear, making hard choices, and having an unyielding belief in our community. My neighbors remind me every day of the importance of generosity, openness, and the power of a nod hello and a little critical feedback. Our city's students model hard work and big dreams; our business owners show relentless energy and creativity. We can take lessons from civic leaders writing in journals, but in New Orleans, we learn from one another each day. As other cities and regions work to model our turnarounds and successes, they should look to engage their communities as we did. These are all of our cities, after all. In New Orleans, a popular t-shirt company prints shirts and stickers with the phrase, "Listen to your City!"—and I believe that's the most important message for all of us.

Notes

1   Michelle Krupa, "New Orleans City Hall Dysfunction Leaves Specialist 'Shocked,'" *Times-Picayune*, March 4, 2011, https://www.nola.com/politics/2011/03/new_orleans_city_hall_dysfunct.html.
2   Mitch Landrieu, "2010 State of the City Address" (speech, New Orleans, July 8, 2010).
3   City of New Orleans, "Mayor Landrieu, City Council Announce 2018 Budget Agreement," news release, December 1, 2017, https://content.govdelivery.com/accounts/LANOLA/bulletins/1c8eef9.
4   City of New Orleans, "Basic Financial Statements: December 31, 2005," July 26, 2007; City of New Orleans, "Basic Financial Statements: December 31, 2006," December 14, 2007.
5   City of New Orleans, "Basic Financial Statements: December 31, 2009," July 30, 2010.
6   City of New Orleans, "Basic Financial Statements: December 31, 2004," June 28, 2005; Tod Wells, acting director, Public Assistance Division of FEMA, to Norman S. Foster, chief financial officer, City of New Orleans, November 5, 2010; Michelle Krupa, "Ray Nagin Wasted $1 Million on Tech Vendor, Inspector General Says," *Times-Picayune,* August 31, 2010.
7   Greg Rattler, senior vice president, JP Morgan Chase, to Byron Poydras, vice president, Bank of New York Trust Company, October 1, 2010; Mitch Landrieu, mayor, City of New Orleans, to Greg Rattler, JP Morgan Chase Bank, October 13, 2011; Bruce Eggler, "New Orleans Sells $200 Million in Bonds to Refinance Firefighter Pensions," *Times-Picayune,* October 12, 2012.
8   Landrieu, "2010 State of the City Address."
9   "City of New Orleans Saves More Than 1.25 Million by Using BuySpeed eProcurement Solution in Katrina's Wake," Periscope Holdings Incorporated, n.d.
10 Landrieu, "2010 State of the City Address."
11 Andy Kopplin to All Departments, Boards, Agencies and Commissions, "Circular Memorandum No. 11-01: Employer Healthcare Adjustments," May 4, 2011; City of New Orleans, "Presentation on the 2010 Budget" (presentation, New Orleans, October 26, 2009).

12 "New Orleans Firefighters Pension Fund Reform Overview," Business Council of New Orleans and the River Region, accessed July 1, 2019, https://www.bcno.org/new-orleans-firefighter-pension-fund-reform.

13 "Independent Auditor's Report: Firefighters' Pension and Relief Fund of the City of New Orleans and Subsidiaries," Duplantier, Hrapmann, Hogan & Maher, L.L.P, December 31, 2014.

14 *Sound the Alarm: New Orleans Firefighter Pension Woes and the Legislative Session* (New Orleans: Bureau of Governmental Research, April 2013), https://www.bgr.org/wp-content/uploads/2017/07/BGR-Pensions-Firefighters_2013.pdf.

15 "NOPD Consent Decree," City of New Orleans, last updated April 15, 2019, https://www.nola.gov/nopd/nopd-consent-decree/.

16 "Orleans Parish Prison Consent Judgment, 12-cv-859, Jones V. Gusman," United States District Court Eastern District of Louisiana, accessed July 2, 2019, http://www.laed.uscourts.gov/case-information/mdl-mass-class-action/oppconsent#nav.

17 Jonathan M. Smith, chief, Special Litigation Section, Civil Rights Division of the Department of Justice, to Marlin N. Gusman, April 23, 2012, http://www.laed.uscourts.gov/sites/default/files/oppconsent/09252012DOJFindings2012.pdf.

18 "Orleans Parish Prison Consent Judgment, 12-cv-859, Jones V. Gusman," United States District Court Eastern District of Louisiana, December 11, 2012.

19 "Revenue and Expenditure Analysis, Orleans Parish Sheriff Office," PFM Group, December 28, 2012.

20 Orleans Parish Sheriff's Office, "2016 Budget," December 16, 2015; Orleans Parish Sheriff's Office, "2015 General Fund Amended Budget," December 16, 2015.

21 Naomi Martin, "Federal Judge Approves Orleans Parish Prison Consent Decree," *Times-Picayune,* June 7, 2013, https://www.nola.com/news/crime_police/article_12368ec8-2d8c-52f8-b74b-703dcbf8324a.html.

22 Orleans Parish Sheriff's Office, "2016 Budget."

23 Ray Nagin, mayor of New Orleans, letter and mayor's budget summary to "fellow New Orleanians," October 30, 2009.

24 Landrieu, "2010 State of the City Address."

25 "A Transformation Plan for City Government," Public Strategies Group, March 2011.

26 Ibid.

27 City of New Orleans, "Mayor Landrieu, City Council Announce Plan to Fix All Streetlights in the City," news release, May 2, 2012, https://www.nola.gov/mayor/press-releases/2012/20120502-streetlight-plan/.

28 Landrieu, "2010 State of the City Address."

29 Ibid.

30 Krupa, "New Orleans City Hall Dysfunction."

31 Bruce Eggler, "Unpaid Furlough Days for New Orleans City Workers Can Start Next Week, Panel Decides," *Times-Picayune,* July 29, 2010, https://www.nola.com/politics/2010/07/unpaid_furlough_days_for_new_o.html.

32 City of New Orleans, "2011 Annual Operating Budget," October 15, 2010.

33 Brendan McCarthy, "N.O. Police Spending Millions on Overtime; Many Officers Taking Home Tens of Thousands," *Times-Picayune,* June 20, 2010, https://www.nola.com/politics/2010/06/post_351.html.

34 Finance Department of the City of New Orleans, "City of New Orleans, Louisiana, Comprehensive Annual Financial Report," December 31, 2015, 77, https://www.nola.gov/accounting/files/comprehensive-annual-financial-report/2015-city-of-new-orleans/.

35 Juan Sanchez, "Mayor Landrieu, Facing House Arrest, Addresses Judge's Decision to Pay Firefighters," *WDSU News,* September 4, 2015, https://www.wdsu.com/article/mayor-landrieu-facing-house-arrest-addresses-judge-s-decision-to-pay-firefighters/3379609.

36 Seth Williams, senior management consultant, PFM Group Consulting LLC, e-mail to the author, July 3, 2019.

37 "Mayor Mitch Landrieu Launches Public Strategy Sessions on Next Year's Budget," *Times-Picayune,* August 2, 2010, https://www.nola.com/politics/2010/08/mayor_mitch_landrieu_launches.html.

38 "NOPD Chief Ronal Serpas Announces 16 New Commanders," *Times-Picayune*, April 1, 2011, https://www.nola.com/news/crime_police/article_e36ad2e4-d9b4-5bf0-9332-2bf615320a73.html.

39 City of New Orleans, "Civil Service Commission Approves Mayor Landrieu's 'Great Place to Work Initiative' and Increases Employee Minimum Wage to $10.10," August 25, 2014, https://www.nola.gov/mayor/press-releases/2014/20140824-great-place-to-work-initiative-approved/.

40 Bureau of Justice Assistance and Police Executive Research Forum, *Compstat: Its Origins, Evolution, and Future in Law Enforcement Agencies* (Washington, DC: Police Executive Research Forum, 2013).

41 "Data Driven Government in Baltimore," Centre for Public Impact, posted March 31, 2016, https://www.centreforpublicimpact.org/case-study/data-driven-government-baltimore/.

42 Mitigating Neighborhood Blight," US Department of Housing and Urban Development, accessed July 1, 2019, https://www.huduser.gov/portal/pdredge/pdr-edge-featd-article-012218.html.

43 Bruce Eggler, "Bar owner's Bentley Is Seized to Pay His New Orleans Sales Taxes," *Times-Picayune,* May 5, 2011, https://www.nola.com/politics/2011/05/bar_owners_bentley_is_seized_t.html.

44 City of New Orleans, "Mayor Landrieu, City Council Announce Plan."

45 City of New Orleans, "2017 Budget Proposal."

46 Ibid.

47 "New Orleans Firefighters Pension Fund Reform Overview."

48 City of New Orleans, "2019 Annual Operating Budget," prepared by Gilbert A Montano, January 1, 2018.

49 "Incarceration Trends, Orleans Parish, LA: Jail Population (counts)," Vera Institute of Justice, accessed July 3, 2019, http://trends.vera.org/rates/orleans-parish-la; "New Orleans: Who's in Jail and Why? The Jail Population Remains Near Historically Low Levels," Vera Institute of Justice, accessed July 7, 2019, https://www.vera.org/publications/new-orleans-jail-population-quarterly-report/new-orleans-whos-in-jail-and-why-second-quarterly-report-2017/the-jail-population-remains-near-historically-low-levels.

50 Mitch Landrieu, "2016 State of the City Address" (speech, New Orleans, LA, June 21, 2016).

51 City of New Orleans, "City Receives Grant from W. K. Kellogg Foundation to Continue to Support Community Health and Wellness in New Orleans," news release, July 11, 2016, https://nola.gov/mayor/news/archive/2016/20160711-w-k-kellogg-foundation-grant/.

52 Landrieu, "2016 State of the City Address."

53 Ibid.

54 City of New Orleans, "BlightStat Report" (PowerPoint presentation, New Orleans, LA, December 16, 2010).

55 City of New Orleans, "Housing for a Resilient New Orleans: A Five Year Strategy," June 2016, https://nola.gov/home/buttons/resilient-housing/.

56 City of New Orleans, "Customer Service Stat Report" (PowerPoint presentation, New Orleans, LA, December 5, 2013); City of New Orleans, "Customer Service Stat Report" (PowerPoint presentation, New Orleans, LA, March 5, 2015).

Transparency and Efficiency in Government Operations: New Orleans Civil Service Reform

Kevin Wm. Wildes, S.J.

Kevin Wildes, S.J., was the first chair of the New Orleans Ethics Review Board. He also served as chair of the New Orleans Public Belt Railroad and the Civil Service Commission. He is University Professor at St. Joseph's University, Philadelphia, Pennsylvania.

It may strike some students of history as ironic, if not contradictory, to talk about civil service reform. The civil service movement was the reform.[1] Some of that skepticism was apparent in the response we received from many city employees when we began exploring the idea of reforming the city's civil service in post-Katrina New Orleans, and it was understandable. The city employees we talked with expressed fear that we would be returning to the colorful days of Governor Huey Long, when political patronage was based on who you knew and not what you knew. They assumed there were only two options: the civil service system they were operating under and the spoils system that existed under Huey Long. Their reaction was further complicated by fear of change. Another important background element was the trauma of Katrina and post-Katrina New Orleans. People in New Orleans had experienced change on almost every level of their lives. Now, for civil servants, there was another change coming, and it seemed to threaten their jobs and their pensions.

Understanding Reform: *Ecclesia semper reformanda est*

With rare exceptions, change is not easy for most human beings and it is even more challenging for systems and groups of people.[2] While many people may see problems in their present circumstances (individually or as part of an organization), it is often easier to live with what you have and what you know rather than to try to make serious changes. Holding onto the current situation, though pathological, may seem safer than moving into the unknown by accepting change.

We certainly encountered resistance to change when we began the effort to reform civil service after Katrina. The US civil service system began its evolution in the late nineteenth and early twentieth centuries when progressive Republicans such as Theodore Roosevelt sought to reform the old spoils systems. The Louisiana patronage system is a great example of how things were done in government before civil service.[3] But people forget that societies, like the human beings who make them up, are dynamic and changing. That means that the systems that serve society ought to change and adjust just as society does. One of the brilliant insights of the authors of the US Constitution is that the document they created can change and evolve to meet the changing needs of the nation.

The Need for Change: Evaluating the Civil Service System

One characteristic of New Orleans is that the past is always present. Many of its citizens, dramatically affected by Katrina, had rarely, if ever, left the city. The exodus of a large portion of the population to other US cities after Katrina, however, helped longtime residents see that there are different ways of running a school system and operating local government. Many people had not noticed that there had been significant developments in the legal and regulatory protections around workers. Between the influence of the past (e.g., Huey Long) and the lack of change in any social system, the aftermath of Katrina was devastating to the psyche of New Orleans city employees.

The effort to understand and evaluate the New Orleans civil service system began with some extensive work that involved looking at other systems and listening to those using the system in New Orleans.[4] In evaluating the civil service system, as it existed, we found from a survey of city employees conducted in 2012 that only 18 percent of employees agreed "that the current city civil service system [was] effective"; 58 percent disagreed. When asked whether the system was "efficient," 17 percent agreed, while almost 60 percent disagreed. The hiring process received even lower marks, and only 29 percent agreed that "poor performance [was] dealt with effectively on [their] team."

Managers and supervisors were equally harsh in their judgments about the system as it existed. Only 16 percent agreed that hiring "occurs quickly enough to meet the needs of [their] department/office"; 5 percent said they were "able to hire the best candidates at the appropriate salary to support the needs" of their department or office; and 15 percent said they were "able to promote qualified employees" when needed. Thirteen percent agreed that the system "gives [managers] the flexibility to create positions of the type and number [they] need," while 23 percent felt that it "allows [managers'] to hire the best candidates for the position."

In addition to the survey, there were interviews with more than seventy-five city employees, managers, and stakeholders, four focus groups (including one with almost all department heads and executive leadership), and half a dozen meetings with top civil service staff. Along the way, the city heard predominantly troubling stories. Under the "rule of three," hiring managers had to choose one of three candidates rated most qualified by the Civil Service Department, based on test scores (if a test is done for that position) and work experience but never on interviews or reference checks. Not surprisingly, after interviews and reference checks, managers often found those top three candidates unsuitable. As one manager explained, "I have been forced to choose between bad, worse, and worst."

Qualifications written by the Civil Service Department were often so rigid that managers could not hire those candidates they considered best suited because, though they may have exactly the experience the manager needs, they do not have the degree or credentials predetermined by civil service staff. The qualifications for web developers, for instance, favor those with the most certifications. But as most people in the IT field know, the best web developers often do not have time to take courses and accumulate certifications; they are too busy learning cutting-edge technology in real time and responding to the high demand for their services.

Another relic of the civil service system was that managers were forced to pay new employees at the bottom of their pay range. One department lost about a quarter of the candidates to whom it made job offers in a span of two years because of this problem. On the survey, a staggering 80 percent of managers agreed that the current system "allows [managers] to set the pay for new hires equal to their knowledge, skills and ability to perform the job well."

Managers were constantly concerned about losing good employees because they could not raise their pay or promote them. Under the system, promotions were based on employees' years of service and roster of training courses taken, most of which employees judged to be irrelevant and not on managers' assessments of their performance. In the survey, less than a quarter of employees agreed with the statement, "Supervisors, managers, and department heads have the ability to promote employees who exhibit outstanding performance." One department had a management analyst with a track record of high performance (as well as a law degree) but could not promote him to the next classification in the job series because people who had taken seven irrelevant training classes trumped him on the list.

In the civil service system as it existed, hiring could take six months or longer, and everything was done on paper. Managers found the written tests for many positions outdated and irrelevant. Paper-and-pencil tests may have made sense for most positions when many government employees were clerks, but those measures have been studied by the US Office of Personnel Management and found to have low correlation with future job performance.

Finally, the employee evaluation system was a waste of time according to virtually everyone we asked. Few managers rated employees honestly because doing so had no upside and multiple downsides, including employee anger, low morale, and time-consuming grievances or appeals. A 2010 study by the George Bush School of Government and Public Service at Texas A&M reported that only 1 out of every 250 employees in New Orleans had been rated unfavorably in the previous seven years. In the 2012 survey, only 12 percent of supervisors claimed to regularly rate employees "unsatisfactory" or "needs improvement."[5]

Both the Bush School report and a more in-depth report by the Bureau of Government Research (BGR) in 2004 recommended fundamental changes in the civil service system. The BGR report summed it up this way:

> Predictably, New Orleans' human resources system suffers from the flaws inherent in a rule-bound and bureaucracy laden system. It is simply too complex and cumbersome, and often too slow, to meet the challenges of hiring and retaining an effective government work force. The system is beset with problems and inefficiencies at every level. In many cases, bureaucratic steps created in the name of merit ultimately worked against the production of the most qualified work force. In addition, efforts to hire and reward high performers are handicapped by a number of failings and systemic problems, including a lack of flexibility in hiring and compensating employees and a meaningless evaluation system.[6]

Problems like these are typical of traditional civil service systems, which were created for industrial-era bureaucracies filled with simple, rote jobs. Many governments have therefore reformed their systems over the past twenty-five years. Half of federal employees, for instance, have been removed from the federal civil service system, and several states have phased out their systems altogether. Many cities have long functioned without civil service systems. Moreover, other cities and states have modernized their rules, eliminating the rule of three, using fewer written tests, giving managers more flexibility to set pay and promote high performers, and creating pay-for-performance systems.

Civil service systems were created for a good reason, and they have largely accomplished their purpose. In our society, many rules and laws have developed in the past fifty years to protect all workers in their place of employment. During that time, however, the civil service system in New Orleans did not reinvent itself. Thus, it contributed to a lowering of employee morale and impeded the implementation of a merit-based system. Rather than evolving with the changing times, New Orleans's civil service system developed and adapted by adding more and more rules that functioned as straitjackets for both employees and their managers. In return for making patronage and political manipulation of employees difficult, the system made good management almost impossible. Managers found it difficult to hire those they wanted, to promote and reward those who performed best, and to fire those who failed to perform. Without these essential tools, public organizations had trouble responding to citizens' needs, and when they did respond, service was often ponderously slow and performance was mediocre at best. Nevertheless, after Hurricane Katrina, despite the lack of rewards inherent in the system, dedicated civil servants performed their duties to the best of their abilities.

The Evolution and Development of a System: The Great Place to Work Initiative

In April 2014, Mayor Mitch Landrieu launched the Great Place to Work Initiative. Acknowledging that the New Orleans personnel system had for decades been in need of modernizing, the mayor announced that the Civil Service Commission had approved a series of reforms that would move "the City of New Orleans into the twenty-first century." Those reforms included an increase in the city employee minimum wage to $10.10 an hour. "Since taking office," the mayor said, "we committed to delivering New Orleans residents a more effective government that responds to their needs." Through the Great Place to Work Initiative reforms, the mayor promised that the city would be "a more attractive place for employees, and our managers will be able to choose the most meritorious and fit candidates from a larger field of qualified candidates."[7]

The Great Place to Work Initiative rule changes offered the following:

Process Improvements
- Leaves in place the same Civil Service protections against hiring candidates who do not possess the knowledge, skill and ability to perform the work the job requires.
- Gives more decision making to the managers who know the work requirements best.
- Allows managers to hire the most meritorious candidate who took the competitive examination and was determined qualified by the Department of Civil Service.
- Increase Civil Service's ability to [post] existing job classifications to speed hiring and sets meaningful performance goals for the personnel function of City government.

- Gives all employees the right to take at least one training per month, regardless of intent to take a promotional exam.
- Evaluate the performance of new employees before their job becomes permanent.

Pay Improvements
- Increases the minimum wage for all City employees to $10.10 per hour.
- Allows department directors to give pay increases within the already-approved pay range for special assignments without prior approval from Civil Service.
- Gives all departments an equal percentage of 2% of their approved budget for performance based pay increases to employees each year. Employees who successfully achieve their objective goals will receive a 1.25% increase and employees who meet their goals and perform excellently will be eligible to receive a 3.75% increase.
- Allows managers use the full approved salary range for jobs with recruitment challenges or candidates with exceptional qualifications. This requires objective justification and oversight.[8]

After the reforms were announced, in my capacity as chair of the New Orleans Civil Service Commission, I announced that the commission was "committed to ensuring merit-based decisions regarding the recruitment, selection, training, evaluation, management and retention of skilled and capable individuals who provide excellent service to the citizens of New Orleans."[9] I felt confident that once the reforms took effect, the city's Civil Service Commission would be more efficient and more supportive of its employees.

Erika McConduit-Diggs, president and CEO of the Urban League of Greater New Orleans, praised the commission for implementing the reforms, expressing the league's strong support for their efforts to "bring about greater diversity within all ranks and city departments." LaTanja Silvester, president of the SEIU Local 21LA, pointed out that the vote signaled that the Landrieu administration "understands that raising the minimum wage so that it can keep up with rising prices on the basic necessities of life is not only a plus for the workers, but also a huge step in the right direction for our great city."[10]

For employees, the changes approved in 2014 allow for merit-based pay increases to those who perform well, higher entrance salaries when necessary to make the city competitive with other cities, more opportunities for relevant and transferable training, and a fairer and more objective approach to evaluations. The rule changes did nothing to weaken the rights employees have to appeal disciplinary actions.

For managers, these improvements allow them far more ability to hire, retain, promote, and reward high performers, to motivate their employees, and to give actionable performance improvement plans to low performers.

For the public, in the coming years these reforms should result in better service, a higher quality of life, and a city personnel system that is a model public service organization.

For the city's elected officials, these reforms should produce a city workforce with higher morale, higher performance, and greater adaptability to change that should in turn yield a public that is more satisfied with their city's government structures.

Changing the rules and processes of civil service in New Orleans was only a first step. The older set of rules and ways of proceeding had created a culture that was stuck in the past and it will take time, with the implementation of the new rules and procedures, for a new culture to emerge and evolve. The staff of the Civil Service Department was inordinately attached to the way things had always been done and they harbored a suspicion of change. Their cooperation will be important to the implementation of the new rules and the development of a new culture. In a broader context, New Orleans is a city in love with the past, whether it was good or bad. In life after Katrina, New Orleans has embraced a new vision of itself to become a city better than it was before the storm. My hope is that that same spirit will be part of the transformation of civil service.

Notes

1   Matthew Schott, "Huey Long: Progressive Backlash," *Louisiana History* 27, no. 2 (Spring 1986): 133–145.

2   The phrase *Ecclesia semper reformanda est* (The Church must always be reformed) comes to mind here. It refers to the conviction of certain Protestant theologians that the church must continually re-examine itself in order to maintain its purity of doctrine and practice. This view was important to our reform efforts in New Orleans because, since the era of Governor Huey Long, many people had seen the Civil Service system as in need of reform.

3   H. Eliot Kaplan, "Accomplishments of the Civil Service Reform Movement," *Annals of the American Academy of Political and Social Science* 189 (1937): 142–147.

4   The research work done by the Bush School at Texas A&M University was supported by the Business Council of New Orleans and the River Region.

5   "Moving Forward: Charting the Future of Civil Service in New Orleans," paper prepared for the Bush School of Government & Public Service, Texas A&M University (Arnold Vedlitz, project advisor), May 2010.

6   Bureau of Governmental Research, *System Upgrade: Retooling New Orleans' Civil Service* (New Orleans: Bureau of Government Research, August 2004).

7   "Civil Service Commission Approves Mayor Landrieu's 'Great Place to Work Initiative' and Increases City Employee Minimum Wage to $10.10," New Orleans, Mayor's Office, August 25, 2014, https://www.nola.gov/mayor/press-releases/2014/20140824-great-place-to-work-initiative-approved/.

8   Ibid.

9   Ibid.

10   Ibid.

The Strange Case of the Seven Assessors

Janet Howard[1]
with Shaun Rafferty[2]

Janet Howard served for fifteen years as president and CEO of the Bureau of Governmental Research, a nonpartisan, nonprofit organization dedicated to making local government in the New Orleans metropolitan area more effective and efficient. She is now the principal of Howard Policy Solutions LLC.

Shaun Rafferty is a lifelong New Orleans citizen and practices law there. He has served on several boards, currently as a member of a charter school board.

Mark Twain supposedly once said that when the world was coming to an end he wanted to be in Cincinnati, since it was twenty years behind the time. He could have delayed his demise even longer by moving to New Orleans, where change comes at a glacial pace. The case of the seven assessors illustrates the point.

New Orleans was, before Katrina, the only parish (county) in Louisiana to have multiple assessors. There were seven. Each of them had his or her own district, and collectively they formed the Board of Assessors. The strange structure was the vestige of times past, with no rhyme or reason in modern times.

It was riddled with absurdities. For example, the assessors' districts varied widely in size, with fewer than seven thousand taxpayers in one and more than seventy thousand in another. It was obviously costly and inefficient to pay seven chief executives when one would do. The assessment budget was approximately double those of parishes with similar numbers of parcels. Yet, because of the expensive top-heavy structure, the assessors' offices in New Orleans had less money to invest in personnel and technology.

The return on this substantial investment was a shoddy system. The offices were understaffed and manned by people with insufficient training. For their methodology, the assessors generally engaged in sales chasing, meaning that they adjusted the assessed value of a property when it sold without addressing changes in the values of other properties. This practice resulted in wide divergences in the assessed values of similar properties and consequently the tax obligations of the owners. Properties that had changed hands recently were taxed at a far higher effective rate than those that had remained with owners for a long time.

The inefficiencies and the lazy assessment practices were bad enough, but the effects of the system were more pernicious. The multiplicity of assessors, all elected, invited an overly cozy relationship between an assessor and his constituents. Property owners routinely met with their

98

assessor to discuss their assessments. Proponents of the system praised this system as a personal touch, but the reality was that the relationship subverted objectivity and corroded the system. It was a nexus that had to be broken.

Despite the obvious problems, the assessment system stubbornly resisted reform efforts. The Bureau of Governmental Research (BGR), a nonpartisan group formed to improve the quality of government in New Orleans, had begun to advocate for the consolidation of the assessors' offices in the 1930s. Its repeated calls for reforms fell on deaf ears until after Hurricane Katrina.

The citizens' attitude toward assessments changed dramatically after Katrina, when an enraged public became actively engaged in reforming systems perceived as obstacles to the city's rebuilding and growth.

The push for change in the assessment arena had multiple participants. This article focuses on the contributions of two of them: BGR and the I.Q. Ticket. BGR, an established institution, worked to educate the public and public officials on the deficiencies in the system. The I.Q. Ticket, a newly formed ad hoc group, sought change through the ballot box. Another key player, the newly formed Citizens for 1 Greater New Orleans, worked relentlessly on the legislature. Its work is discussed in this issue in a separate article dedicated to it. While the stories are presented separately, they are intertwined.

Laying the Groundwork

The unfairness of the assessment system began to move into the public spotlight before Katrina. Following up on its earlier work, BGR marked the end of the millennium by issuing a major report describing shortcomings in assessment practices. Among other things, the report identified flaws in the ratio studies performed by the Louisiana Tax Commission, the state's oversight body for assessments, to determine whether local assessors were doing an accurate job. The problems with the methodology were masking the extent of inaccuracies and inequities.

In a quiet move that infuriated the assessors, the city's technology officer put all assessments on the new city website. This small move had a big effect. For the first time, voters could easily compare their assessments to others. A property owner could see that his neighbor, with a finer house, had a lower assessment. The inequity of it became plain and well-understood.

In 2004, the local newspaper, the *Times-Picayune,* published a devastating exposé of the system. The paper estimated that the assessors were valuing properties on average at 41 percent below sales prices. The Louisiana Tax Commission subsequently hired independent appraisers to review residential assessments in Orleans. It found that on average assessments were 25 percent below fair market value and ordered a citywide assessment of residential properties.

In the spring before Katrina, BGR issued a report entitled *Unfair Assessments, Excessive Exemptions.* Using a range of estimates, the report illustrated the impact of underassessments on tax rates and city finances. It demonstrated that correcting the problem would allow for a significant drop in tax rates without adversely affecting revenues. The report also brought the topic down to a more personal level by demonstrating how underassessments resulted in different tax rates for similarly situated property owners.

Shortly after Katrina, the assessors themselves provided a perfect example of how the seven-assessor system contributed to unfairness. Three of them cut property valuations in undamaged parts of their districts by as much as 50 percent. The other four did not. As a result, some taxpayers would receive significant tax cuts, while others similarly situated would not. As BGR pointed out in the release that brought the situation to the public's attention, the action of the three Santa Clauses would actually cause the taxes of the latter group of taxpayers to rise higher than they otherwise would have.

Reform Efforts Get Under Way

In the first legislative session following Katrina, legislators introduced two bills to replace the seven-assessor system with a single assessor. Representatives of BGR, Citizens for 1, the president of the city's largest real estate agency, and others made the trek to Baton Rouge to speak in favor at the committee hearing. Following their testimony, the bills were unceremoniously killed by a margin of two votes. Two of the negative votes were cast by immediate family members of two of the assessors.

That normally would have been the end of the matter, but the times had changed. Citizen complacency had given way to anger. Back in New Orleans, Shaun Rafferty channeled his rage by spending Saturday drafting a memo called "The 'I.Q.' (I Quit) Ticket." It began by neatly outlining the problems and an ingenious solution.

Statement of Problem:

- Orleans Parish's property tax assessment system, with seven independent, elected, paid assessors, wastes money, enriches a few and creates grossly inequitable assessments.
- The Louisiana Legislature has just proven again that it cannot sensibly address the problem.
- Under the Louisiana constitution, a reform system involving the abolishment of offices cannot take effect until the incumbents' terms end. The upcoming election of assessors in April will delay the effective date of a reform system for four years.

Solution: Let the voters decide by turning the upcoming election of assessors into a referendum on replacing the system.

How: Reputable individuals should run for each of the assessor positions on a unified "I.Q." Ticket.

Pledge: Each candidate would pledge:

- To resign as assessor immediately upon enactment of a reform system.
- Actively to promote enactment of a reform system.
- To serve as a volunteer, refusing pay.
- Pending the successful enactment of reform legislation, to work with the other assessors immediately to establish an *ad hoc* city-wide system of fair, consistent assessments.

Rafferty sent the memo to a number of like-minded people. The response was immediate and positive. By Tuesday, he had in place a limited liability company with a diverse board that included bankers, a former city attorney, a tax lawyer, a retired businessman, and the president of the city's largest real estate agency.

Momentum gathered almost immediately. By Friday, February 17, a week after the committee vote, the group had an all-hands meeting. It discussed how to raise money, how to gather candidates, and how to hire a political consultant. One member reached out to the *Times-Picayune* and within a week the group had made front-page news. "If you can't get the Legislature to do what you want, go around it," was the lead. The article went on to explain the plan: that the I.Q. candidates would pledge to work from within the system to achieve an effective consolidation immediately.

Gathering Candidates

The plan would not work without a candidate for each of the seven districts, and there was very little time to assemble the ticket. The qualifying period closed on March 3. In the end, seven wonderful people stepped up to devote countless hours and subject themselves to the rigors and the slings and arrows of running for public office. They were all successful, professional individuals with management experience committed to making the City of New Orleans a better place to live and work. They had no political agenda other than eliminating the unfairness and excessive costs of the existing system. They all deserve honorable mention:

- Charlie Bosworth, a former television news reporter with a great understanding of the public relations of a campaign
- Maria Elliott, the development officer at Trinity Episcopal Church (Maria agreed to join us on Ash Wednesday, saying that she always thought one should do something extra rather than give up something for Lent.)
- Errol George, a young man with significant experience in local politics
- Chase Jones, a young family man and a salesman for the local National Basketball Association franchise (Chase lived in the modest Irish Channel and, thanks to the system, had a higher assessment on his modest shotgun double than some owners of grand houses in the neighboring Garden District.)
- Nancy Marshall, a litigator at Deutsch, Kerrigan & Stiles, a prominent downtown New Orleans law firm
- Ron Mazier, a real estate professional who knew the subtle drag the system applied to the real estate market
- Jackie Shreves, a long-time civic activist from the Lakefront

The candidates all marched down to the clerk's office Friday afternoon just before closing time to qualify. Each had given "I.Q." as a nickname to identify them as reform candidates.

The Campaign

On the day he agreed to run, one candidate suggested that Rafferty read *The Late George Apley* by John Phillips Marquand, a Pulitzer Prize winner in the 1930s. The book spoofs the efforts of a pompous Brahmin trying to navigate Boston urban politics. While the I.Q.ers certainly did not resemble George in his pomposity, they learned that politics is not for the faint of heart.

The first alarm came early. As the group repaired to Café Adelaide to celebrate, Rafferty received a call giving him heads-up on a problem with the potential to kill the effort before it even got started. Two senior politicos who had seen the qualifications on the Secretary of State website were saying that the use of the I.Q. moniker violated a state statute that prohibits political candidates from using nicknames identifying them with a particular political position or cause. The politicos claimed that the violation would disqualify the candidates from running at all.

Rafferty spent the weekend researching the matter and trying to arrange litigation support in case it was needed quickly. And indeed it was. The prediction was followed by lawsuits seeking to disqualify the I.Q. candidates on the basis of the nicknames. A young litigator from a major law firm stepped in to represent the candidates pro bono. He did an outstanding job. The courts barred the nicknames from the ballot but allowed the candidates to run.

The I.Q. moniker turned out to be a problem in more ways than one. The initials, which stood for "I Quit," had been borrowed from an antismoking campaign that had run on television decades before. But they could also be interpreted as a reference to the measure of intelligence. The first thing the steering committee's political consultant told them was that the name and concept would play poorly among those voters who distrusted good government groups, particularly ones who claimed to be smarter than others. By the time the consultant made his sensible observation, the name had already gained currency. If it was a strategic mistake, it was not the last.

The campaign received significant financial support from a number of generous civic-minded people and companies. Nevertheless, the same donors were also supporting the other significant post-Katrina reform efforts in education and on the levee boards. Their ability to support the I.Q. Ticket allowed only for a shoestring campaign.

While the goal of the I.Q. Ticket was simple—to end a wasteful and unfair assessment system—the novel approach was difficult to explain and sell to the public and the press. The group had to dispel the whiff of elitism emanating from the name, promote unknown candidates, explain how the I.Q. assessors would accomplish their mission if all were elected, explain what would happen if they did not win all seven races, and address the biggest issue of all: Will the one assessor system cause my property taxes go up?

The complexity was reflected in the group's position paper, which ran to three pages of bullet points:

- To dispel any notion that "I.Q." was elitist: "'I.Q.' stands for 'I Quit politics as usual.'"
- To comfort voters that the job would get done: "We will develop unified, written, consistent policies and procedures for assessing properties throughout Orleans parish based on recommendations from the Louisiana Tax Commission. The elected 'I.Q.' candidates will serve as a Board of Directors without pay. We will hire one experienced qualified Deputy Assessor to carry out the statutory duties of the office."

- To tout the unknown candidates: "The 'I.Q.' candidates are seven successful, professional individuals with management experience who are committed to making the City of New Orleans a better place to live and work. They have no other political agenda except to eliminate the unfairness and excessive costs of the existing seven Assessor system."

- Deal with the obvious chance that the ticket would not win all seven races: "All elected 'I.Q.' candidates will perform the duties for their respective districts in accordance with our platform. We will continue to work towards consolidation of the seven Assessors' offices into a single office. If only one 'I.Q.' candidate wins it is still possible that a majority of the New Orleans voters will have voted for the 'I.Q.' Ticket and consolidation. This vote sends a message to legislators that their constituents want the opportunity to vote for consolidation. Every vote for a candidate who favors consolidation is a step towards one assessor and every member of 'I.Q.' who is elected is one more district which will be fairly assessed."

- And to address the biggest issue of all: "Will the one-assessor system cause my property taxes go up? Not necessarily. Under the current system, some people pay more than their fair share while others pay little or no tax. The law requires that all property be assessed at fair market value. When all the properties in Orleans Parish are fairly assessed, the millages MUST be rolled back and the overall impact to the taxpayers of Orleans Parish will be revenue neutral, so some taxpayers may actually pay less tax under a fair assessment system. Every property owner will wind up paying only his or her fair share."

Clearly, these plans and impacts did not lend themselves to sound bites. Conveying them to the voter would be challenging at any time, and even more so when citizens were reeling from the flooding.

The complexity and novelty of the idea proved a stumbling block when it came to obtaining the endorsement of two key local entities, the *Times-Picayune* and the Alliance for Good Government. Both got stuck on the mechanics of what would happen if the ticket did not win every race. The *Times-Picayune* gave a squirrelly almost-endorsement, demurring from a full one because there were "too many questions" about the effort. Almost was not good enough. Critically, it meant that the listing of endorsed candidates appearing on the front page of the paper on election day would not include the I.Q. candidates. Losing those endorsements cost dearly.

On the night of the primary vote, the I.Q. group gathered at a hotel to await the results. Toward the end of the evening, Rafferty's high-school-age son, who was watching his computer intently, looked up to say that with a minute left, the I.Q. Ticket was down, and the other team had the ball. Nancy Marshall, the candidate for the uptown district, had won. But in the First and the Fourth Districts, where there were multiple candidates, the incumbents had over 50 percent of the votes with only two precincts outstanding. The reformers waited for a miracle from those two for almost an hour. Then the results came in: both I.Q. candidates had made it into runoffs. Thank Goodness! A third candidate had come close to unseating the incumbent in her district in a two-person race, receiving 46 percent of the vote, but the other I.Q. candidates had been shellacked.

Essentially, the I.Q. Ticket received a positive vote in areas where the concept was able to penetrate and resonate, but a negative vote in all others. Maybe if they had had more time and money. Maybe if those endorsements had come through. Then again, perhaps if Katrina had not happened, the notoriously status quo voters of New Orleans would not have been willing to try such a quirky idea.

The two I.Q. candidates who had barely made it into the two runoffs lost their races in the general election, leaving Nancy Marshall as the only reformer on the otherwise hostile Board of Assessors. Her first official act was to raise the assessment on her own home.

Although the I.Q. Ticket had failed to garner enough assessor positions to implement its reforms, it had substantially advanced the issue by presenting a solid reform plan, keeping the issue before the public in a high-profile manner, and making a far better showing in the elections than any neophyte group had any right to expect. It had also gained access to the inner working of the less-than-transparent Board of Assessors.

The Aftermath

The issue of consolidation came before the legislature in the legislative session that followed the election, with multiple bills being introduced. This time the outcome was different. The legislature voted to send a constitutional amendment to the voters for their consideration. To become law, the amendment had to be approved by both a majority of voters in New Orleans and a majority of voters statewide.

Citizens for 1 took the lead in the tough lobbying effort to get the legislature to act and the voters to approve the constitutional amendment. As noted earlier, those efforts are described in the article by Ruthie Frierson.

The amendment passed in the fall of 2006 with 70 percent of the vote in Orleans Parish and 78 percent statewide. But since the assessors had just been elected, the consolidation could not be implemented until 2010. Fortunately, unlike some other post-Katrina reforms with delayed implementation, the consolidation occurred as scheduled.

As BGR pointed out in its analysis of the constitutional amendment, consolidating assessors did not guarantee accurate assessments, but it was a necessary precondition. There was no hope without that step. Thanks to the efforts of a dedicated, diverse group of people, that important step was taken.

Recreation Reform: Leveling the Playing Field in Post-Katrina New Orleans

Arnie D. Fielkow[1]
with Mithun B. Kamath[2]

<UNFN>[1]*Arnie D. Fielkow served on the New Orleans City Council from 2006 to 2011. He is now CEO of the Jewish Federation of Greater New Orleans.*

[2]*Mithun B. Kamath served from 2013 to 2018 as an assistant district attorney at the Orleans Parish District Attorney's Office. He is now director of Governmental Affairs & External Partnerships at the Jewish Federation of Greater New Orleans.*

Between 2000 and 2005, I was in charge of every aspect of the New Orleans Saints' non-football operations, from ticket sales to corporate sponsorships to lease negotiations for the Superdome. By spring 2007, though, by some combination of fate, determination, and maybe a little naiveté, I found myself in charge of legislatively repairing the City of New Orleans' entire system of recreation. I quickly discovered that this was no small task.

To add some context: I moved to New Orleans in 2000 to become executive vice president of the Saints. Five years later, Hurricane Katrina struck the Gulf Coast, changing the lives of many thousands of people living in New Orleans and along the coast, including my family and me. For many long months afterward, I was unsure of what to do next. In all that time, while my mind wandered far and wide considering the direction in which my professional life might be headed, I never gave a thought to abandoning the adopted hometown with which my family and I had fallen in love. I soon realized that I did not have to support the city's rebuilding merely by living there but that I could play an active role in that recovery by running for an at-large seat on the New Orleans City Council. In May 2006, I won that seat, and, at my request, I was appointed chair of the Council's Youth and Recreation Committee. I asked for that assignment because of my sincere belief in the power of sports to unify diverse individuals and groups. I thought that recreation, as much as any other government program, had a chance to help bring New Orleans back. By fall 2006. I was working to put back together the pieces of a recreation department that had been deteriorating for decades even before Katrina. Restoring the recreation department was as important to me in the wake of Katrina as the rebuilding of actual infrastructure.

The New Orleans Recreation Department (NORD) was created by ordinance in 1946 as a department directly under the purview of the mayor of New Orleans. For many years, NORD was the epitome of a well-run municipal agency, even inspiring a United States Supreme Court

Justice to cite it as "the most progressive" recreation department in the country.[1] Continually underfunded and understaffed, though, NORD was in such a dire state when I arrived on the city council sixty years later that the equipment looked as though it had been on the department's first purchase order. To make matters worse, the quality of recreation in New Orleans showed an undeniable racial disparity—NORD-owned facilities and programs (used primarily by African American residents) were very different from those owned and operated by private organizations (used primarily by white residents), such as the Carrollton Boosters Club, to which my own three sons belonged. The irony of the Carrollton Boosters facilities when I joined the city council was that they were located in the middle of Hollygrove, one of the poorest neighborhoods in the city. Compared to the private groups, NORD was not financially or organizationally sound, as was readily apparent in the poorly maintained fields, the old uniforms and equipment, and the coaches, who had the best of hearts and intentions but little to no formal training. Even before Katrina, but especially after, this disparity gnawed at me personally and professionally. My colleagues on the Youth and Recreation Committee and I sought to make the system more fair and to ensure that the city's recreation services were rebuilt to a standard well beyond the one in which they had wallowed before the storm.

It all started with input from citizens. If there was any silver lining to Hurricane Katrina, it was the colossal increase in vigorous citizen participation in government—an essential component of a government that works well for its constituents—and that included recreation. With no particular agenda in mind, we set out to hear about the way that the city had run NORD over the years from the people that knew the issue best—those who used (or least attempted to use) the department's limited resources.

We also called committee meetings to hear from NORD's administrators about what they were doing in the short- and long-term to improve citizens' access to recreation activities. It was not the sexiest post-Katrina recovery issue on which I was working, and the hearings themselves were not always pretty either. They put on display a severe dysfunction that was exemplified by the department's nonsensical approach to its facilities' hours of operation and the high turnover of the leadership of NORD, which had twelve different directors between 1978 and 2008.[2] But that was the point—we wanted and needed to get into the nitty gritty of the policies and operations to determine, for example, why there were weeds all over our city's playgrounds. Much of what we learned revealed to us what a city should not be doing with its recreation department.

Finally, we learned a great deal from Baton Rouge. Our neighbor to the west is often chided for being New Orleans lite, but, we discovered, when it came to recreation services, Baton Rouge was miles ahead of us. BREC, the acronym given to the recreation program in East Baton Rouge Parish, had won several awards, and we were lucky to be able to turn to it as a model for best practices.

The recommendations we received were many and varied, but over the course of numerous public hearings and listening sessions between 2007 and 2008, the one thing that we heard time and again was that recreation in New Orleans needed proper funding. We found, however, that citizens were not asking for blank checks or allocations well out of proportion with the city's budget but were asking only for the bare minimum amount they believed the city should have been devoting to NORD all along. For example, between 1985 and 1991—following the oil bust of the mid-1980s—NORD's annual budget was cut from $6.2 million to $2.2 million, which in

2010 dollars amounted to a cut from $12.5 million to $3.5 million, a staggering decline.[3] The challenges were pushing for recreation as a priority when there were so many other rebuilding priorities facing City Hall and then cutting through the red tape to access whatever funds were available. I certainly did not envy the position in which Mayor Ray Nagin and his team, as well as the state and federal governments, found themselves in the aftermath of the storm, but I was disappointed by the many roadblocks they all put up as we on the committee tried to make progress on the provision of recreation services. Delays were often instituted in the name of fiscal responsibility, but I suspect many had more to do with lack of political will and, sadly, lack of appetite for reform. The Nagin administration and the Federal Emergency Management Agency (FEMA) were frustratingly unwilling or unable to coordinate logistics and stalled on the most basic of repairs and constructions despite my pleas and those of others for urgency—even when the funds were supposedly there for the taking.[4]

Partly for that reason, one recommendation piqued my interest more than the others—it was suggested that New Orleans simultaneously address the structural and the financial issues associated with recreation by moving key pieces of NORD out of city government, with its inherent politicization and unpredictability. Proponents believed that administration of recreation services by a quasi-independent board and CEO as part of a "public-private partnership," still accountable to city government and with council oversight but not completely beholden to the mayor or any other individual, would result in increased efficiency, and moreover, that less of a reliance on limited and discretionary public funds in favor of corporate and other private funds would result in a more stable budget year after year. It was a revolutionary idea but one that I immediately believed had merit. After all, since post-Katrina New Orleans had become a laboratory for so many other innovative ideas—the education system most notable among them—why not recreation, too, if the idea was feasible? And what did we as a city have to lose? In July 2008, almost three years after Katrina, the nonprofit organization Greater New Orleans Afterschool Partnership formally presented the Youth and Recreation Committee with the proposal to revamp recreation in New Orleans with a public-private partnership model similar to BREC in Baton Rouge. As I said at the committee hearing (and still believe today), NORD was not in need of a Band-Aid but in need of a major overhaul, and in my mind the public-private partnership was the solution.[5]

With the end goal now clearly defined, a smooth approval and implementation process was imperative. By the time of the proposal, I had my legs under me as a public official, and I was confident that I could lead the recreation effort legislatively—and yet one of the best decisions I made in the entire process was to build an all-star team of private sector advocates to work with me. In the attorney Bobby Garon (also a personal friend whose sons played sports with mine), the Entergy CEO (and former University of Notre Dame football player) Rod West, and Roy Glapion Jr., a successful businessman whose father had also been a champion for high-quality recreation in New Orleans, I had beside me an array of well-known, well-respected, and well-spoken professionals who were passionate about creating equitable opportunities for New Orleans youth. They generously agreed to volunteer their time to lead a citizens advisory panel (CAP) so that reform of the city's recreation programs could be a grassroots-driven rather than top-down project.

The CAP was tasked with figuring out important questions related to governance and financing, and after many public meetings it submitted its recommendations to the city council in August 2009. The panel called for the creation of a commission to lead the city's recreation programs, with monetary support coming jointly from the city budget and a fundraising foundation that would have its own board of directors. Under the CAP's plan, some commission members were to be appointed by the mayor, some by the city council, and some from other organizations—in contrast to the model used since 1946 that placed all control with the mayor. All meetings of the independent commission and its committees and all those of the fundraising foundation were to be open to the public, in line with the bottom-up approach that resulted in the reform proposal in the first place. In addition, the panel suggested that the duties of the parks department be merged with those of the recreation department so that the commission would also be in charge of the city's recreation facilities.

With the report filed, one would assume that the CAP's work was done—but I am proud to say that Bobby, Rod, Roy, and I went on to hold public meetings every month and separately meet with numerous neighborhood associations and residents to solicit further input, and we even created a website for that purpose.[6] Not content just to lobby my fellow councilmembers and other public officials to support the proposal, I relished discussing the reform plan with the coaches, parents, and others most closely affected by NORD's decline. I was heartened by the community's enthusiasm for our efforts to make the city's recreation system work and make it work for everyone. It was truly a grassroots movement in which all New Orleanians should take pride.

On citizen input, I would be remiss if I did not mention that there was certainly a vocal minority in support of the status quo. Those citizens unquestionably had every right to participate in the process, and I valued their opinions. They tended to focus on the privatization of a function that had always been a municipal responsibility and questioned whether racial and geographic disparities in the provision of recreation services would persist or even grow. Current NORD employees were also worried about losing their jobs. In my answer I would often reference my own sons' excellent experiences at Carrollton Boosters and ask detractors whether they thought the current NORD system was comparable. Dedicated private funding sources and continuity in leadership, I argued, could do more to reduce the inequities in different neighborhoods' facilities and equipment than anything the city could do on its own. Furthermore, I said, there would be more recreation jobs and other opportunities in New Orleans under the proposed initiative.

With keen awareness of these policy arguments for and against, my council office took the lead in the translating the CAP's report into proposed law—the city charter amendments and ordinances that would bring about the recommended reforms. On June 1, 2010 (in no small part because of my concerted lobbying, I like to think), the city council unanimously approved a package of measures that created the new, semi-autonomous New Orleans Recreation Development Commission (NORDC) and accompanying NORD Foundation, and newly sworn-in mayor Mitch Landrieu signed off shortly thereafter.[7] Moreover, because of Mayor Landrieu's commitment to increase the city's budget allocation for recreation, it was determined that a property tax increase was not necessary, at least for the time being. Then, in early September, the council unanimously agreed on the impending commission's makeup and composition—it would consist of thirteen members, including the mayor and two other high-level administration officials, one councilmember, leaders from the Recovery School District and the Orleans Parish School Board, the chairman of the City Planning Commission, one private citizen from each of the five council districts with expertise in or experience with recreation, and a representative of the NORD Foundation.[8] It was a promising start but not nearly the end, since all changes to the city charter also require voter approval. NORDC was scheduled to be placed on New Orleanians' ballots in October 2010.

Meanwhile, I was thrilled to have overwhelmingly won re-election in February 2010, especially because it meant that I would be able to continue the push for recreation reform from my bully pulpit. Despite the "mandate" that some thought I had earned because of my relatively painless re-election, though, I felt that the NORDC vote was also a referendum on my first term. As such, I spent much of that summer and fall on the stump for the NORDC campaign—talking to voters and pitching the reform proposal, hearing their feedback, and requesting endorsements such as the ones garnered from the weekly business newspaper *New Orleans CityBusiness* and the good government organizations Citizens for 1 Greater New Orleans and the Bureau of Governmental Research. In many respects, the campaign for recreation reform was among the most meaningful labors of love of my entire council tenure, and going to the playgrounds to urge coaches and parents to give recreation reform a chance provided me with some of the best moments of my public life.

In the end, I could not have dreamed of a better result. On October 4, 2010, the city charter amendment passed with a whopping 74 percent of the vote. Furthermore, in the 2011 city budget, Mayor Landrieu followed through on his funding promise to double the city's allocation to recreation to approximately $10 million.[9] Although the mayor did not go as close to total overhaul as I and some of the other reformers would have liked, they were certainly delighted when the NORDC champion Roy Glapion Jr. was tapped to be the first chair of the new commission. Furthermore, the first CEO, Vic Richard—though a product of the old NORD system—embraced the public-private model. Vic thrived over the course of a successful tenure that lasted until 2018, exactly the type of leadership stability that we envisioned.

In addition to Bobby, Rod, and Roy, there are countless individuals inside and outside government that have earned my eternal gratitude for their essential leadership in the NORD reform process. Among them are my city council staff members, whose hard work, intellect, and dedication made me a better advocate for this new recreation system for New Orleans. I firmly believe that they represent the best of city government, and without them NORDC would never have come to fruition. I would also like to take this opportunity specifically to thank the people of the great city of New Orleans for entrusting me with the enormous challenge of reversing the downward decline of our city's recreation system for years to come.

Today, more than nine years after the public vote, the NORDC system is certainly not perfect and has a way to go to achieve the heightened quality and equality we set out to provide to all New Orleanians. I am comforted, though, every time I drive by one of the many facilities that has been built or renovated in diverse neighborhoods all over town with the help of FEMA, the City of New Orleans, and the NORD Foundation and its steady source of financial assistance—facilities such as Wesley Barrow Stadium in Pontchartrain Park, which was rebuilt to host the Major League Baseball Urban Youth Academy (New Orleans is the only city without an major league baseball team to have such an academy).[10] I am also comforted every time I hear that the city's recreation system has earned a new award for excellence—such as the national accreditation it received in 2017 for the first time since such a recognition became available nearly twenty-five years earlier.[11]

I was deeply involved in many issue areas during my six-year stint in public service, but the most near and dear to my heart, and the most rewarding, was recreation reform. My goal was, and still is, equity for all throughout the recreation system, and I am optimistic that the city is headed in that direction. I believe that the recreation overhaul will have reached its full potential when all New Orleans youth and seniors, irrespective of neighborhood or race, will have the first-class recreation experience my own children enjoyed. I am looking forward to the day when a game between a Carrollton Boosters team and a NORDC team can be played at either team's facility without anyone noticing any difference.

Notes

1   Richard Thompson, "NORD Has Gone from 'Progressive' to 'Terrible," nola.com, January 24, 2010, https://www.nola.com/news/politics/article_5462e4a9-6d5f-5d6f-b7c0-85f794df6cbf.html.

2   Bruce Eggler, "New Orleans Recreation Vote Is Saturday," nola.com, September 29, 2010, https://www.nola.com/news/politics/article_095c3417-9e47-5a1c-a852-f45c55133c1c.html.

3   Ibid.

4   David Hammer, "N.O. Council Committee Demands Quick Fix at 15 Parks," nola.com, June 20, 2008, https://www.nola.com/news/article_6d109854-273e-53f3-878e-8b741ca87ec3.html; David Hammer, "City Council, Nagin Administration Spar over Unspent Recovery Money for Derelict Playgrounds," nola.com, March 25, 2009, https://www.nola.com/news/article_03032d05-f668-5622-8bbe-2e9c51d0fb4b.html; Martha Carr, "FEMA Pledges to Try to Speed Up Reimbursement for N.O. Playgrounds, but NORD Repairs Remain in Limbo," nola.com, April 8, 2009, https://www.nola.com/news/article_bd01f9a7-439c-5fdc-83e9-fecd88f3fcb7.html.

5   Michelle Krupa, "Recreation Department Reforms to Go before New Orleans City Council," nola.com, July 23, 2008, https://www.nola.com/news/article_347447fd-bea0-50f3-8402-b62b773b74c4.html.

6   "NORD's New Web Site Designed to Get Residents Involved," nola.com, October 26, 2009, https://www.nola.com/news/politics/article_1d3c6748-ae03-5bd1-bfa1-77a3dc9a7188.html.

7   Bruce Eggler, "Voters Will Decide Future of New Orleans Recreation Department," nola.com, June 2, 2010, https://www.nola.com/news/politics/article_fc80de47-6d18-5866-aee3-7d5ec946f72c.html.

8   Bruce Eggler, "Makeup of Proposed New Orleans Recreation Commission Endorsed," nola.com, September 3, 2010, https://www.nola.com/news/politics/article_72221f2e-3d49-517e-8b93-23d53544d47c.html.

9   Gordon Russell, "Doubling of New Orleans Recreation Department Budget on Track for Next Year," nola.com, September 29, 2010, https://www.nola.com/news/politics/article_d70bbcaf-df5a-5c7d-8942-4b80b44f7fe3.html.

10 Bruce Eggler, "City Council Approves MLB Youth Initiative for Barrow Stadium," nola.com, July 8, 2011, https://www.nola.com/news/politics/article_6413e108-de38-5547-8d6e-319ba90f1f14.html; Trey Iles, "Politicians, Players Get a Kick Out of Refurbished Wesley Barrow Stadium," nola.com, August 27, 2015, https://www.nola.com/sports/article_22bc638c-a699-52cc-9fb2-713925161948.html.

11 Beau Evans, "New Orleans Recreation Department Earns National Accreditation for First Time," nola.com, September 26, 2017, https://www.nola.com/archive/article_414b3c86-c264-5829-be07-ee46bb7b7ca9.html.

Reinventing the New Orleans Public Education System

David Osborne

David Osborne directs a project on education reform at the Progressive Policy Institute. This article is excerpted from his latest book, Reinventing America's Schools: Creating a 21st Century Education System.

If we were creating a public education system from scratch, would we organize it as most of our public systems are now organized? Would our classrooms look just as they did before the advent of personal computers and the internet? Would we give teachers lifetime jobs after their second or third years? Would we let schools survive if, year after year, half their students dropped out? Would we send children to school for only eight and a half months a year and six hours a day? Would we assign them to schools by neighborhood, reinforcing racial and economic segregation?

Few people would answer yes to such questions. But in real life we don't usually get to start over; instead, we have to change existing systems.

One city did get a chance to start over, however. In 2005, after the third deadliest hurricane in US history, state leaders wiped the slate clean in New Orleans. After Katrina, Louisiana handed all but seventeen of the city's public schools to the state's Recovery School District (RSD), created two years earlier to turn around failing schools. Over the next nine years, the RSD gradually turned them all into charter schools—a new form of public school that has emerged over the past quarter century. Charters are public schools operated by independent, mostly nonprofit organizations, free of most state and district rules but held accountable for performance by written charters, which function like performance contracts. Most, but not all, are schools of choice. In 2019, New Orleans' last traditional schools converted to charter status, and 100 percent of its public school students now attend charters.

The results should shake the very foundations of American education. Test scores, school performance scores, graduation and dropout rates, college-going rates, and independent studies all tell the same story. During the first decade of these reforms, New Orleans improved its schools faster than any other city in the United States.[1] This improvement would be impressive enough on its own, but it occurred in a district in which 85 percent of the students were African American and a similar percentage were low income.

This revolution occurred in large part through the efforts of one unlikely heroine.[2] Leslie Jacobs was born into New Orleans' small Jewish community in 1959. In 1992, seized with "passion and naïveté"—her words—she ran for a seat on the Orleans Parish School Board.[3] In a district with a majority of African Americans, she went door to door, often in public housing projects. And she won.

It is hard to describe how bad the New Orleans schools were at the time. In crumbling buildings, teachers napped during class, students roamed the halls at will, and fights were common. Some principals' jobs went to the mistresses of top district officials or to those who bribed the right administrator. If someone failed as a principal, he or she was kicked upstairs, into the central office.[4] A 2004 study showed that one in four adults in the city had not completed high school and four in ten were unable to read beyond an elementary school level.[5]

Jacobs pushed her colleagues on the board to "reconstitute" failing schools—replace their principals and teachers and start over. But they stonewalled her. After four years of frustration, Governor Mike Foster appointed her to the state Board of Elementary and Secondary Education (BESE, like the cow). There she pushed through an accountability system: statewide standardized tests; school performance scores, based on test scores, attendance rates, and graduation rates; help for schools with low scores, in the form of money and consultants; and forced reconstitution of schools rated failing for four years in a row.

The new tests were given every year from third through eighth grades, and high school students took graduate exit exams (GEEs). Students had to achieve at least a "basic" (grade-level) score in English language arts or math and an "approaching basic" score in the other subject to move from fourth to fifth grade and eighth to ninth. To graduate, high school students had to pass the GEE. In 2000, only one in four public school students in New Orleans scored basic or above on the new tests.

Jacobs's epiphany came in 2003 when the valedictorian at New Orleans' Fortier High failed the GEE, despite making five attempts. "When she failed and couldn't walk across that stage and get her diploma, there was no civil rights protest, there was no religious protest, business protest, civic leadership protest—there was a deafening silence," Jacobs remembers. She decided it was time for something radical: a special school district to take over failed schools, a new idea in education reform circles.

Unfortunately, her brainchild required a constitutional amendment, which necessitated a two-thirds vote in the legislature, then a simple majority on a statewide ballot. The governor and his staff convinced the legislature, and Jacobs led the statewide campaign. The Orleans Parish School Board, the city council, and the teachers' union all came out against the amendment. "But I had served an African American district," Jacobs says. "I had walked the district; I answered my phone. I knew parents wanted good schools for their kids; I had no doubt about it." The amendment passed by close to 60 percent—statewide and in the city.

The new district had a lot of New Orleans schools to choose from: Fifty-four of the state's seventy-three failing schools were in the city.[6] In its first two years, the RSD took control of five New Orleans schools, turning them over to charter operators.[7]

On August 29, 2005, Katrina roared in and the levees gave way. New Orleans Public Schools was already broke when Katrina hit; the board was searching for a $50 million line of credit so it could meet payroll. On September 15 it put all employees on unpaid disaster leave.[8] Soon afterward it announced it was not reopening any schools that academic year. Jacobs met with State Superintendent Cecil Picard and insisted that they do something. Her solution: a bill to require that the new RSD take over all New Orleans schools that had performance scores below the statewide average. The RSD would reopen them all as charter schools, she said.[9]

State legislators from both parties were so fed up with the Orleans Parish School Board

(OPSB) that they passed the bill. In November, with one stroke of her pen, Democratic governor Kathleen Blanco swept more than a hundred empty schools into the RSD.[10] With no plans to reopen schools and no money to rehire anyone, the OPSB voted in December to permanently lay off its seventy-five hundred employees.[11]

Louisiana's senior senator, Democrat Mary Landrieu, learned that the US Department of Education had almost $30 million of unspent charter startup money, and she persuaded Secretary Margaret Spellings to make most of it available for new charters in New Orleans.[12] The new money enticed even the OPSB to begin chartering its schools.

When charter applications began to roll into the RSD, its leaders asked the National Association of Charter School Authorizers to vet them, to make sure those approved had a good chance of producing high-performing schools. To their chagrin, the association recommended only six of forty-four applicants in the first round.[13] But quality was important to Jacobs and her colleagues, so they swallowed hard and chartered only six schools. That meant the RSD somehow had to open its own schools—three of them that spring of 2006, more in the fall—with no fund balance to draw on, no principals lined up, and no teachers.

To top it off, State Superintendent Cecil Picard, who had been ill, passed away in February 2007. The state board appointed Paul Pastorek, a New Orleans attorney who had served with Jacobs on BESE, as state superintendent. He immediately hired Paul Vallas to run the RSD. Vallas had run school districts in Chicago and Philadelphia, where he managed a portfolio of some forty contracted schools, fifty-six charter schools, and more than two hundred district-run schools. He had learned the value of handing authority over budget and personnel to the schools but holding them accountable for results.[14]

"My game plan was to create a system of either charter or charter-like schools—traditional schools with charter-like autonomy," Vallas told me.

"Rather than try to restore what was there, we would select school providers—and they didn't have to be charters, they could be old schools—based on the quality of their application. And then give all the schools the independence and autonomy they would need so that the structure of the schools—how they hired, the length of the school day, length of year, the operational plans— would really be designed to benefit kids." The central office would play a support role, providing the buildings, the materials, and the accountability.

"All the schools would be up for renewal every five years, including traditional schools"— and if they were not performing, they would be closed down. "You would be prequalifying or incubating new school providers or identifying top performing schools that were ready to take on other schools or expand their clusters, so you would turn the weak performing schools over to the strong performing schools."

While BESE accepted every charter application its screeners approved, Vallas and his staff worked hard to make the schools the RSD operated succeed. They treated the "direct-run" schools as much like charters as possible, though teachers who survived three years automatically got tenure, under state law.

It was an uphill battle. When Vallas first arrived, in the spring of 2007, less than half the kids were showing up for school.[15] More than 90 percent of the RSD's students lived in poverty, the vast majority being raised by single parents or grandparents.[16] "So you take deep poverty and then you compound that by . . . the physical, psychological, emotional damage inflicted by the hurricane," he told the *New York Times*. "It's like the straw that breaks the camel's back."[17]

After a couple of years, it became obvious that charters were outperforming RSD-run schools, especially at the high-school level. Motivated parents were flocking to the charters; the RSD-operated high schools became dumping grounds for those paying less attention and for students dropping in and out of school. Their average entrant was four years below grade level, and every year almost half their students were new.[18] So Vallas and Pastorek embraced the obvious solution: turn all RSD schools in the city into charters.

Partnering with New Schools for New Orleans—a nonprofit that helped charters get started—the RSD landed a federal Investing in Innovation grant for $28 million, to replace failing schools with high-performing charters. As the city's strongest charters took over failing RSD-run schools, a transition began from mostly single charters to charter management organizations, each with a handful of schools.

"Paul Vallas was our Gorbachev," Jacobs says. "He came in and was willing to give up his power and control. He could have created a mini school district; instead, he wound down the RSD-run schools, which was very hard to do. Every year he had to lay off people, downsize his budget, because he ran fewer schools. He deserves phenomenal credit for that."

Another key player was Senator Landrieu. As a rule-bound bureaucracy, the Federal Emergency Management Agency (FEMA) refused to fund anything but strict replacement of what had been there before the storm: a clock for a clock, a desk for a desk. Yet New Orleans' schools had been woefully outdated. Senator Landrieu fought for two years to convince the Bush administration to agree instead to provide a lump sum payment of more than $1.84 billion to rebuild all the city's schools. Finally she had to push a change in the law through Congress, but she prevailed.[19]

The FEMA money, along with Community Development Block Grant funds, allowed the RSD and OPSB to finance their $2 billion master plan, which should eventually reconstruct or renovate every public school in New Orleans, while reducing the number of permanent school facilities from 127 before Katrina to 87.[20] "The FEMA lump sum made the master plan possible," Landrieu says, "and the master plan made the transformation of New Orleans' schools possible, because charters finally had access to reliable capital funding for their facilities."

The Results

Before Katrina, 62 percent of New Orleans students attended a school with a performance score in the bottom 10 percent of the state. By 2018, only 8 percent did.[21]

Before Katrina, roughly half of public school students in New Orleans dropped out, and fewer than one in five went on to college.[22] In 2015, 76 percent graduated from high school within five years, a point above the state average.[23] In 2016, 64 percent of graduates entered college, six points higher than the state average.[24]

The fastest progress took place in the RSD schools. Because the OPSB was allowed to keep only those schools that scored above the state average, the failing schools were all in the RSD. In the spring of 2007, only 23 percent of students in those schools tested at or above grade level. Seven years later, 57 percent did. RSD students in New Orleans improved almost four times faster than the state average.[25] (The state adopted a new standardized test in 2015, so scores are no longer comparable to those of the previous decade.)

Stanford University's Center for Research on Education Outcomes (CREDO) studied charter school results between 2005–2006 and 2011–2012. Charter students in New Orleans gained nearly half a year of additional learning in math and a third of a year in reading, every year, compared to demographically similar students, with similar past test scores, in the city's nonchartered public schools.[26]

Douglas Harris, an economist at Tulane University, created a research center to investigate education reform in New Orleans. He and his team have looked into every possible explanation for the improvements, and in the process have proven that they are just what they appear: the result of profound reforms. They examined whether demographic changes in the city could have contributed to the improved test scores and concluded that, at most, demographics accounted for only 10 percent of the difference between progress in New Orleans and progress in other districts hit by the storm. But because New Orleans students experienced more trauma and disruption than those in the other districts, they added, "The factors pushing student outcomes down were at least as large as the population changes pushing them up."

"We are not aware of any other districts that have made such large improvements in such a short time," Harris concluded.[27]

Winning Political Battles

It is one thing to deliver results. It is quite another to win the hearts and minds of a majority of voters. Race is a wound that festers beneath the surface of virtually every issue in New Orleans.

By the time Katrina hit, the black community still harbored deep distrust of the white power structure. When the school district laid off its seventy-five hundred employees—three-quarters of them black—it triggered enormous anger. The available data suggest that only a third of the former OPSB employees landed jobs with the OPSB, the RSD, or charters, though another 18 percent found jobs in other parishes.[28] The public school population had fallen dramatically, after all, and 30 percent of OPSB teachers who applied to the RSD failed its basic skills test.[29] To make matters worse, blacks had to watch white reformers at the state board and the RSD take over the schools and white charter operators and teachers flood the city. By 2015 African Americans still made up only 51 percent of school leaders and roughly half the teaching force, down from 71 percent of teachers before the storm.[30]

Today, however, a solid majority of New Orleanians supports the reforms. The Cowen Institute for Public Education Initiatives does a poll every year. In 2009, only 31 percent of public school parents said the schools had improved since Katrina. Two years later 66 percent believed the schools had improved.[31] In April 2016, 63 percent of voters surveyed in New Orleans agreed with the statement: "Public charter schools have improved public education in New Orleans." Among African Americans, 57 percent agreed. Three-quarters of those surveyed supported public-school choice (72 percent of African Americans), and 62 percent thought it had had a positive impact on the quality of education (52 percent of African Americans).[32]

In 2016, after a Democrat hostile to charters won the governorship, Jacobs and her allies decided it was time to move control over New Orleans' charters back to the OPSB. They drafted a set of principles that most local leaders signed onto, then a bill that easily passed the state legislature. All RSD schools in the city returned to the locally elected school board on July 1, 2018.

Why the New Orleans Model Works

Traditional public-school systems centralize authority, organize in hierarchies, use rules to control behavior, avoid competition, treat those they serve as dependents not customers, and operate cookie-cutter schools for most children. In the Information Age, these bureaucracies are dinosaurs. They are too slow, too rigid, too inward-looking, and too indifferent to the quality of their performance.

What can these traditional school systems learn from New Orleans' startling turnaround? Based on several decades of research on bureaucratic transformation in the public sector, I believe its success rests on several fundamental changes in organizational DNA.

Decentralizing Operational Control to the School Level

Most charters in New Orleans are either independent or part of a charter network with only a few schools. Even KIPP (the Knowledge Is Power Program), the largest with eight schools, lets its principals make most of the decisions, as long as they are faithful to a handful of philosophical tenets. So school leaders—not superintendents—make the key operational decisions in New Orleans.

Ask any charter principal why the new model works, and you will hear the same story: we can hire good teachers, fire mediocre ones, and spend our money in whatever way works best for our kids. In traditional districts, most hiring, budget, and curriculum decisions are made at central headquarters, and it is virtually impossible to fire a teacher who has tenure.

While controlling hiring and school budgets are the two greatest advantages, freedom from school districts' other rules is also important. Even seemingly insignificant rules can have a profound effect. At the RSD school where he had taught, one charter principal told me, "We couldn't keep kids after school for detention, because an RSD rule said all kids had to go home in a yellow bus." That one rule undermined the school's ability to enforce discipline. At the charter "we can do that, plus have Saturday school."

Creating Different Schools for Different Kids and Letting Families Choose

Children learn differently, they come from different backgrounds, they are interested in different things, and they thrive in different environments, so putting them all in cookie-cutter schools is profoundly unfair to most of them. We need different learning environments to meet the needs of different children, and in urban areas, that is very doable.

In New Orleans, there are now "no excuses" schools, with a laserlike focus on getting poor, minority children into college. There are schools with a special focus on science and math, technology, creative arts, and language immersion. There is a Montessori school. There are many schools that use blended learning and some that embrace project-based learning. There are two high schools that offer the demanding International Baccalaureate program, one military and maritime high school, and three alternative high schools for kids who are far behind or over-age or who have dropped out or been expelled. Several diverse-by-design schools have opened, with deliberately integrated student bodies. And a new career-tech high school opened in 2017, followed by a career-tech center available to students from any public high school.

In a system like this, it makes no sense to force a student to attend any particular school. Hence no one in New Orleans is assigned; every family chooses. All schools are required to provide transportation for their students.

To make the choice process easier, the RSD in 2012 launched a computerized enrollment system, "OneApp," and the OPSB joined a year later. Families list up to twelve choices, in order, and a computer program matches students with available seats. Siblings get preference, and in K–8 schools half the seats are reserved for kids from fairly wide zones around the schools. The RSD set up three centers around the city to help parents trying to decide which schools to list.

Creating Consequences for Performance

When families choose, public dollars follow their children, so school operators are in direct competition for funds. The more students they attract, the more funds they have. But the consequence that motivates principals, teachers, and charter boards even more than losing students and funds is the threat of closure if students are not learning enough. Everyone knows their job is on the line if students aren't learning, so they usually pull together and do what it takes, no matter how difficult.

Nolan Grady taught math for more than forty years at O. Perry Walker High School. "You as an individual teacher, you can't be stagnant, not in this day of charters," he told me. "You have to constantly reflect, review, and improve. You don't have the job security you had with the old system. That's a hard pill, but it's a reality. It makes you work harder."

Elected school boards rarely close failing schools—in any district—unless they are in fiscal crisis and have no choice, because closing a school is often political suicide. Turnout in school board elections is typically around 10 percent, so when teachers and their unions get upset, their votes usually carry the day. Hence board members who anger them know they are risking defeat.

In a charter system, however, closures are easier, because usually only one school protests. Other school operators welcome the opportunity to compete to run a school in the vacated building. In New Orleans, parents, alumni, and staff at a few schools have protested closures, particularly when communities were invested in their local high school. But in most instances, there has been little resistance. By 2017, at least twenty-two charters had closed or changed hands.[33]

In sum, no one has a right to operate or work at a school for life. Such rights are contestable: the steering body has the power—and the political independence—to award the school building to a competitor with a superior track record.

Closing failing schools accomplishes two things. It keeps all adults in a charter school on their toes, motivates them to solve whatever problems are undermining student performance. And it improves the mix of schools by weeding out the worst ones.

Closure works best when failing schools are replaced by stronger schools, as has been the norm in New Orleans. When Douglas Harris's group at Tulane studied the impact of closures, they found that students in failing schools had gained significant ground two years after their school was closed or taken over by a charter. "The positive effects of closure and takeover in New Orleans explain 25 percent to 40 percent of the total effect of the New Orleans post-Katrina school reforms on student achievement," they concluded. (On top of that, imagine the benefits for future students, who never have to attend the failing school.)[34]

Jay Altman, co-founder of the city's first charter school, puts it well: "If we can keep an accountability system and say, 'Here's the bar, and it's set high, and if you can't meet it, someone else is going to run your school,' New Orleans could become the only city in the country where every kid goes to a good school."

Changing School Cultures

Children tend to meet the expectations of the adults in their lives, and for too long in New Orleans, those expectations were set woefully low. Charter schools have reset them. Most aim from day one at college as the goal for every student. They put college banners in the hallways and classrooms, name each homeroom after the teacher's college, and call each class by the year it will graduate from college. They also put tremendous stress on a series of school values. Signs about the values cover the walls, many with brief sayings from famous people.

Motivation is the key to learning. A motivated student can learn almost anything; an unmotivated student will learn almost nothing. Too often, the adults in public schools assume their students arrive with motivation; little effort goes into creating it. But that assumption is false in high-poverty communities, where many students see no reason to graduate from high school. Hence charter leaders often view motivating students as their first task. "It's huge," Gary Robichaux, another charter pioneer, says. "We won't hire someone who thinks our kids don't want to learn—that's their job, to create that motivation. Traditional teachers' colleges don't train their teachers to do that, but in high-poverty schools, it's everything."

Building a Talent Pipeline

Creating excellent public schools in a poor community is not easy. According to Leslie Jacobs, the RSD's biggest problem has been finding effective school leaders. Almost everyone in the charter school world agrees that school leaders are a critical element of success. "The right leader is everything," Robichaux says. "Even with good systems, the school will fail if the leader is not strong, not motivating, not good at discipline."

New Schools for New Orleans and others have invested heavily in developing effective school leaders. They have also imported talented teachers, through Teach For America and the New Teacher Project (called TeachNOLA in the city). Both programs are selective, accepting only the brightest candidates, and studies have consistently shown that their teachers outperform graduates of the state's teachers' colleges.[35]

Creating Clarity of Purpose by Separating Steering and Rowing

What truly sets New Orleans apart is the governance system. The RSD's job—and now the OPSB's—is simply to steer: to set direction, solve system-wide problems, enforce compliance with the few rules that govern the schools, and replace failing schools. The district rarely operates schools.

In a typical system, the district employs all principals, administrators, teachers, aides, nurses, custodians, and lunchroom workers—sometimes even bus drivers. The elected school board often becomes politically captive of its employees, many of whom belong to unions and almost all of whom vote in school board elections.

Before Katrina, everyone who worked in the New Orleans Public Schools would probably have agreed that the schools' foremost purpose was to educate children. But other, more pressing purposes kept interfering—all related to the needs of adults. Board members needed patronage positions, so they could win votes by finding people jobs. They also needed campaign contributions from vendors, who needed contracts. The teachers' union needed better pay and benefits for teachers. And teachers needed job security.

Today, doing what's best for children is foremost. The districts' core purpose is student achievement. If schools put adult interests first and student achievement suffers, they are replaced. Teachers are kept on if they can educate kids and let go if they can't. Principals are kept on if their schools educate kids and let go if they don't. The needs of administrators, teachers, unions, and school bus operators do not override the academic needs of children.

When districts operate many schools, they get sucked into rowing: leaders spend their time and energy worrying about hiring teachers, assigning them to schools, negotiating union contracts, making sure the buses run on time, and dealing with broken water mains or vacation schedules or even scandals in the schools. They often run from crisis to crisis, losing sight of their core purpose.

And few principals in traditional schools have the autonomy necessary to define clear missions, hire their own people, and get the job done. Most have little control over their budgets or personnel and no mission other than operating a traditional, cookie-cutter school. Too often their real purpose becomes self-preservation, which means not rocking the boat. They are governed by "the rule of the ringing telephone"—if they minimize complaints to the school board and superintendent, by minimizing change, everyone will do fine.

Everyone except the kids, that is.

Success is rare when a large school district tries to steer and row at the same time. "Any attempt to combine governing with 'doing,' on a large scale, paralyzes the decision-making capacity," the management sage Peter Drucker wrote long ago. Successful organizations separate top management from operations, he taught, so top management can "concentrate on decision making and direction." Operations are run by separate staffs, "each with its own mission and goals, and with its own sphere of action and autonomy."[36] That is precisely the model New Orleans has created: the school board and superintendent steer, but they use independent organizations, each driven by a clear mission and goals, to operate schools.

In this new paradigm, district administrators become skillful buyers of educational programs. They learn how to measure and evaluate schools. They conduct on-site reviews of each school every year and a high-stakes review when charters come up for renewal. They shift their supply to meet the needs of their students—replacing schools that fail, replicating schools that succeed, and opening new schools to meet new needs. And they spend their time addressing systemwide needs, such as special education and equity of access to quality schools.

In short, they *steer*.

Notes

1 See Douglas N. Harris, "Good News for New Orleans," *Education Next* 15, no. 4 (Fall 2015), https://www.educationnext.org/good-news-new-orleans-evidence-reform-student-achievement/.

2 Leslie Jacobs's background is from author interviews with her in March through September 2011, email communications in 2011 and 2015, and interviews with others in New Orleans.

3 All quotations without endnotes are from interviews with the author.

4 On New Orleans schools before Katrina: Sarah Carr, *Hope Against Hope: Three Schools, One City, and the Struggle to Educate America's Children* (New York: Bloomsbury, 2013), 120; Cowen Institute for Public Education Initiatives (hereafter cited as Cowen Institute), *The State of Public Education in New Orleans: Five Years after Hurricane Katrina* (New Orleans: Cowen Institute, Tulane University, 2010); "Board Games," *Gambit* (July 23, 2013): 14, available at https://issuu.com/gambitneworleans/docs/july2313/4?ff&e=1818998/4132284; and interviews with Leslie Jacobs, Anthony Amato, and others.

5 "A Brief Overview of Public Education in New Orleans, 1995–2009," New Schools for New Orleans, 2009.

6 Nelson Smith, *The Louisiana Recovery School District: Lessons for the Buckeye State* (Washington, DC: Thomas Fordham Institute, January 2012), 4.

7 Jaime Sarrio, "Georgia Looks to New Orleans Model for Rescuing Schools," *Atlanta Journal-Constitution*, February 17, 2015.

8 Supreme Court of Louisiana, ruling "*Eddy Oliver, Oscarlene Nixon and Mildred Goodwin v. Orleans Parish School Board* on Writ of Certiorari to the Court of Appeal, Fourth Circuit, Parish of Orleans, 2014-C-0329 Consolidated With 2014-C-0330," October 31, 2014, www.lasc.org/opinions/2014/14C0329cw14C0330.opn.pdf.

9 Interviews with Leslie Jacobs and Paul Pastorek, 2011.

10 Ibid.

11 Supreme Court of Louisiana, *Eddy Oliver*.

12 Interviews with Leslie Jacobs, 2011.

13 Interview with Leslie Jacobs, March 2011.

14 Interviews with Paul Vallas, 2011.

15 Ibid.

16 Adam Nossiter, "A Tamer of Schools Has Plan in New Orleans," *New York Times*, September 24, 2007.

17 Ibid.

18 Interviews with Paul Vallas, 2011.

19 Interview with Mary Landrieu, June 2017.

20 "Louisiana's Turnaround Zone: Answering the Urgency of Now," Recovery School District, January 2011, 6.

21 "New Orleans by the Numbers," New Schools for New Orleans, 2019, http://www.newschoolsforneworleans.org/wp-content/uploads/2019/04/NSNO-New-Orleans-by-the-Numbers-Spring-2019.pdf.

22 The high school graduation rate in 2005 was 56 percent, according to "Brief Overview of Public Education in New Orleans." New Schools for New Orleans, 2009. But another 4.5 percent of students dropped out in grades seven and eight in 2004–2005, according to Educate Now! ("Orleans Parish Public Schools Drop Outs: 2004–05 Compared to 2008–09, 2009–10 and 2010–11," https://educatenow.net/wp-content/uploads/2012/04/Dropouts_Summary_All_Orleans_04-10.xls.pdf.). Hence, about half of all students

graduated at the time. Only 37 percent of graduates went on to college, according to Leslie Jacobs, "By the Numbers: Student and School Performance," EducateNow!.net, August 22, 2015, https://educatenow. net/2015/08/22/by-the-numbers-student-and-school-performance-3/#more-6135/. This means less than 20 percent of all students went on to college.

23 Leslie Jacobs, "Reflection on 2015," Educate Now!.net, January 3, 2016, http://educatenow.net/2016/01/03/reflecting-on-2015/.

24 Louisiana Department of Education, 2015–2016 report card for "Orleans All" (Orleans Parish + RSD New Orleans Schools), *Louisiana Believes* (website), www.louisianabelieves.com/data/reportcards/2016/.

25 Data from Louisiana Department of Education, *Louisiana Believes* website.

26 CREDO, "Urban Charter School Study: Report on 41 Regions 2015" (Stanford, CA: Center for Research on Education Outcomes, 2015).

27 Harris, "Good News for New Orleans."

28 Jane Arnold Lincove, Nathan Barrett, and Katherine O. Strunk, "Did the Teachers Dismissed after Hurricane Katrina Return to Public Education?" Education Research Alliance, May 31, 2017.

29 Erik W. Robelen, "Desperately Seeking Educators," *Education Week*, February 21, 2007, https://www.edweek.org/ew/articles/2007/02/21/24orleans.h26.html.

30 Leslie Jacobs, "By the Numbers: Who Is Leading Our Schools?," Educate Now!.net, August 9, 2015, at https://educatenow.net/2015/08/09/by-the-numbers-who-is-leading-our-schools/; Danielle Dreilinger, "New Orleans' Katrina School Takeover to End, Legislature Decides," *Times-Picayune*, May 5, 2016; Nathan Barrett and Douglas Harris, "Significant Changes in the New Orleans Teacher Workforce," Education Research Alliance, Tulane University, August 24, 2015, http://educationresearchalliancenola.org/files/publications/ERA-Policy -Brief-Changes-in-the-New-Orleans-Teacher-Workforce.pdf.

31 Cowen Institute, "K–12 Education through the Public Eye: Parents' Perceptions of School Choice," Cowen Institute Research Brief, December 2011, www.coweninstitute.com/wp-content/uploads/2011/12/Public-Opinion-Poll- 2011-Final1.pdf.

32 Kate Babineau, Dave Hand, and Vincent Rossmeier, "What Happens Next? Voters' Perceptions of K–12 Public Education in New Orleans," Cowen Institute, April 2016, www.coweninstitute.com/wp-content/uploads/2016/04/Cowen -Institute-2016-Poll-FINAL.pdf.

33 Danielle Dreilinger, "A First in 7 Years: Low Scores Won't Close Any New Orleans Schools," *Times-Picayune*, December 23, 2015.

34 Whitney Bross, Douglas N. Harris, and Lihan Liu, "Extreme Measures: When and How School Closures and Charter Takeovers Benefit Students," Education Research Alliance, October 17, 2016, http://educationresearchalliancenola.org/files/publications/Education-Research-Alliance-New-Orleans-Policy-Brief-Closure-Takeover.pdf.

35 See, for instance, "Louisiana Study Rates TNTP-Trained Teachers as Exceptionally Effective for Fourth Consecutive Year," The New Teacher Project, October 3, 2011, https://tntp.org/news-and-press/view/louisiana-study-rates-tntp-trained-teachers-as-exceptionally-effective.

36 Peter F. Drucker, *The Age of Discontinuities* (New York: Harper Torchbooks, 1978), 233.

Criminal Justice Reform

The New Orleans Criminal Legal
System: A Flowing River

William C. Snowden

William C. Snowden is the director of the Vera Institute of Justice in New Orleans. He previously served as a public defender in Orleans Parish.

No man ever steps in the same river twice, for it's not the same river and he's not the same man.
—Heraclitus

Ask anyone from New Orleans and they will tell you the city has not been the same since the storm. Although the city has persevered through many storms and hurricanes in its three-hundred-year history, this particular storm—Hurricane Katrina—is notorious for the transformation it brought to New Orleans in the years that followed.

The makeup, culture, and rhythm of New Orleans have changed, but so too have the various systems that give the city its tempo—particularly the criminal legal system. Hurricane Katrina was a disaster that revealed deficiencies, abnormalities, and injustices in the New Orleans criminal legal system. Some responses to these revelations were criticized and some were supported, and what we have today in 2020—fifteen years after the storm—is a city that is not the same.

To understand the change in the city's criminal legal system, we will start by looking at how the Vera Institute of Justice (Vera) came to work in New Orleans, then we will review Vera's involvement in various efforts to reduce the jail size—in population and in structure. Finally, we will list some lessons learned since Vera began its work in New Orleans.

Vera to New Orleans: The Backstory

When New Orleans Council member James Carter called the president of Vera, Michael Jacobson, for help in 2006, the two had never met. In the aftermath of Katrina, Carter, newly elected to the city council, would soon make criminal justice his central issue.

The tenor of New Orleans at the time was to rebuild various systems, including education, housing, and infrastructure, to pre-Katrina levels. As a defense attorney, Carter was familiar with the criminal legal system and its failings. He recognized the desperate need for New Orleans to avoid rebuilding the pre-Katrina system and began to reimagine what local justice could look like. Thus, along with his fellow councilmember Shelley Midura, he reached out to Vera for assistance.

Vera is a nonprofit organization that drives change in justice systems to ensure fairness, promote safety, and strengthen communities. It was started in New York City in 1961 with a focus on demonstrating, through the Manhattan Bail Project, that New Yorkers who were too poor to afford bail but had significant ties to their communities could be released from jail and still make their court dates. Vera has evolved to address a multitude of issues in our criminal legal system.

Today, Vera works in more than forty states, with its main office in New York City and other offices in Los Angeles, New Orleans, and Washington, DC. Vera works with local, state, and national government officials as well as community leaders to create change within the criminal legal system, employing a combination of research, data analysis, community engagement, technical assistance, and project management.

Vera's first task on arriving in New Orleans in 2006 was to assess the landscape and determine the steps New Orleans needed to take to develop a criminal legal system that was more just, reliable, and effective. That assessment included interviews with members of the New Orleans City Council, Criminal District Court judges, the district attorney, the chief public defender, the sheriff, the chief of police, and other justice system leaders as well as nonprofit research and advocacy organizations. Vera also analyzed the available data on the system's operation after the storm.

This assessment produced Vera's 2007 report "Proposals for New Orleans' Criminal Justice System: Best Practices to Advance Public Safety and Justice." This report identified areas that needed to be improved and made recommendations that were eventually adopted by the New Orleans City Council. The adoption of these recommendations demonstrated the city's commitment to a well-functioning criminal legal system and signaled the flow of changes to come.

Vera was adamant that the city lead this reform. And they did. With the guidance of Vera and support of a local philanthropic organization, Baptist Community Ministries, Carter organized a two-day retreat with all the city leaders to encourage them to commit to implementing the reforms the criminal legal system needed. At the end of the retreat, all of the leaders signed on in support of and commitment to the reforms. Later, the Criminal Justice Leadership Alliance came together to lead these reforms. The alliance comprised many of the same justice system leaders present at the retreat.

Vera also made a commitment to the city by opening and staffing its own local office in New Orleans in 2008. Diverging from its typical approach to jurisdictional assistance, which involved making phone calls, sending e-mail messages, and flying in New York staff, Vera made New Orleans one of its homes and hired local New Orleanians. Having Vera staff physically present, and made up of people from New Orleans, was a vital way to maintain the energy and direction of the reform strategies and their implementations.

An Oversized Jail

In August 2005, the month Hurricane Katrina hit New Orleans, the average monthly jail population was recorded at more than sixty-five hundred inmates.[1] It cannot be overstated how monumental this number is. Compared to nine other areas in the country, Orleans Parish—which is the same as the City of New Orleans—was an outlier (see Figure 1).[2]

Figure 1. Ten most incarcerated US jurisdictions, 2005; jail
incarceration rate per 1,000 residents (Bureau of Justice Statistics,
"Jail Inmates at Midyear 2007," US Census Bureau, 2008)

Orleans Parish ("parish" is used instead of "county" in Louisiana), for decades, consistently had incarceration rates significantly higher than those of other cities. The local jail, Orleans Parish Prison—so named though it was a jail, not a prison—unlike typical jails, housed more than just pretrial inmates. The system, however, which allowed the sheriff to be paid per inmate per day, provided a financial incentive to fill the jail.

The inmate population comprised juveniles and adults and was made up of people with different categorizations and at different stages of their journey through the system. Among the inmates were those who were in felony pretrial or misdemeanor or traffic pretrial, those who were in custody for competency restoration, those charged with violating parole or probation, those held on local warrants or for other jurisdictions for extradition, those sentenced to Orleans Parish Prison, and state inmates sentenced to Department of Corrections time. The practice of housing state inmates in local jails is unique in Louisiana and was abundant in Orleans Parish.

This variety of people in the jail was a main contributor to its bloated size. Because of reforms instituted over the past eleven years, the average monthly jail population has been reduced significantly.

In the summer of 2019, fourteen years after the storm, New Orleans was averaging a monthly population of between eleven hundred and twelve hundred inmates. The jail is no longer the same—in size or structure. The population and size reduction was a product of many strategies, including the halting of plans to expand the jail size, the creation of the New Orleans Pretrial Services Program, and a growing movement for bail reform. These strategies are discussed in the following sections, which highlight Vera's involvement in a few of the many strategies to reduce the jail population.

Jail-Bed Cap of 1,438

One of the most significant strategies undertaken to reduce the jail population was to build a smaller, centralized jail to replace the ones destroyed by the storm. Before Katrina, the local jail was made up of twelve facilities spread out within a half-mile radius, each of which had inmates when Hurricane Katrina hit August 28, 2005. According to the sheriff's self-reported numbers, the inmate population of 7,520 was divided as follows: Community Corrections Center (1,280 inmates), Conchetta (408 inmates), Fisk School Work Release (200 inmates), House of Detention (825 inmates), Orleans Parish Prison (831 inmates), Rendon (200 inmates), South White St. Juvenile Facility (288 inmates), Templeman Phase 1 (840 inmates), Templeman Phase 2 (890 inmates), Templeman Phase 3 (1,204 inmates), Templeman Phase 4 (234 inmates), and Templeman Phase 5 (320 inmates). Compared to national averages, the city's average monthly jail population in 2005 should have been about 1,200 people. Instead, it was six times the average size it should have been the day the storm hit.

As the city recovered during the first year after Katrina, makeshift jails were erected to house inmates temporarily until there was a developed plan for a new, more permanent structure. In 2010, the City Planning Commission reviewed a proposal that the Orleans Parish sheriff, Marlin Gusman, submitted to the New Orleans City Council to build a new jail complex that would house up to 5,832 people. According to the sheriff, this was the size needed to replace the facilities that were lost by the storm, though at the time the jail population was about 3,400.[3]

Vera had different projections. After the sheriff's report was made public, Vera helped bring together the Orleans Parish Prison Reform Coalition, the Workers Center for Racial Justice, the New Orleans Coalition on Open Governance, and other community groups to organize the community demand for the city to commit to a smaller and safer jail.

As the sheriff's proposal was nearing a vote in city council, Vera helped persuade Stacy Head, a council member, and Susan Guidry, chair of the City Council Criminal Justice Committee, to delay the vote. Vera and local criminal justice community organizations also informed the Mayor's Office that New Orleans did not need or want a massive jail.

With the vote on the sheriff's proposal delayed, Mayor Mitch Landrieu assigned his first deputy mayor, Andy Kopplin, to review the proposal with a convening of the Criminal Justice Working Group. After meeting with Vera and other experts, as well as community leaders, this group concluded in its resolution: "If specific policy reforms are fully implemented, New Orleans would need approximately 1,485 beds to house local inmates by the year 2020."[4] On the recommendation of the Criminal Justice Working Group, the city council approved construction for only one of the sheriff's proposed housing facilities with 1,438 beds. The council also called for the decommission or demolition of the other facilities.

New Orleans Pretrial Services

The issue of pretrial services comes right back to that same question: Who should be in jail? And who can safely be at home?
—Judge Calvin Johnson (Ret.), Orleans Parish Criminal District Court, 2014

When Vera did its 2007 assessment of the New Orleans criminal legal system, it immediately highlighted the absence of a pretrial services program.[5] Without such a program, the judges were not receiving the information they needed to help them determine the potential flight risk or risk to public safety of defendants brought before them during bail hearings.

According to the Louisiana Code of Criminal Procedure §230.2, an accused person must be brought in front of a magistrate judge or commissioner within forty-eight hours of their arrest.[6] This hearing is called a first appearance. At the first appearance, the magistrate judge or commissioner will decide three things: whether or not probable cause exists for the person's arrest, whether or not the person qualifies for a public defender, and what type of bail the person should receive.

The outcome of the first appearance is critical to the person charged with a crime. Depending on the type of bail and one's financial circumstances, the decision could mean the difference between sitting in jail and getting out and keeping one's job, one's apartment, custody of one's children, and so on. At the time, New Orleans did not have a risk assessment process to assist the judges in determining who could be safely released from jail and who should be considered for detention.

Vera developed and launched the first New Orleans Pretrial Services program for the city in April 2012, and it was fully implemented in 2013.[7] The plan was for Vera to start, develop, and operate the program until it could be spun off to another nonprofit or government agency. New Orleans Pretrial Services (NOPTS) produced reports with scores correlating with risk levels to give the judges additional information to consider when deciding whether to detain or release a defendant. The scores were based largely on an individual's criminal history, or lack of criminal history, and employment and residential stability.

NOPTS helped recommend defendants, on the low-end of the risk spectrum, for their nonfinancial release (a recognizance bond). That, in turn, helped reduce the jail population. Unless one had a private attorney calling in a favor from a judge, being released on one's own recognizance was almost unheard of before NOPTS and before the storm. Vera helped normalize this practice.

When NOPTS was introduced, the judges of the Orleans Parish Criminal District Court were pessimistic about it. Many judges dismissed the value such risk assessments could offer during their bail-setting hearings. Nonetheless, in March 2017, the city handed the program over to the Criminal District Court, with the oversight of the Supreme Court, and the court adopted it as its own. The risk assessment instrument now used by the court is the Public Safety Assessment process from the Laura and John Arnold Foundation. The transition to this instrument represents a significant change in the court and their desire to effectively contribute to reducing pretrial detention.

Ending Financial Injustice

Anyone who studies the criminal legal system in New Orleans will quickly recognize the significant weight money plays on the scales of justice. In 2017, Vera looked at the extraction of wealth from poor, often black and brown, communities in New Orleans through bail, fines, and fees and submitted a report titled "Past Due: Examining the Costs and Consequences of Charging for Justice in New Orleans." This report found that in 2015 New Orleanians paid $4.7 million to bail bond agents, $1.7 million in bail bond fees to government agencies, and $3.8 million in conviction fines and fees.[8]

When a money bail is set at a person's first appearance, the person generally has two options: pay the full amount in cash to the court or pay a percentage to a bail bond agent. There are other forms of bond, but a majority of the types assigned in New Orleans are cash or commercial surety. When the full amount of bail is paid in cash, the money is returned minus the assessed government fee. When a bail bond agent is used, the percentage paid is not returned. For example, according to the Vera report, on a $10,000 bond, a person would pay a New Orleans bond agent a 10 percent premium, or $1,000, plus a 3 percent fee, or $300, which gets passed on to the government, and a separate flat government fee of $44, for a total of $1,344. When the person pays $1,300, excluding the flat government fee, the person will not get any of that $1,300 refunded regardless of the outcome of the case.

The 3 percent fee is divided among the government actors present in the courtroom. The court gets 1.8 percent, the district attorney gets 0.4 percent, the public defender gets 0.4 percent, and the sheriff gets 0.4 percent. The judge who sets the bail amount and receives a portion of the bail fee has a financial conflict of interest according to a 2018 decision by federal judge.

Generally, the purpose of bail is to ensure public safety and to ensure that the person returns to court. Research demonstrates, however, that people actually do not need to put up money to ensure that they will come back to court or not get rearrested. In jurisdictions that do not use money bail, people released through nonfinancial means have similar rates of court appearance and of no new arrests as those who are released through money bail.[9]

As cited in "Past Due" in 2017 and in a 2019 report discussed later, on any given day in New Orleans, three out of ten people were in jail not because they were a threat to public safety but because they were too poor to afford bail. This financial injustice happens at the start of a case, with money bail, and it occurs also at the end of the case, with fines and fees. A majority of the New Orleanians sentenced in 2015 were ordered to pay fines and fees totaling $3.8 million.

The "Past Due" report helped expose the inequitable ways money was being injected into the criminal legal system. Advocates seized on these findings and brought two successful lawsuits against the Orleans Parish courts, both decided in 2018.

In the first of these, *Caliste v. Cantrell*, the federal court ruled it was unconstitutional to detain a person on money bail without determining their ability to pay, and that it was a conflict of interest for the local court to make a bail amount determination when they benefit financially from fees on bail bonds.[10] In the other case, *Cain v. City of New Orleans*, a federal court ruled that it is unconstitutional to incarcerate a person because of their inability to pay fines and fees and that it is a conflict of interest for the courts to be the one determining the same person's ability to pay.[11]

Vera is often able to position itself to collect and report on data revealing injustices within the criminal legal system. Although we do not bring litigation ourselves, we often are in spaces where our findings help lay the framework for lawsuits, as we did in the *Cain* and *Caliste* cases.

According to the lawsuits, the judges no longer can rely on the revenue generated from bail fees or conviction fees. The city provided the judges with funds to fill the gap created by the lawsuits in 2018 and gave them a full budget for the subsequent fiscal year. Following these lawsuit decisions, the city is in a unique moment to replace the money bail system with one that does not include money as part of the calculus to determine whether someone is detained or released. Such a determination should be based on an assessment of a person's potential threat, or lack of a threat, to public safety.

Seizing the moment created by the federal lawsuit decisions, Vera came out with a report in June 2019, "Paid in Full: Ending Money Injustice in New Orleans," which includes a host of recommendations. If the twelve recommendations are adopted, the jail population could see a reduction of between approximately 304 and 687 people.[12]

Money bail does not keep us safe. "Paid in Full" advocates for the replacement of money bail with a decision-making framework anchored in public safety. It also argues for the elimination of conviction fees. Since the court has been fully funded by the city, it no longer needs to rely on the revenue previously generated by money bail and conviction fees.

The lawsuits and the report will not automatically change the behavior of the judges. But the report does give advocates, nonprofit organizations, and community members a blueprint laying out the necessary changes the judges need to make. Vera will continue to work with the judges, the community, and city leaders to replace money bail and end conviction fees with a more equitable and safety-promoting system.

Lessons Learned

The people of New Orleans were very protective of their city after Hurricane Katrina. Its greatness had been rocked by a devastating storm leaving its infrastructure fractured, its residents displaced, and its future uncertain. New Orleans is a true treasure in the United States with a rich sense of history and pride. When national organizations, such as Vera, offered services during the recovery, they were not always immediately welcomed by the community.

Some of the pushback Vera experienced was due to the way the organization was rocking a boat floating on self-interest. In New Orleans, for-profit systems were used to being the sole beneficiary of government contracts. Because Vera is a nonprofit organization, it was perceived as a threat to these business opportunities, particularly with the creation of the NOPTS program. At a city council meeting in 2012, many members of the community came out in support of NOPTS. Others, however, spoke out against it and resisted Vera's work in New Orleans.[13]

Resistance rooted in entrenched interests is often difficult to overcome. The lesson learned in New Orleans is that the way to overcome this resistance is through maximizing engagement with a variety of long-standing community organizations and government leaders. Many community organizations got behind Vera and its plans and recommendations, as did strong government leaders on the city council, such as Stacey Head and Susan Guidry, and in the Mayor's Office, such as Andy Kopplin, who drove the transformation envisioned for the New Orleans criminal legal system with Vera's assistance.

In the years since that particular city council meeting, Vera has built its reputation with the New Orleans community as a trusted expert in the space of reform in the criminal legal system. Thirty-two local community organizations signed on endorsing and supporting the recommendations of the 2019 report "Paid in Full" to end financial injustice in New Orleans. This trust was built slowly, the product of meetings, partnerships, and recognition that justice reform is a collaborative process and that Vera had an important role to play in that movement.

Conclusion

In August 2005, other cities' jail populations were dwarfed in comparison to New Orleans'. The unconscionable size of the jail population in the city was a symptom of a cancer of injustice that had spread throughout the criminal legal system. Hurricane Katrina revealed many of these injustices.

The city rightly takes pride in the way it has significantly reduced its jail population. But despite this reduction, the racial disparities are nearly the same today as they were before Katrina. The population of New Orleans is about 60 percent black, 30 percent white, 5 percent Latinx, and 3 percent Asian, yet black males, on average, make up 80 percent of the jail population.[14] This figure highlights work that still needs to be done.

New Orleans is not the same as it was when Vera arrived in 2006. The mayor has changed, the city council has changed, and the justice issues have changed. Vera is proud of the way we have been able to contribute to its transformation by envisioning a society that respects the dignity of every person and safeguards justice for all New Orleanians.

Notes

1   Paige M. Narrison and Allen J. Beck, "Prison and Jail Inmates at Midyear 2005," *Bureau of Justice Statistics Bulletin*, May 2006, https://www.bjs.gov/content/pub/pdf/pjim05.pdf.

2   Figure 1 is reproduced from Judge Calvin Johnson (Ret.), Mathilde Laisne, and Jon Wool, "Justice in Katrina's Wake: Changing Course on Incarceration in New Orleans," Vera Institute of Justice, November 2015, https://storage.googleapis.com/vera-web-assets/downloads/Publications/justice-in-katrinas-wake-changing-course-on-incarceration-in-new-orleans/legacy_downloads/justice-in-katrinas-wake.pdf.

3   "Smaller, Safer, and More Secure Jail," Orleans Parish Sheriff's Office, http://www.opcso.org/ppt/presentation20101018.pdf, accessed November 25, 2019.

4   New Orleans Criminal Justice Working Group Resolution on Executive Order 10-06, https://thelensnola.org/wp-content/uploads/2010/12/jail-working-group-resolution.pdf, accessed November 25, 2019.

5   "Proposals for New Orleans' Criminal Justice System: Best Practices to Advance Public Safety and Justice," Vera Institute of Justice, June 2007, https://storage.googleapis.com/vera-web-assets/downloads/Publications/proposals-for-new-orleans-criminal-justice-system-best-practices-to-advance-public-safety-and-justice/legacy_downloads/no_proposals.pdf.

6   Louisiana Code of Criminal Procedure 230.2, Justia US Law, https://law.justia.com/codes/louisiana/2011/ccrp/ccrp230-2/, accessed November 25, 2019.

7   "New Orleans Pretrial Services" (video), Vera Institute of Justice, https://www.vera.org/research/new-orleans-pretrial-services, accessed November 25, 2019.

8   Mathilde Laisne, Jon Wool, and Christian Henrichson, "Past Due: Examining the Costs and Consequences of Charging for Justice in New Orleans," Vera Institute of Justice, January 2017, https://storage.googleapis.com/vera-web-assets/downloads/Publications/past-due-costs-consequences-charging-for-justice-new-orleans/legacy_downloads/past-due-costs-consequences-charging-for-justice-new-orleans.pdf.

9   Michael R. Jones, "Unsecured Bonds: The As Effective and Most Efficient Pretrial Release Option," *Pretrial Justice Institute*, October 2013, https://pdfs.semanticscholar.org/5444/7711f036e000af0f177e176584b7aa7532f7.pdf.

10   Adrian Caliste, et al. v. Harry E. Cantrell, 329 F.Supp.3d 296 (2018), https://www.leagle.com/decision/infdco20180807e72.

11 Alana Cain, et al., v. City of New Orleans, et al., 327 F.R.D. 111 (E.D. La. 2018), https://www.leagle.com/decision/infdco20180803935.

12 Jon Wool, Alison Shih, and Melody Chang, "Paid in Full: Ending Money Injustice in New Orleans," Vera Institute of Justice, June 2019, https://storage.googleapis.com/vera-web-assets/downloads/Publications/paid-in-full-a-plan-to-end-money-injustice-in-new-orleans/legacy_downloads/paid-in-full-report.pdf.

13 Tyler Bridges, "Squabble over Pre-Trial Program Erupts as Hearings Plow Forward," *The Lens*, November 13, 2012, https://thelensnola.org/2012/11/13/pre-trial-program-debated/.

14 See the New Orleans City Council Criminal Justice Committee website at https://council.nola.gov/committees/criminal-justice-committee/.

Reconnecting the Broken Post-Katrina New Orleans Criminal Justice System

Graymond Martin

Graymond Martin has been the First Assistant District Attorney for Orleans Parish, Louisiana. In that capacity, he led an effort to build stronger between police and district attorneys.

When Hurricane Katrina struck New Orleans and the levees protecting the city gave way in August 2005, an already struggling and weakened criminal justice system collapsed in spectacular fashion.

Damage within New Orleans extended far beyond the loss of physical infrastructure. The city's population was depleted by more than half. For those who remained or returned within the first year, spirits were crushed, uncertainty abounded, and the hard work of restoration was riddled by anxiety, conflict, opportunism, and battles for precious resources.

Longtime judge Leon Cannizzaro Jr., appalled at the near-complete dysfunction of the local criminal justice system, entered and won the race for Orleans Parish district attorney (OPDA). In November 2008, because of the urgency and enormity of the task ahead, he assumed the unexpired term of his elected predecessor, Eddie Jordan, who had resigned under clouds of scandal in October 2007.

Cannizzaro took office more than three years after the flood waters had receded but found his new agency's building still uninhabitable. While the OPDA's office had received three to four feet of flood water and had been designated by the Federal Emergency Management Agency (FEMA) as a high-priority critical infrastructure, what should have been a fairly easy restoration hadn't begun. Instead, residual moisture from the flood had festered for years, exacerbating the damage caused by inundation.

Their home office still in shambles, prosecutors were working on plastic picnic tables and folding chairs inside donated temporary office space in a downtown high-rise across from City Hall. The location was more than a mile and a half from the Criminal District Courthouse, New Orleans Police Department headquarters, the Orleans Parish Sheriff's Office, and the partially restored Orleans Parish Prison. Assistant district attorneys had limited space for witness interviews and were forced to carry large seafood boxes containing case files to their personal vehicles and then up the stairs of the criminal courthouse. The walk began from wherever they could find parking, first come first served.

Such logistical difficulties were only the beginning of prosecutors' troubles, soon to be compounded by the shortcomings of sister agencies.

The sheriff's office struggled to properly serve court notices and subpoenas and to bring detainees from the parish jail, so there was no assurance a defendant would appear at scheduled court hearings. Evidence custody could be an issue if a trial was scheduled and then postponed, because the NOPD's Central Evidence and Property Room would provide evidence to OPDA investigators but not always take it back. On the rare occasions that both defendant and evidence arrived in court at the same time, the absence of an essential witness to whom sheriff deputies failed to timely serve a subpoena could force unwanted continuances. Each misstep along the way increased the likelihood of case files, evidence, or even witnesses being lost or misplaced. Too many moving parts, it seemed, were moving in wrong directions.

Reconfiguring the operations of a single inefficient law enforcement agency is daunting enough, so imagine the challenge when the entire criminal justice system is disrupted and hobbled by multi-agency dysfunction. Three years removed from the city's great flood, a complete makeover was needed, and it would require unprecedented cooperation and effort from all stakeholders.

Post-Katrina rehabilitation was desperately needed on two fronts: the myriad issues related to cases pending when the levees failed, and those of the newer, post-flood cases brought by police.

Cases in the former category were beset by difficulties, such as lost or damaged evidence, victims and witnesses who had relocated around the country (often without forwarding contact information), and defendants who were incarcerated but dispersed and difficult to locate. Defendants who were at-large when the waters rose often simply disappeared, hoping their case files were misplaced. If their case files had been located on the ground floor and were water-logged, sometimes their hopes were realized.

Newer cases posed their own problems, introduced as they were into an overwhelmed, barely functional system. The simple logistics of working space, evidence storage and retrieval, records management, process service, and difficulty locating defendants, victims and witnesses likely were not being solved with ad hoc solutions.

Restorative measures also were road-blocked by the poor recent history between the DA's office and the NOPD. New Orleans' per-capita murder rate had swelled to eight times the national average during a period of finger-pointing and feuding between District Attorney Jordan and police department leadership. Police complained that the prior DA would not prosecute viable cases. The DA staff countered that police would not conduct thorough and timely investigations to produce prosecutable cases.

Violent offenders soon realized the dispute between the agencies meant that only a minimal number of murder cases were going to be prosecuted. New Orleans' streets produced sarcastic mentions of the "60-day murder" penalty—the time then allotted under state law for a suspect to be arrested and detained, then released if the state had by then failed to institute prosecution. Police often failed to provide investigative reports sufficient to support a prosecution within the specified time, so cell doors were flung open. Defendants still could be indicted in a state where murder charges do not prescribe. But there was no meaningful tracking system to pursue matters once a defendant won his pretrial release.

The acrimony between police and prosecutors boiled over in 2006, when more than three thousand of these Article 701 releases effectively terminated prosecutions of cases, including murders. New Orleans' mayor threatened to have District Attorney Jordan investigated for malfeasance. City council members and civic groups called for the DA's resignation. The community expressed outrage at the system's inability to hold violent offenders accountable for their criminal acts. The business community finally intervened, funding a soft landing for the DA in the private sector in exchange for his resignation and pledge not to seek re-election in 2008.

It was against this dire backdrop that Cannizzaro took over as the city's top prosecutor in November 2008. He immediately set about evaluating the deficiencies of the DA's office, as well as those of other agencies negatively impacting the performance of the DA's office. He declared that the OPDA no longer would allow underperforming partners in the criminal justice system to lower the bar for the prosecutors' office. But he also ordered a stop to public criticism of the police, so that the relationship between the two critical law enforcement partner agencies might be repaired.

Cannizzaro sought to emphasize prosecutions of the most serious and violent crimes. After finding that misdemeanor violations consumed more than 40 percent of the Criminal District Court's docket, and that simple possession of marijuana made up about 60 percent of those misdemeanor cases, the new DA in 2009 asked the city council to adopt a municipal ordinance for the prosecution of minor weed possession in municipal court. The council initially balked, so Cannizzaro used his own authority to unilaterally transfer marijuana possession cases to municipal court under state jurisdiction. The move immediately freed up about 25 percent of the criminal district court docket, and eventually the city council adopted a full range of municipal law violations that moved the bulk of misdemeanor cases to the municipal court.

With the criminal district court docket now leaner, Cannizzaro turned his attention to refilling it with the most serious cases of violent crime. He asked the NOPD to begin a cold-case review of some 450 murder cases for which prosecution had previously been declined and lobbied the city council to double the size of the department's homicide unit to assist with the task.

Police, however, were not immediately on board with the new DA's workhorse ways. NOPD Superintendent Warren Riley, maintaining his antagonism toward the DA's office, actually declined the additional resources. So the council instead funded the hiring of six investigators to work six months for the DA's office, reviewing as many of the 450 cold murder cases as they could.

The group got through 150 cases, determining that 75 merited prosecution. But in a little more than half of those cases, the investigators found the murder suspects had themselves already been killed in subsequent homicides. Retribution killings are a hallmark of New Orleans' meanest streets.

About thirty-five remaining cases, refused years earlier, were resurrected and indicted, resulting in about twenty-seven convictions. It was the start of Cannizzaro's campaign against the city's murderous offenders that has seen more than seven hundred New Orleans killers successfully prosecuted in his first ten-plus years as DA.

The campaign required another innovation to put the "60-day murder" penalty to rest, and it would require a new bridge of trust, respect, and cooperation between the DA's office and NOPD headquarters. A new protocol was negotiated between Cannizzaro's office and the NOPD's Homicide Division, entitled, "Homicide arrest to indictment in 60 days." Both agencies pledged to improve communication to enhance the likelihood that a homicide arrest would develop into a prosecutable case.

Cannizzaro's office provided an on-call assistant DA and victim-witness coordinator who would accompany a senior investigator to homicide scenes, whether or not an arrest had been made. This protocol allowed for immediate interaction between the DA's office and potential witnesses and the victim's surviving family and demonstrated to detectives the DA's commitment to prosecuting these important cases. The protocol required investigators and prosecutors to meet within ten days to discuss a homicide case and to meet again within ten days of an arrest for case review and evaluation. Homicide detectives were obligated to submit a complete report to prosecutors within twenty-eight days of an arrest.

That report would become the subject of a charge conference, a weekly meeting between case-level investigators and prosecutors and their supervisors, where determinations would be made about whether cases were ready for prosecution. Previously, these conferences were being held at the deadline of a suspect's release under Article 701. If the investigation was complete and sufficient for prosecution, it was accepted. If the investigation was incomplete or deficient in some way, it was refused. And under previous DA administrations, that would be that.

The new protocol required police and prosecutors to begin discussing within a month of arrest what problems or deficiencies a case might have, affording time to correct such faults through further investigation. Many cases now are reviewed between three and five times in the charge conference setting before a charging decision is made.

This repeated interaction has allowed for more thorough and complete investigations that are more likely to result in indictments and convictions. Where under the previous administration, about 50 percent of homicide cases were being refused and forgotten by the DA's office, Cannizzaro's office now accepts homicide cases for prosecution about 90 percent of the time and achieves conviction in those cases at an impressive 95 percent rate.

Rebuilding the relationship between the DA's office and NOPD not only has enhanced the performance of the city's criminal justice system but undoubtedly has made New Orleans a safer city. This cooperative effort to aggressively prosecute serial homicide offenders has contributed substantially to the historically low homicide rates of which New Orleans currently boasts.

Rising from Katrina's Ashes but Still in Crisis: Public Defense in New Orleans

Derwyn Bunton

Derwyn Bunton is a national leader and advocate for public defense and equal justice. He is chief public defender for Orleans Parish, Louisiana. Before becoming chief, he was a civil rights litigator and executive director for what is now the Louisiana Center for Children's Rights, the nation's first stand-alone juvenile defense provider.

When we least expect it, life sets us a challenge to test our courage and willingness to change; at such a moment, there is no point in pretending that nothing has happened or in saying that we are not yet ready. The challenge will not wait. Life does not look back.
—Paulo Coelho, *The Devil and Miss Prym*

New Orleans' nickname "Big Easy" was based on the "anything goes" perception of the city. Feeding this perception was a sense of lawlessness, that New Orleans was a place where the rules changed depending on who you were and who you knew. So when Hurricane Katrina hit the city in August 2005 and tossed everything around—flooding mansions and missions, damaging the Superdome and supermarkets—the storm challenged old perceptions and presented unique challenges. Katrina made at least one thing clear: New Orleans could no longer wait for change, pretend nothing happened, or look back. The city's survival depended on its ability to move forward.

One of the greatest challenges to New Orleans' ability to move forward was its criminal legal system, especially the public defense system. For decades before Katrina, the public defense system in New Orleans—like others throughout Louisiana—was "plagued by negligent attorneys who provide[d] haphazard and deficient representation." Orleans Parish Prison, for example, was packed with more than six thousand people, most of whom had no representation once Katrina hit.[1] Fragile and underfunded, the New Orleans public defense system lacked the ability to even try to respond to the crisis of Katrina. All but four staff members were terminated immediately after the storm. Like most social institutions in New Orleans, however, public defense in New Orleans had been targeted for reform multiple times before Katrina, with few positive results.

Katrina was uniquely devastating, producing a national outcry and causing local embarrassment. Now palpably visible, the unjust status quo was deemed unacceptable. At the time, I and a group of like-minded leaders stood ready with time, passion, and capacity to seize the moment to effect reform. While opposition to reform remained alive, it was critically wounded, as millions in and outside New Orleans could see how the system they had supported and defended all these years had failed. With reform opponents weakened by the storm, New Orleans started accepting changes to its public defender system.

I begin this article with a brief history of public defense in New Orleans, outlining the well-documented injustices and dysfunction plaguing public defense before and immediately after Katrina and describing the efforts that were made to cure the ills of the system. I then discuss the efforts by reformers in the years after Katrina to create a more just, fair, and equitable public defense system. In the final section I discuss outcomes and the lessons learned from the efforts to transform public defense in New Orleans and the challenges that remain as the struggle for equity and fairness in our public defense system continues.

Public Defense Pre-Katrina: History, Structure, and Struggle

History

Nearly 250 years ago, a civil disturbance broke out in a territory on the verge of revolution. An unjust monarch maintained an occupying force of soldiers, and in late March 1770, eight of these soldiers fired on civilians, killing five and wounding six others. The territorial government returned indictments for murder, and the penalty for conviction was death. After several attempts, the soldiers—unpopular and poor—could find only one lawyer to handle their case. That lawyer represented the soldiers and their captain and achieved acquittals for all but two of the soldiers, who were found guilty of lesser offenses. All escaped the death penalty.

The civil disturbance became known as the Boston Massacre. Six years later, that territory declared its independence, and the United States of America was born. That lawyer who represented the unpopular and abandoned soldiers free of charge (or at least at a price too small for history to remember) went on to become the second president of the United States, John Adams—perhaps the first great public defender.

The principle that no person accused of a crime should face the government without counsel is an American value that predates our republic.

The right to counsel is rooted in the Sixth Amendment to the United States Constitution as part of the Bill of Rights, adopted in 1789. It is one of the original ten amendments, forming the foundation of the United States. It reads, "In all criminal prosecutions, the accused shall enjoy the right to . . . the Assistance of Counsel for his defense." The right to counsel was initially interpreted to mean that those who wished to have counsel, and who were able to afford counsel, would not be denied the right to have representation in criminal cases in both state and federal court.[2]

The United States Supreme Court, however, did not order states to provide counsel for the poor facing criminal prosecution until after the passage of the Fourteenth Amendment to the US Constitution in 1868.[3] The Fourteenth Amendment made the US Bill of Rights applicable to the states—but not all at once. The Supreme Court systematically, gradually, and selectively made the Bill of Rights applicable to the states through the Fourteenth Amendment.

In 1963, the Supreme Court decided *Gideon v. Wainwright*.[4] This case made the Sixth Amendment applicable to the states, guaranteeing poor people counsel in criminal cases. In

Gideon, the Supreme Court wrote: "The right of one charged with crime to counsel may not be deemed fundamental and essential to fair trials in some countries, but it is in ours."[5] Robert F. Kennedy remarked: "If an obscure Florida convict named Clarence Earl Gideon had not sat down in his prison cell . . . to write a letter to the Supreme Court . . . the vast machinery of American law would have gone on functioning undisturbed. But Gideon did write that letter, the Court did look into his case . . . and the whole course of American legal history has been changed."[6] *Gideon* is the seminal case on the right to counsel in the United States. It is the reason we have public defenders representing poor people around the country.

Structure

In 1966, in response to *Gideon*, Louisiana created indigent defender boards, divided into forty-one judicial districts. Under local control and funded by court fines and fees paid by people accused of crime (largely traffic tickets), these boards (known as IDBs) were tasked with providing competent counsel for people too poor to afford a lawyer on their own.[7] In 1974, the right to counsel was codified in the new Louisiana state constitution, recognizing the right to counsel and other rights of men and women accused in criminal proceedings. The Louisiana Constitution of 1974 specifies: "The legislature shall provide for a uniform system for securing and compensating qualified counsel for indigents."[8]

Louisiana's statewide user-pay public defender funding scheme is unique in the United States. Louisiana's entire criminal legal system depends on fines and fees generated by (or at least assessed against) poor people moving through the system. In the beginning these fines and fees were the sole source of revenue for public defender offices around the state. Every other part of the criminal legal system received supplemental funds directly from the state or local government or both. It took the Louisiana State Legislature twenty years after ratification of the 1974 Constitution to provide supplemental state funding to public defense—at a woefully low level.[9]

Before Katrina, the IDB in New Orleans was known as the Orleans Indigent Defender Program or OIDP. At the time Katrina hit New Orleans, it was an office that comprised between forty and fifty contract, part-time attorneys handling a large percentage of the new criminal cases moving through the New Orleans criminal justice system—more than a hundred thousand cases in 2004. If the lawyers handled only half the workload, it meant a caseload average of a thousand new cases per lawyer—part-time. Such caseloads were excessive by any measure.[10] For a couple of decades before Katrina, the OIDP and the entire state public defender system received constant and consistent national criticism.[11]

Struggle

The Louisiana and New Orleans public defender system was targeted for reform many times by social justice advocates and frontline public defenders.[12] One of the most heavily publicized efforts to reform public defense in Louisiana and New Orleans occurred in the early 1990s. An overworked and underresourced public defender, Rick Tessier, appeared in court, stood up, and told Judge Calvin Johnson of the Orleans Parish Criminal District Court he was unable to proceed.

Tessier asserted that he was ineffective at the outset and to move forward would deprive all his clients of their Sixth Amendment rights. Judge Johnson halted proceedings and ordered hearings and briefings to determine whether the public defender system was structurally ineffective. After testimony from multiple practitioners and experts, Judge Johnson found Tessier and the public defender system unconstitutional at its inception. The district attorney appealed and the case was ultimately decided by the Louisiana Supreme Court.[13] In *State v. Leonard Peart*, the Louisiana Supreme Court declined to provide any systemic relief, finding instead that public defender services in that section of court were unconstitutional because of excessive workloads.[14] So the disparities and ineffectiveness continued from district to district and section to section.[15]

Peart was emblematic of the challenges public defense reform advocates faced before Katrina. Decision makers were reluctant to make systemic change—what some organizers call a fear of too much justice—while at the same time pretending the unfairness, inequity, and injustice either did not exist or was confined, contained, or episodic. Reformers, however, were steadfast. Efforts were launched in the courts and in the legislature to improve public defense in New Orleans and throughout Louisiana. Each shortfall, half win, and failure drew more intellectual capital to the cause and gave advocates experience. The various efforts also provided hope as we saw incremental improvements in structure.[16]

Through it all, OIDP lawyers fought hard, but even the most skilled were fighting with their hands tied. Structurally, the OIDP provided little more than speed bumps on the way to jail and prison for the poor and overwhelmingly African American clients moving through the system. Because a person in jail was not considered a case until the district attorney decided to accept the case, often a person who could not afford a lawyer sat in jail after an arrest for more than two months before he or she was sent to a courtroom and assigned a public defender.[17]

Part-time lawyers were assigned to courtrooms rather than clients. The terrible incentives created by this system were threefold. First, the system caused lawyers to care more about pleasing—or at least not angering—judges than clients. Second, lawyers prioritized completing the day's court docket over worrying about clients' substantive cases. Third, because OIDP lawyers were part-time (and poorly paid), more attention was given to their private—paying—clients.

The OIDP had no meaningful investigative resources, no organized training, and no money for experts or adequate administrative support. The chief source of OIDP income was traffic tickets—the nation's only statewide user-pay criminal justice system. OIDP attorneys were forced by oppressive caseloads and poor funding to brutally triage cases, making quick decisions about which cases were worth fighting. Innocent clients pleaded guilty rather than face charges represented by an understaffed and underresourced public defender. Because of this history, before Katrina, Louisiana became a national leader in exonerations and incarceration.[18] The Department of Justice, Bureau of Justice Assistance, in its 2006 report on the OIDP, confirmed the problems of the New Orleans court-centered, resource-starved public defense system: "There appeared to be little accountability within the office. There were no client files or any other records or data, save a monthly tabulation of cases closed and how they were closed (e.g., trial, plea, dismissal). There is no phone number for the office, and clients cannot come to the office. We were told that attorney evaluations seem to be passive, based on judicial satisfaction with the attorneys assigned to their court. There is no supervisory evaluation of public defenders on such core skills as communication with clients, recognition of legal issues, or trial preparation."[19]

The National Legal Aid and Defender Association also assessed public defense in New Orleans after the storm. It too found that public defense in New Orleans before Katrina was probably systemically unconstitutional. The report reads: "Pre-Katrina, the public defense system in New Orleans was not obligated to adhere to any national, state or local standards of justice resulting in public defenders handling too many cases, with insufficient support staff, practically no training or supervision, experiencing undue interference from the judiciary, all the while compromising their practices by working part-time in private practices to augment their inadequate compensation."[20]

Public Defense Post-Katrina: Reform, New Structure . . . and Struggle

When thousands of men and women in orange jumpsuits were forced by the flood waters of Katrina to find safety on an overpass under the New Orleans sun, their massive numbers provided vivid evidence of decades of overincarceration, failed criminal justice policies, and cumulative injustice. The columnist David Brooks put it this way: "[Hurricane Katrina] wash[ed] away the surface of [New Orleans] society, [and] expose[d] the underlying power structures, the injustices, the patterns of corruption and the unacknowledged inequalities."[21] Public defense in New Orleans was one of these exposed injustices and unacknowledged inequalities. Still, advocates in New Orleans who dreamed of a better and more just city saw in post-Katrina New Orleans an opportunity to rebuild the criminal legal system with justice and fairness as its cornerstones. Critical to any fair and just criminal legal system is public defense.

Reform

The pre-Katrina struggles in New Orleans built an infrastructure of reformers and developed intellectual capital to move public defense forward. Thus, in the aftermath of the storm, with the New Orleans criminal legal system in full collapse, I and other reformers began to work for change.[22]

We met in Springfield, Louisiana, on May 10 and 11, 2006, to discuss the crisis in public defense. We all agreed that reform was long overdue and that funding and structural reform were necessary.[23] Also at that meeting was Ronald Sullivan, a Yale Law School professor and former director of the District of Columbia public defender program whose knowledge about best practice for public defense left us with a vision, renewed hope, and sense of purpose.

A month earlier, Chief Judge Calvin Johnson (the judge responsible for the *Peart* decision) persuaded the local IDB members to resign and appointed an entirely new board, tasked with reforming the system.[24] I was part of that new board. We hired Sullivan to help organize the reformed OIDP and launched a state reform effort, using the debacle caused by Katrina as a reason to reform the structure of public defense. Among the many leaders of this effort was the Louisiana State Bar Association president, Frank Neuner, who played a major role.

Structure and Struggle

OIDP was reborn as the Orleans Public Defenders Office (OPD). With a budget of $2.8 million in federal relief funds, the new board set about remaking public defense in New Orleans. The Bureau of Justice Assistance report asserted, however, that real reform would cost millions more.[25] Under Sullivan's direction, we mandated attorneys to work full-time on behalf of poor people in New Orleans. We added Jon Rapping, the former training director for public defender programs, to train a new class of attorneys.[26] We also mandated lawyers be assigned to clients— not courtrooms—based on levels of experience and competence. It was a seismic cultural shift. It drew a seismic response.

The post-Katrina confrontations between OPD and the old guard were extraordinary. Many in the criminal legal system simply wanted their old system back. The Orleans Parish District Attorney even charged an OPD investigator with kidnapping for daring to interview a young witness in the course of her investigation.[27] This was a response to professional defense investigation—routine in other jurisdictions but foreign (and therefore illegal) in New Orleans. The charges were later dropped.

Opponents to reform seemed to be as numerous as proponents. Perhaps most formidable among the opponents were Criminal District Court judges, most of whom either very publicly attacked the board or remained silent while others did.[28] The chief tool used to try to rein in our independent board: contempt. Acting individually and as a group, Criminal District Court judges routinely found our new independent board and lawyers in contempt.[29] After demanding to remain present with the lawyer he supervised and the client OPD represented, Stephen Singer, the OPD chief of trials, was placed in a compliance hold and dragged out of the courtroom by deputies—after the court's order of contempt.[30] Before Katrina, the criminal bench exercised significant control over the OIDP board, selecting members who catered to the wishes of the judges rather those of the clients. After Katrina, with the appointment of an independent board, the judges resisted the loss of control and, without more structural reform, attempted to regain control as soon as Judge Johnson's term as chief judge expired. We responded by filing suit in federal court in May 2007.[31]

Deeper structural change was brewing, though. In the 2007 legislative session, legislation designed to change the structure of public defense statewide was making its way through the Louisiana State Legislature. HB 436, sponsored by Representative Daniel Martiny, aimed to create a more independent state board with more authority (and more funding) to regulate public defense practice. Important to us, if passed, the legislation would immediately eliminate local IDBs, consolidating their power in the position of chief district defender. The chief defender in place at the time of passage would assume the powers of the IDB, and in the future, the chief district defender would be chosen by the newly created Louisiana Public Defender Board—reasonably immune to and independent of the local judiciary and political pressures.[32]

In August 2007, the Louisiana Public Defender Act (Act 307) became law, and Christine Lehman assumed the role of chief defender. A new public defender office, chosen by the reform-oriented board, was now all but guaranteed. Act 307 eliminated the IDBs, mooted our lawsuit, and remade the structure of public defense in Louisiana and New Orleans—for the better. Act 307 created a new Louisiana Public Defender Board, which required membership from diverse constituencies, eliminated local boards, set standards for practice, and removed judges from the decision-making process regarding type of service delivery or selection of the chief defender.[33] It also gave more money to public defense and gave the Public Defender Board the ability to hold districts accountable for how they deliver public defense services in Louisiana.

Public Defense Pre-Katrina: Outcomes, Lessons, and the Road Ahead

Outcomes

When the dust settled, OPD emerged as an independent, client-centered, full-time public defender office with better training and more resources. New, progressive public defender leaders created an office more capable of living up to the promise of *Gideon*, granting all of us the right to effective counsel. In *Gideon*, the US Supreme Court states that public defenders are fundamental to the existence of justice in our criminal courts: "The right of one charged with crime to counsel may not be deemed fundamental and essential to fair trials in some countries, but it is in ours."[34] Obstacles and challenges continue, however, to prevent our criminal legal system from achieving fairness, justice, and equity.

Fourteen years after Katrina, OPD remains underresourced and understaffed. The state reforms of 2007, while laudable, failed to change the structure of our user-pay criminal legal system. Hard-fought structural and policy reforms can be fully realized only with adequate funding and resources, and the system in place today is inadequate, unreliable, and unstable.[35] For example, OPD is currently restricting public defender services for the fourth time in fourteen years.[36] Thus, we have poor people waitlisted for an attorney and staff laid off or put on furlough; we lack investigative and expert funds, and funding for conflict case representation is inadequate. These issues are largely products of Louisiana's user-pay criminal legal system. Fueling the criminal legal system on fines, fees, and costs from poor people caught in the system yields inadequate, unpredictable, and unreliable revenues, rendering public defenders incapable of providing professional, ethical, constitutional representation for the poor.[37] More work is needed to ensure that *Gideon* and the reforms of the past fourteen years are not hollow. To that end, OPD strives to live up to its responsibilities in our criminal legal system: defend innocence, fight for clients, and hold power accountable.

Lessons

Despite great disparities between the funding and resources for our office and those for other criminal justice agencies, public defense in New Orleans is exponentially better than it was before Katrina. OPD is now a local partner in managing jail population, increasing public confidence in the criminal legal system, reducing wrongful convictions, maintaining system accountability, and ensuring that justice is done. OPD attracts national recognition for its strength, tenacity, and commitment to excellent representation. For example, OPD won the Southern Center for Human Rights, Frederick Douglass Human Rights Award in 2009.[38] In bestowing that award, the same organization that had deemed public defense in New Orleans an unconstitutional disaster (even before Katrina) now recognized OPD as a champion of civil and human rights. Among the most prestigious honors OPD received was the 2015 American Bar Association/National Legal Aid and Defender Association, Clara Shortridge Foltz Award.[39] As it had for the Frederick Douglass award, OPD, declared one of the best public defenders in the nation, earned praise from an early critic.[40]

The New Orleans community respects and supports OPD, recognizing that justice for poor people means something and requires a champion to make it mean something. OPD has little in common with the old OIDP. Evidence of OPD's acceptance within the community as a champion of justice for poor people came on December 16, 2014, when, more than 250 people answered our call to protest the 2004 shooting death of Michael Brown Jr. in Ferguson, Missouri, and other police shootings.[41] Our community stood with us to highlight the injustices seen every day in New Orleans criminal courts and our willingness to bear witness and fight. We essentially emptied the courthouse for this demonstration, and no one was held in or even threatened with contempt. Community recognition and support is also evidenced by the number of people who show up each year for OPD's Second Line for Equal Justice.[42]

The Road Ahead

Hurricane Katrina split all our lives into before and after. Katrina challenged us to not just survive but change. Fourteen years later, OPD is now evidence of how the most entrenched and intransigent places can reform. For the moment, however, that work is incomplete. For the reform effort to continue, stakeholders and decision makers must make structural changes to our user-pay system. The fight for public defense reform provides a blueprint. I am in my tenth year as chief defender for Orleans Parish, but I have worked on behalf of the poor and vulnerable all my professional life—more than twenty years. This journey of public defense reform has taught me some important lessons.

Remember your failures and who failed with you. Those same people, if committed, will be around when the time is right and change is most needed. They are the intellectual (and physical) muscle needed to make change a reality—the people learning the same tough lessons from previous efforts. For example, the chair of the reform-minded board put together by Judge Johnson was Denise LeBoeuf, a superb lawyer and veteran of many legal and legislative battles fought in the effort to change how the criminal legal system in Louisiana operates.[43]

Find the opportunity in every moment. Katrina was devastating. It forced me to move to Shreveport, Louisiana, after short stints in Tennessee and Texas. Maintaining a reform mindset was critical to my not giving up on New Orleans. Katrina forced humility on our community that sowed the seeds for change. But just as easily we might have given into destructive despair.

Recruit new allies. Particularly after Katrina, as we endeavored to strengthen and build on reform, new stakeholders joined in the call for reform. But reform really started in those moments after the storm and in the new local board. The new reform board members were partners from prestigious firms: Harry Rosenberg and Kim Boyle from Phelps Dunbar, and Phil Wittmann from Stone Pigman Walther and Wittmann. The education each of these new board members received turned them into advocates for change in their respective communities.

Continue to educate yourself and others on the issues. Information is powerful. Our reform was armed with reports and a history of litigation and legislative efforts that helped us persuade stakeholders that change was necessary and urgent. Knowing the history and having all the facts allowed us to point to third-party opinion and research to prove we were on the right side of history and the issues.

Media work and strategy are powerful tools. The incredible work done by journalists over the past decade and a half has been invaluable in educating stakeholders, decision makers, and the public. The work of the media highlighting the problems of real people in the criminal legal system, publicly calling out unfairness, and exposing years of neglect prompted people to pay attention and demand action.

Our reform successes and failures in post-Katrina New Orleans make it impossible to pretend that nothing happened or that nothing can be done. Katrina taught us that the stakes are too high to say we are not ready. Our reform journey continues.

Notes

1 Ann M. Simmons, "The Nation: Justice on Katrina Time; Hundreds, if Not Thousands, Languish behind Bars without Their Day in Court," *Los Angeles Times*, December 12, 2006.

2 D. Majeeda Snead, "Will Act 307 Help Louisiana Deliver Indigent Defender Services in Accordance with the 6th Amendment Right to Counsel Mandate?," *Loyola Journal of Public Interest Law* 9, no. 158 (2008).

3 The Fourteenth Amendment, which was ratified on July 9, 1868, provided in part: "All persons born or naturalized in the United States, and subject to the jurisdiction thereof, are citizens of the United States and of the State wherein they reside. No State shall make or enforce any law which shall abridge the privileges or immunities of citizens of the United States; nor shall any State deprive any person of life, liberty, or property, without due process of law; nor deny to any person within its jurisdiction the equal protections of the laws."

4 *Gideon v. Wainwright*, 372 US 335, 344 (1963). The court found that "in our adversary system of criminal justice, any person haled into court who is too poor to hire a lawyer, cannot be assured a fair trial unless counsel is provided to him." Thus, the right to counsel in felony cases was deemed necessary in our concept of ordered liberty, fundamental fairness and due process.

5 Ibid. at 796.

6 "Address by Hon. Robert F. Kennedy, Attorney General of the United States, before the New England Conference on the Defense of Indigent Persons Accused of Crime," Parker House, Boston, MA, November 1, 1963.

7 Snead, "Will Act 307 Help Louisiana?," 160.

8 "When any person has been arrested or detained in connection with the investigation or commission of any offense, he shall be advised fully of the reason for his arrest or detention, his right to remain silent, his right against self incrimination, his right to the assistance of counsel and, if indigent, his right to court appointed counsel. In a criminal prosecution, an accused shall be informed of the nature and cause of the accusation against him. At each stage of the proceedings, every person is entitled to assistance of counsel of his choice, or [one] appointed by the court if he is indigent and charged with an offense punishable by imprisonment. The legislature shall provide for a uniform system for securing and compensating qualified counsel for indigents." Louisiana Constitution art. I, § 13.

9 Ed Greenlee, "Feature: Justice in Louisiana: Indigent Defense: The Louisiana Indigent Defense Assistance Board," *Louisiana Bar Journal* 50, no. 97 (August/September 2002) (noting the assistance board's inadequate statewide budget of $7.5 million to supplement local public defender offices).

10 Norman Lefstein, *Securing Reasonable Caseloads: Ethics and Law in Public Defense* (American Bar Association Standing Committee on Legal Aid and Indigent Defendants, 2011). In 1973, the National Advisory Commission on Criminal Justice Standards and Goals (NAC), established and funded by the

federal government, recommended annual maximum caseloads for public defense programs. The NAC's recommendations had—and continue to have—significant influence in the field of public defense with respect to annual caseloads of public defenders. Specifically, the NAC recommended that annual maximum caseloads "of a public defender office should not exceed the following: felonies per attorney per year: not more than 150; misdemeanors (excluding traffic) per attorney per year: not more than 400; juvenile court cases per attorney per year: not more than 200; Mental Health Act cases per attorney per year; not more than 200; and appeals per attorney per year: not more than 25."

11 Fox Butterfield, "Few Options or Safeguards in a City's Juvenile Courts," *New York Times*, July 22, 1997 ("Welcome to the Orleans Parish Juvenile Court, considered by many lawyers and children's rights advocates to be the most troubled juvenile court system in the country."); Stephen B. Bright, "Counsel For The Poor: The Death Sentence Not for the Worst Crime but for the Worst Lawyer," *Yale Law Journal*, May 1, 1994, 1887–1890 ("A public defender in New Orleans represented 418 defendants during the first seven months of 1991. During this time, he entered 130 guilty pleas at arraignment and had at least one serious case set for trial on every single trial date during the period. In 'routine cases,' he received no investigative support because the three investigators in the public defender office were responsible for more than 7000 cases per year. No funds were available for expert witnesses. The Louisiana Supreme Court found that, because of the excessive caseloads and insufficient resources of the public defender office, the clients served by this system are 'not provided with the effective assistance of counsel the [C]onstitution requires.'"); Brett Barrouquere, "Money Sets Fate of Bills***Justice Reform Victim of Finance," *Baton Rouge Advocate*, May 26, 2003 ("'My feeling is that the system there is in crisis,' [David Carroll, director of research and evaluation for the National Legal Aid and Defender Association in Washington, D.C.] said. 'We have real issues with the quality of representation going on down there.'"); Sasha Polakow-Suransky, "I Plead the Sixth," *American Prospect,* July 25, 2002 ("In a corner, Victor Papai, the head of indigent defense at the juvenile court, shares a 4-foot-by-10-foot office with a staff of six part-time attorneys. Each handles close to 800 cases per year—four times the federally recommended annual caseload for full-time juvenile defenders. But when I enter, Papai is alone playing solitaire on his computer.").

12 One of the best chronologies of reform efforts is found in a case considered at least a partial victory by reformers, *State v. Citizen.*04-1841 (La. 04/01/2005); 898 So. 2d 325. In *Citizen*, after documenting decades of underfunding for public defense, the Louisiana Supreme Court decided courts have the power to halt prosecutions where resource disparities render the proceedings unfair—and thus unconstitutional.

13 *State v. Peart*, 621 So. 2d 780 (La. 1993).

14 Ibid. at 789. The court concluded that, to be effective, "the lawyer not only possesses adequate skill and knowledge, but also that he has the time and resources to apply his skill and knowledge to the task of defending each of his individual clients."

15 "An example of these disparities is documented in a report on the American Bar Associations' Hearings on the Right to Counsel in Criminal Proceedings. One witness reported that in Calcasieu Parish 83% of the cases revealed nothing that suggested the public defender ever talked to his client outside of the courtroom. It reported that often what happened was that 'on the morning of the trial, the public defender [would] introduce himself to his client, tell him the 'deal' that has been negotiated, and ask him to 'sign here.'" Snead, "Will Act 307 Help Louisiana?," 164.

16 "The legislature has taken steps to remedy the critical state of indigent criminal defense in Louisiana since our warnings in *Peart*. For instance, it created the statewide Indigent Defense Assistance Board in 1997, via La. R.S. 15:151. In 2003, the legislature, by separate but identical House and Senate resolutions (HR 151; SR 112), created the Louisiana Task Force on Indigent Defense Services, effective January 12, 2004, to study the problem and make an initial report no later than March 1, 2004. The legislature has constituted the Task Force as a blue ribbon committee whose members range from the Governor to the Chief Justice of this Court. It is not [p. 14] clear whether the 2003 Task Force ever made its report, but this year, by concurrent resolution (SCR 136), the legislature voted to continue the Task Force, directing it to report on its findings together with specific recommendations no later than April 1, 2005. We assume that, given the obvious deficiencies in funding from the State to satisfy its constitutional mandate in La. Const. Art.

I, § 13, this Task Force will work diligently to formulate specific recommendations on April 1, 2005, to address these problems and that the legislature will act quickly to promulgate these, or other, appropriate solutions." *State v. Citizen* at 336.

17   The time spent in jail while the district attorney (D.A) decides whether or not to accept a case is known locally as "doing D.A. time." The D.A. has 45 days to decide on a misdemeanor, 60 days on a felony, and 120 days on a serious felony. See La. Code. Crim. Pro. Art. 701 et seq. The practice of not assigning or appointing an attorney until after a case is accepted by the D.A. (while a person sits in jail) is still a widely implemented policy in public defender offices throughout Louisiana. This practice is used to save scarce, inadequate resources.

18   Emily Maw, "'When They See Us' and Louisiana," *Times-Picayune*, June 23, 2019. ("Nationally, Louisiana has the second-highest per capita rate of proven wrongful conviction. New Orleans far and away leads US cities in the rate at which it wrongly convicts people, largely young black men. And because of Louisiana's draconian sentencing, most of the state's wrongly convicted were sentenced to life without parole, or death.")

19   Department of Justice, Bureau of Justice Assistance, *An Assessment of the Immediate and Longer Term Needs of the New Orleans Public Defender System* (Baton Rouge: Louisiana Public Defender Board, 2006).

20   National Legal Aid and Defender Association, *A Strategic Plan to Ensure Accountability and Protect Fairness in Louisiana's Criminal Courts* (Washington, DC, 2006).

21   David Brooks, "Brace Yourself for the Next Torrent That Opens the Wounds of Race, Class," *Detroit Free Press*, September 2, 2005, op-ed.

22   Laura Parker, "City's Public Defender System Troubled before Katrina; Activists, Lawyers, Feds See a Chance to Fix New Orleans' Judicial Problems," *USA Today*, May 23, 2006. ("The Southern Center for Human Rights, an Atlanta-based public interest law firm, sent attorneys and staff members to New Orleans in March. In a scathing report, the center concluded that even before Katrina, overwhelmed public defenders in New Orleans generally 'did not visit crime scenes, interview witnesses, check out alibis, did not procure expert assistance, did not review evidence, did not know the facts of the case even on the eve of trial, did not do any legal research and did not otherwise prepare for trial.'")

23   Snead, "Will Act 307 Help Louisiana?," 170.

24   Gwen Filosa, "Indigent Defense Board Sworn In: Members Face Task of Rebuilding System," *Times-Picayune*, April 27, 2006.

25   Nicholas L. Chiarkis, D. Alan Henry, and Randolph N. Stone, *An Assessment of the Immediate and Longer-Term Needs of the New Orleans Public Defender System* (report prepared by the BJA National Training and Technical Assistance Initiative Project at American University, 2006), available at http://lpdb.la.gov/Serving%20The%20Public/Reports/District%20Reports.php; Laura Maggi, "Indigent Office in for Nearly $3 Million: But It's a Drop in the Bucket, Officials Say," *Times-Picayune*, May 12, 2006.

26   In 2014, Jonathan Rapping received the MacArthur "Genius" Grant for his work to change the culture of public defense. "Jonathan Rapping," MacArthur Foundation, https://www.macfound.org/fellows/925/, accessed December 31, 2019.

27   Sarah Covert, "Charge Undermines Aggressive Indigent Defense," *Times-Picayune*, August 4, 2009, op-ed.

28   Melissa Block, "New Orleans Judge Slams City's Justice System," *All Things Considered*, NPR, April 2, 2007. ("Indigent defense in New Orleans is unbelievable, unconstitutional, totally lacking the basic professional standards of legal representation and a mockery of what a criminal justice system should be in a Western, civilized nation.")

29   Gwen Filosa, "Defender, Investigator Found in Contempt: They Tried to Interview Children in Rape Case," *Times-Picayune*, July 16, 2009; James Gill, "Fight Looms for Control of Indigent Defense," *Times-Picayune*, April 25, 2007, op-ed ("Since the indigent defender board was reconstituted after Katrina, it has asserted the right and the duty to represent clients without political or judicial interference, as both state law and American Bar Association standards require. This has come as quite a shock to the judges, who under the old system called all the shots, with predictable consequences for the constitutional rights

of poor defendants."); Laura Maggi, "Public Defender Office Leader Jailed: Judge Says More Attorneys Needed to Cover Juvenile Cases," *Times-Picayune*, January 10, 2007; Laura Maggi, "Indigent Staff Rise Is Ordered: Judges Say Office Not Competently Run," *Times-Picayune*, November 11, 2006 ("They let that system stand for years and years without a peep," [Denise LeBoeuf, chair of the Orleans Indigent Defense Board, said], "I'm pretty suspicious that this is all done for the altruistic benefit of poor people.").

30 Gwen Filosa, "Lawyer Handcuffed in Clash with Judge: Public Defender Freed after Hour of Detention," *Times-Picayune*, May 13, 2008.

31 Once Judge Johnson ceased being chief judge, the new chief judge, Raymond Bigelow, a staunch opponent to reform, tried to dismantle the reform-minded board, replacing four of us (myself included). We responded by filing suit. See Laura Maggi, "Suit Filed over Indigent Defense: Judges Vote to Pull 4 Members off Panel," *Times-Picayune*, May 5, 2007. ("'The attempted removal of four members of the present board and replacing them with other people is nothing more than an attempt to interfere with the management decisions by what is, by any measure, an outstanding indigent defender board,' said Herbert Larson, the attorney for the board.")

32 Snead, "Will Act 307 Help Louisiana?," 171.

33 Ibid.

34 *Gideon v. Wainwright*, at 796.

35 Matt Sledge and Bryn Stole, "Supreme Court Panel Urges Revamp of Louisiana's 'User Pay' Criminal Justice System, but Implementing It Will Be Hard," *Baton Rouge Advocate*, April 18, 2019.

36 Matt Sledge, "Orleans Public Defenders to Cut Services, Freeze Hiring in Face of Revenue Shortfall," *Baton Rouge Advocate,* May 5, 2019. ("It's not a new problem. The agency's recurring budget crises led to large-scale layoffs in 2012 and a waiting list for representation in felony cases in 2015 and 2016.")

37 Derwyn Bunton, "When the Public Defender Says, 'I Can't Help,'" *New York Times*, February 19, 2016.

38 "Frederick Douglass Awards Dinner: Recent Awardees," Southern Center for Human Rights, https://www.schr.org/frederick_douglass_dinner_recent_awardees, accessed December 31, 2019.

39 "Clara Shortridge Foltz Award," National Legal Aid & Defender Association, http://www.nlada.org/about-nlada/nlada-awards/clara-shortridge-foltz-award-biennial, accessed December 31, 2019. ("[The award] commends a public defender program or defense delivery system for outstanding achievement in the provision of indigent defense services. The achievement may be the result of an effort by the entire program, a division or branch or a special project. This award is co-sponsored by NLADA and the American Bar Association Standing Committee on Legal Aid and Indigent Defendants. Established in 1985, this award was named for the founder of the nation's public defender system. Foltz, California's first woman lawyer, introduced the 'Foltz Defender Bill' at the Congress of Jurisprudence and Law Reform in Chicago in 1893.")

40 "Created in the wake of a complete criminal justice system failure following Hurricane Katrina, OPD has become the benchmark for public defense in Louisiana. OPD represents nearly 20,000 people each year; has made significant advances in juvenile mitigation, bond advocacy, and mental health representation; and laid the groundwork to reduce recidivism with diversion and alternatives to incarceration programs." "2015 Recipient," available at ibid.

41 Helen Freund, "Public Defender's Office Joins in National Protest Movement: Attorneys to Gather on Courthouse Steps," *Times-Picayune*, December 16, 2014; Ken Daley, "Public Defenders Stage Protest on Inequality in Justice System: 'It's A Conversation We Have To Have,'" *Times-Picayune*, December 17, 2014 ("More than 250 lawyers, clients and supporters of the Orleans Parish Public Defenders' office staged a silent, 4 1/2-minute protest on the steps of the city's criminal courthouse Tuesday, symbolically objecting to what their chief termed the daily inequities levied upon overwhelmingly minority suspects and defendants in New Orleans and around the nation.").

42 Mark Hertsgaard, "New Orleans Public Defender Turns Away Felony Cases: Derwyn Bunton, the Crescent City's Public Defender, Has Refused to Accept Serious Felony Cases, Claiming That Underfunding Means His Office Can't Do Its Job," *Daily Beast*, November 25, 2016. ("Gathered before him were about 200 people who had marched across town in a 'second line' parade, a beloved New Orleans musical ritual that

has helped generations of African Americans preserve their cultural identity and sense of community in the face of racial injustices dating back to the days of slavery. 'Equal Justice For All' read one of the protest signs that bobbed above the crowd beneath bright blue skies. 'Fund Public Defenders Now' urged another.")

43 A bio of Denise LeBoeuf is available on the ACLU website at https://www.aclu.org/bio/denny-leboeuf, accessed December 31, 2019.

Community Demand for Change and Accountability: A History of Court Watch NOLA, New Orleans' Community Courtwatching Program

Simone Levine

Simone Levine served as counsel in the Office of Independent Police Monitor of the City of New Orleans. She is now CEO of Court Watch NOLA.

Without strong watchdog institutions, impunity becomes the very foundation upon which systems of corruptions are built.
—Rigoberta Menchu Tum, Nobel Prize Laureate

The criminal justice system, like any other system, is run by insiders: prosecutors, judges, deputy sheriffs, police, clerks, private defense, and public defenders. But system outsiders—victims, witnesses, criminal defendants, and the community in general—have the power to demand respect from that same system and to demand that the system work for them. System insiders have no monopoly on the knowledge and the power to shape the criminal justice system. In the words of the legal scholar and now judge Bibas Stephanos:

> A great gulf divides insiders and outsiders in the criminal justice system. The insiders who run the criminal justice system—judges, police, and especially prosecutors—have information, power, and self-interests that greatly influence the criminal justice system's process and outcomes. Outsiders—crime victims, bystanders, and most of the general public—find the system frustratingly opaque, insular, and unconcerned with proper retribution. . . . The gulf clouds the law's deterrent and expressive messages, as well as its efficacy in healing victims; it impairs trust in and the legitimacy of the law. . . . The most promising solutions are to inform crime victims and other affected locals better and to give them larger roles in criminal justice.[1]

But once community members educate themselves, they are able to harness the system and make themselves a group that, in order to function, the system must interact with respectfully, constitutionally, and with deference.

Court Watch NOLA believes the criminal justice system has gone astray. Some system insiders

150

believe we are too conservative. Other system insiders believe we are too progressive. The truth is that Court Watch NOLA is neither. Court Watch NOLA is just you and I. We are community, we are New Orleanians. And we know that the criminal justice system has gone astray because it is no longer listening to us, the community: a community that has been victimized, a community that has witnessed, a community that has been arrested.

What is Court Watch NOLA not? Court Watch NOLA is not afraid. Court Watch NOLA is not afraid of confronting public officials who do not represent the community's interest. The outgoing special agent in charge of the FBI for Louisiana, Jeff Sallet, said of corruption in Louisiana: "People don't want to give up corrupt public officials, often because they're afraid of the consequences."[2] Court Watch NOLA is not willing to stand by corrupt public officials because of a previous alliance or friendship, societal standing, or some desire of future favor. Court Watch NOLA is not concerned with being attacked by public officials who refuse to listen to the community and who continue to work according to outdated standards with their eyes closed and their fingers in their ears. The only fear Court Watch NOLA holds is not sufficiently educating voters to ensure that we have political representatives that will hear and represent our voice.

Court Watch NOLA was created (for the second time) in 2007. We are thirteen years old, and with that many years under our belt, we are one of the longest-standing courtwatching programs in the country.[3] We are not participatory defense. We do not advocate for the defense, nor do we try to ensure that any one defense attorney does a better job of defending the interests of her or his client. We are not participatory prosecution. We will not argue that someone should get the maximum amount of prison time. We are objective, and we never take positions on individual cases. Instead, we look at trends in the data we collect as court watchers in open court. If we examine individual cases, it is only for the larger purpose of looking at the aggregate trend.

We are Court Watch NOLA. We are normal community members like you, and we began to monitor criminal court because we wanted to take the court back from system insiders. We wanted to make sure that the courts are accountable to us, to people who vote (and to those who are barred from doing so), to people who demonstrate, to those held hostage by the criminal court system. We are more than a hundred people a year who go into court. Sometimes we are described as an army of yellow clipboards. And everything changes when we are in court. Judges, prosecutors, defense attorneys, and police all act differently when we walk into court with our yellow clipboards. We are outsiders to the criminal justice system, and the system was not created to support outsiders, to listen to outsiders, or to meet the needs of outsiders. Most of us do not understand the insider language, and frankly, we are not meant to understand that language. But increasingly we are being heard, and the language is starting to change. It has not been without a fight.

This article outlines the history of Court Watch NOLA, New Orleans' long-standing court-monitoring program and premier criminal court watchdog group. It outlines the data that Court Watch NOLA's court watchers first collected and the criminal justice atmosphere (national and local) that allowed Court Watch NOLA to mature, change, and grow. This article outlines the reforms the community demanded after Hurricane Katrina and the reforms demanded by New Orleanians today.

The Beginning and the Storm

Court Watch NOLA started in the chaos that was the aftermath of Hurricane Katrina, one of the waves of reform groups created during this period to change the way New Orleans' public officials would serve the city. Court Watch NOLA joined the Office of the Independent Police Monitor,[4] the Office of the Inspector General,[5] the Crime Coalition,[6] and others to bring accountability to the larger government systems of New Orleans. For many of these new organizations, the New Orleans criminal justice system was the target of change. A common refrain after the storm was, "Katrina sort of ripped off the Band-Aid—it removed the pretension that the system was working."[7]

Many things changed with Hurricane Katrina. The damage caused by Katrina was sizeable. The criminal court took in twelve feet of water, badly damaging case files and evidence stored in the basement.[8] In the end, only 10 percent of evidence was lost. But it took between five hundred thousand dollars and one million dollars and a full year to restore all the evidence that had been flooded in the basement of the Orleans Parish Criminal District Court.[9]

Orleans Parish sheriff Marlin Gusman did not evacuate inmates from the Orleans Parish Prison before the storm, explaining that he could never have persuaded other sheriffs to house thousands of inmates.[10] The Orleans Parish Prison building was not badly damaged during the storm, but like the Criminal District Court building, Orleans Parish Prison was flooded after the storm when the levees broke.[11] Sewage began to back up and emergency generators were destroyed, causing the prison to lose lights and air circulation in ninety-degree weather.[12] Without the use of the generators, the electronic cells could no longer be opened or closed.[13] When the water rose chest-deep on the first floor, guards engaged in "vertical evacuation," forcing inmates who faced traffic and other minor offenses into cells on the higher floors with those who faced murder and rape charges.[14] When the Louisiana Department of Corrections arrived with boats, it carried inmates to an elevated overpass on the nearby interstate and ferried prisoners day and night to other jails around the state.[15] Many of the inmates who were caught in the flooding in Orleans Parish Prison and later evacuated to jails across the state of Louisiana faced only minor misdemeanor and traffic offenses.[16] Later, when Orleans Parish court officials attempted to find these inmates to start court proceedings, they often failed.[17] Sheriffs could provide no proper records for these inmates because "they just poured out of those flooded jails."[18] It was reported that eight thousand detainees awaited proceedings without courts, trials, or lawyers for up to a year.[19] Inmates languished for months in local jails "doing Katrina time," serving long past their sentences without ever receiving a judicial hearing.[20] Louisiana courts suspended habeas corpus for six months.[21]

The storm had a devastating effect on the District Attorney's Office building, with the first floor taking on three to four feet of water.[22] Flooding caused the destruction of many records, and the District Attorney's Office was unable to return to its building for many years.[23] Prosecutors first worked from home and later at three tables in a downtown hotel before moving into a nightclub, where they remained until May 2006.[24] When the tax base of the city collapsed, the District Attorney's Office laid off approximately fifty employees, including all investigators. At one point, it could not even pay its phone bill.[25]

The Orleans Indigent Defender Program, funded primarily by the revenue from traffic tickets (and already extremely underfunded before the storm), laid off twenty-five of its thirty-five attorneys for budgetary reasons.[26] Slowly, key reformers dedicated untold time to help represent the thousands of defendants stranded across the state and rebuilt the Public Defender's Office into a system that began to approach the standards of constitutional representation.[27]

Post-Katrina and the Community Response

Hurricane Katrina struck New Orleans on August 29, 2005.[28] The United States has rarely experienced such a rapid and complete collapse of local law enforcement, a district attorney's office, the indigent defense system, jails, and criminal courts.[29] The first criminal bench trial was held more than eight months after the storm, on March 31, 2006.[30] The first jury trial was held more than ten months after the storm, on June 5, 2006.[31] During the subsequent four months, approximately fifteen jury trials were held, despite the existence of three thousand pending cases.[32] A year after the storm, prison officials, public defenders, and law school clinic students continued to locate hundreds of inmates who had seen neither a lawyer nor a judge since the storm.[33] The criminal courthouse did not reopen until June 1, 2006.[34] Before that, judges presided over cases at Hunt Correctional Facility or the New Orleans Greyhound Bus Station (equipped as a jail) until December 2005 and then for a short while in the federal courthouse.[35]

Crime in New Orleans went up, and while some city officials argued that the crime *rate* had not increased—since the lower post-Katrina population made the per capita crime rate much larger than the same number of crimes would have at pre-Katrina population levels—the New Orleans community grew angry and frustrated with the lack of official response to crime.[36] Mayor Ray Nagin, New Orleans' third African American mayor, publicly responded that most of the crime was "black on black crime."[37] Nagin's response was widely seen as a bid for the return of tourism dollars and an attempt by the mayor to hide his head in the sand.[38] Reports of gang activity based on turf wars and drugs became widespread, increasing the general fear of the city's residents.[39] While some in law enforcement were careful to point out that this criminal activity did not involve traditional gangs,[40] such finite points were lost on the general population.[41] Witness intimidation was frequently cited as both a cause for the continuation of violent crime and a rationale for unsuccessful prosecutions.[42] By the end of 2016, New Orleans was the nation's homicide capital, according to FBI statistics, with 63.5 slayings per 100,000 residents, an increase over other contenders such as Gary, Indiana, and Detroit.[43]

In early June 2006, in what would later be known as the Central City massacre, five teenagers were shot dead; the killings were the worst the city had seen in a decade.[44] Killed were Marquis Hunter, age nineteen; his brother, Arsenio "Lil Man" Hunter, age sixteen; Warren "Luv" Simeon, age seventeen; Iraum Taylor, age nineteen; and Reggie "Putty" Dantzler, age nineteen.[45] The Central City massacre led Governor Kathleen Blanco, at the request of Mayor Nagin, to order the National Guard and the State Police into the City of New Orleans.[46] In July 2006, District Attorney Eddie Jordan arrested Michael Anderson for the quintuple murder but in October 2007 dismissed the charges (without telling the victim's family beforehand), explaining that the evidence was contradictory and that their star witness could not be found.[47] This move led to more discontent against the already very unpopular African American district attorney, and Jordan quickly reindicted Michael Anderson after the New Orleans Police Department "found" the star witness that the district attorney supposedly failed to locate.[48] When the next district attorney, Leon Cannizzaro, who was white, was elected by majorities of both black and white voters,[49] he made history by securing the death penalty against Michael Anderson, New Orleans' first death penalty in twelve years.[50] The fact that District Attorney Cannizzaro had efficiently and effectively prosecuted and returned a verdict in this high-profile case during his first eight months in office provided relief to many New Orleanians, both white and black.[51] Only later in 2010, when the case against Anderson was overturned, did it come to light that District Attorney Cannizzaro's office had not turned over key evidence to either the court or the defense.[52] In 2016, the US Attorney's Office stated in a federal court filing that the New Orleans drug kingpin Telly Hankton, not Michael Anderson, had committed the Central City massacre.[53] While hindsight seems to indicate that Eddie Jordan's hesitation to prosecute Michael Anderson was appropriate, hesitation over the reliability of evidence was not welcome to New Orleanians at the time. New Orleans was being barraged by violent crime and the city's population was infuriated.

In January 2007, an estimated five thousand people staged a historic rally against violent crime in New Orleans.[54] The participants, a diverse group, staged the largest demonstration New Orleans had seen since the civil rights era.[55] In the words of veteran news journalist Gordon Russell, "The 2007 crime rally was the most significant protest of its kind I've seen in 20 years as a journalist in New Orleans." "Thousands of people attended and dozens spoke. It was a completely citizen-driven event—in fact, public officials mostly weren't given a chance to speak."[56] The rally was organized by the victim-rights group Silence Is Violence[57] after two prominent New Orleanians were shot and killed. Dinerral Shavers, an African American drummer for the Hot 8 Brass Band, who was a father and a high school teacher, was shot to death while driving in the 6th Ward with his family.[58] Helen Hill, a white Canadian filmmaker who had moved to New Orleans after the storm, was killed in her home in Faubourg Marigny. Her husband, who was also shot while hiding in the bathroom holding the couple's baby, survived.[59] Public anger exploded over these high-profile murders. New Orleans had already seen nine killings in the first eight days of the year.[60] The crowd marched to City Hall and called for the resignations of Mayor Nagin, District Attorney Eddie Jordan, and Police Superintendent Warren Riley.[61] Glen David Andrews, prominent trombonist for the Hot 8 Brass Band, spoke at the rally and thundered at Mayor Nagin, "Get on your job"[62] but also admitted to the thousands in the crowd that as an African American man, he was "scared to death of the police."[63] Andrews had reason to be scared of the New Orleans Police Department. Later that fall he was arrested by the police for simply marching in a memorial second line; the criminal charges were dropped only months later.[64]

Two years after the January 2007 demonstration against violent crime, Silence Is Violence held another rally "to express their disgust over the continuing violence in New Orleans, the nation's most murderous city."[65] The names of all the people murdered in the city in the past year were read out loud.[66] Rather than calling for the resignations of any public officials, the demonstration's organizers announced that the newly elected district attorney, Leon Cannizzaro, would be among those gathering on the steps of City Hall.[67] The organizers asked "citizens to pause and ponder the city's seemingly intractable crime problem, then make a personal effort to improve the community."[68] The tone had changed by 2008, and community outrage at some public officials had diminished.

The Movement toward Reform

This was the beginning. In 2007 New Orleans was starting to get back on its feet and try to make sense of the ruins around it. In the middle of the post-Katrina chaos, James Carter was elected to the first New Orleans City Council seated after Hurricane Katrina.[69] Carter, the second African American to serve as a New Orleans city councilman in District C, a historically diverse district, would go on to become the first African American criminal justice commissioner in New Orleans' history.[70] In 2006, and after the storm, Carter held town halls to, in his words, "better understand the problems New Orleans community faced."[71] An African American woman (whose name is lost to history) approached Carter at a town hall in Algiers and proposed a community courtwatching project that would bring accountability to criminal court.[72] The project would show the judges, the prosecution, the defense lawyers, the police, and the sheriff that they were being watched and they would be held accountable.[73] Carter approached Michael Cowan—a white academic who had founded Common Good, a group comprising different community organizations focused on rebuilding the city—to discuss starting a courtwatching group in New Orleans.[74] Carter had already begun working with Cowan and other leaders in the white civic and business community to coordinate the creation of the Office of the Independent Police Monitor inside the Office of the Inspector General.[75]

While it always takes a community to get large-scale programs off the ground, it is indisputable that the Office of the Independent Police Monitor would never have been created had it not been for Councilmember Carter.[76] New Orleans became one of the first and remains one of the only cities with an independent office responsible for receiving community complaints of police abuse and monitoring the use of police force used against the civilian community. The Office of the Independent Police Monitor was created as part of the larger Office of the Inspector General but with independent decision-making powers.[77] The Office of the Inspector General was created to investigate municipal agency corruption.[78] While the African American community largely supported the creation of the Office of the Independent Police Monitor, the white community supported the creation of the Inspector General's Office. Carter worked with leaders of white New Orleans, including Michael Cowan of Common Good, the Business Council, and Citizens for 1 Greater New Orleans, to ensure that the combined Inspector General/Independent Police Monitor's office was voted into the New Orleans City Charter by the people of New Orleans.

In many ways Carter was ahead of his time. As a public official, he attempted to institutionalize a method to fight the many ways the African American community, either as criminal defendants or as crime victims, suffered at the hands of the criminal justice system. Issues of inequality remained inextricably tied to the aftermath of Katrina. Orleans Parish's pre-Hurricane situation was equally bleak, however, just less obvious to the rest of the country. New Orleans' pre-Katrina population was 67 percent African American, 28 percent below the poverty line, and 22 percent without their own transportation.[79]

When he came up with the concept of a courtwatching group, Carter saw the purpose of such a group as bringing accountability to the public officials of New Orleans criminal courts in two major areas:

1. the disparate treatment of African Americans in the criminal courts compared to their white counterparts, and

2. the stiffness of penalty for nonviolent compared to violent felony offenses.[80]

Overall, Carter believed that the transparency provided by a courtwatching program would create a better criminal justice system, leading to a safer city for all without regard to race, color, or creed.[81] These are the issues Carter remembers deliberating before speaking to Cowan about the courtwatching concept.[82] Cowan credits Carter as the creator of the current Court Watch NOLA concept.[83] But Carter did not go on to play a part in coordinating the Court Watch NOLA organization, aside from speaking to the community about the concept,[84] because he saw government as having no role to play in coordinating the creation of a courtwatching program.[85]

To say that Carter faced an uphill battle in putting his concepts into practice is an understatement. Carter remembers facing resistance from in the African American community in his efforts to gain legitimacy for many of his concepts,[86] though it was often the African American community that stood to gain the most from many of those ideas. Carter reached out to Cowan and other white leaders in the community with his idea of creating a courtwatching program, his objective emanating squarely from the African American community's experience, in part because Carter and Cowan had already been working together to ensure that the Office of the Independent Police Monitor and the Office of the Inspector General was successfully voted into the New Orleans City Charter.

Court Watch NOLA did not model its initial objectives on Carter's concept of examining racial inequalities and sentencing disparities between nonviolent and violent crime. Instead, just as it does now, Court Watch NOLA as a community program took its energy from where the community was the loudest and the most outraged, where the community had started to organize as a popular movement. At the time, community outrage was pitted against the upsurge of violent crime.

In New Orleans, great minds think alike even if such minds come from different worlds, backgrounds, and perspectives. While Carter was speaking to his African American constituency about a courtwatching group and conferring with Cowan, a vibrant and determined civic group, largely comprising successful white women, began to convene and ask the pivotal question of how the community could keep the criminal courts accountable. Citizens for 1, Greater New Orleans (Citizens for 1) started as and remains today a nonpartisan, nonsectarian grassroots initiative formed to fight for the consolidation of the levee boards and assessor system after Katrina; the group's universal demand was for a government "that is open, honest, transparent and accountable."[87] The crime-victim advocate and current Court Watch NOLA advisory board member Patti Lapeyre, an early member of Citizens for 1, recounts the story of a group of Citizens for 1 members gathering information for months and bringing the courtwatching concept back to the Citizens for 1 executive board.[88]

The concept of courtwatching is as old as the courts themselves. Books have been written about prominent criminal trials and the role of the community/audience that makes up the fabric of New Orleans history.[89] In fact, Court Watch NOLA had already been created (for the first time) back in the 1980s.[90] Jerome Goldman, a successful entrepreneur who became concerned about the lack of accountability of criminal court public officials and the high rate of violent crime in New Orleans, created the first Court Watch NOLA.[91] Goldman approached the Metropolitan Crime Commission,[92] one of the few organizations in 1980s New Orleans that focused on the criminal courts and the larger criminal justice system.[93] At the time that the first Court Watch NOLA had begun in the late 1980s, Rafael Goyeneche, a young white former assistant district attorney from District Attorney Harry Connick's office, was just starting to work at the Metropolitan Crime Commission.[94] Jerome Goldman provided the commission with the funds to create New Orleans' first formal courtwatching program.[95] But the Metropolitan Crime Commission was forced to discontinue the program eighteen months after it was created, for lack of funding.[96]

The fact that two different groups believed that a courtwatching program could be created in post-Katrina New Orleans points to the confidence New Orleanians had that it would be community alone that would give courts the accountability they needed, for New Orleanians to regain confidence in the larger criminal justice system.

What is certain is that Citizens for 1 put an enormous amount of groundwork into creating Court Watch NOLA as an organization; without that groundwork, Court Watch NOLA would not have been created at that time in New Orleans. From May 2006 until February 2007, several pioneering women, including but not limited to Barbara Bush, Ann Rabin, Linda Roussel, Hope Goldman Meyer, Nicole Spangenberg, Erin Hangartner, and Zully Jiminez, came together to start meeting with criminal justice stakeholders.[97] This was the beginning of Court Watch NOLA. It is sound planning on the part of any new not for profit but especially a court watching group to meet with stakeholders before launching the concept.[98] Every week for nine months this industrious group met with various criminal court judges and others, including District Attorney Eddie Jordan and his successor, Leon Cannizzaro.[99] For twenty years, one member of the group, Zully Jiminez, had been the assistant to District Attorney Harry Connick, Eddie Jordan's immediate predecessor.[100] According to one Citizen for 1 member, Jiminez was the driving force behind the group's ability to meet with criminal justice stakeholders.[101] Patti Lapeyre began attending task force meetings at the Louisiana State Supreme Court, gaining entrance through John Casbon, an early friend of Court Watch NOLA.[102] Around this time, Nicole Spangenberg met with Mothers Against Drunk Driving, not to copy its model, but to understand it better.[103] Nolan Marshall, who was working for Common Good at the time, began to work with Citizens for 1 to help get Court Watch NOLA off the ground.[104] Together Lapeyre and Marshall wrote letters to all judges, councilmembers, and other stakeholders, informing them of the creation of Court Watch NOLA.[105] "Very early on," Marshall reports, "we wanted to make sure we were devising a program that was accepted by the judges, that wasn't seen as overly critical of any specific aspect of what folks were observing. It was not supposed to be a criticism and review of only judges—we wanted to look at everyone: public defenders, prosecutors, defense attorneys. The question was how do we devise that, how do we achieve that?"[106]

The concept of courtwatching was also discussed at the second or third meeting of the New Orleans Crime Coalition, a group formed to think through how to stop violent crime.[107] The New Orleans Crime Coalition was beginning to look at every aspect of the criminal justice system and trying to determine how to restart the gears of the criminal justice system to combat violent crime.[108] At the time Court Watch NOLA was being discussed, the Crime Coalition was made up of Citizens for 1, the Metropolitan Crime Commission, Common Good, Crime Stoppers, the Police and Justice Foundation, the Business Council of New Orleans, and the Urban League.[109] "The whole system," according to Cowan, "was being broken up and ripped apart at the time. We knew that we could not just look at the police department, that we needed to also look at the judges. Every part of the criminal justice system was in the hole and Court Watch NOLA was the response to the judiciary. There was a light being shed."[110] Carter made formal presentations to Common Good and the New Orleans Crime Coalition. In both presentations he did not refer to his specific objectives for the program or the data he envisioned the program should collect. Instead, he spoke of the overarching concepts of community accountability over the courts in an effort to ensure that the universal concept for the program was accepted by the larger (white) community that could put the courtwatching program into effect.[111]

In the months before Court Watch NOLA hired its first executive director, Marshall, Cowan, and a small group of Citizens for 1 members met with Councilmember Carter and Mayor Nagin.[112] Lapeyre remembers hearing Mayor Nagin tell this group of mostly women that it would be "too dangerous" for volunteers to watch court and that instead he could have cameras installed in the court.[113] Lapeyre responded, "No disrespect to you but this is a grassroots effort, and it's not going to be government run."[114] Lapeyre and the others she was working with refused Mayor Nagin's offer of governmental help, a rule to which the group still adheres today.[115] Court Watch NOLA was launched in February 2007 with initial seed money provided by the Business Coalition, Citizens for 1, and Common Good.[116]

In 2007, Rafael Goyeneche also provided much-needed help in getting Court Watch NOLA off the ground.[117] "Rafe spoke very eloquently," Cowan reports, "about the problems that judges caused in the system, the inefficiencies that judges caused, and the need to hold these judges accountable."[118] In 2007, the Metropolitan Crime Commission themselves began issuing reports that examined the performance of the New Orleans criminal justice system through the police department, the District Attorney's Office, and the judiciary.[119] The Metropolitan Crime Commission reports continue to examine agencies through the lens of efficiency data, looking at the district attorney's felony arrest-to-conviction rates, each felony judge's average numbers of pending cases, the rate of backlogged cases, and median case-processing time.[120] Goyeneche was a strong force in ensuring that Court Watch NOLA exclusively examine efficiency data in the New Orleans Criminal District Court.[121] Goyeneche and the Metropolitan Crime Commission mentored Court Watch NOLA as it got on its feet, providing it office space before the Court Watch NOLA board member Ellen Yellin, who is still a Court Watch NOLA board member, procured the organization its credentials as a 501(c)(3) not-for-profit organization.[122]

Another early pioneer of Court Watch NOLA, Hope Goldman Meyer, was invited by Goyeneche to be on Court Watch NOLA's first board of directors.[123] Meyer, whose father had created the courtwatching project with the Metropolitan Crime Commission in the 1980s, had already been working for months with Patti Lapeyre and Citizens for 1 to get Court Watch NOLA off the ground.[124] Meyer, who is still an advisory board member, represents the continuum between the traditions of courtwatching in the 1980s and the project we have today.[125] She was overjoyed to be involved with the re-creation of Court Watch NOLA, stating, "It makes perfect sense to hold people in power accountable, and in New Orleans it is one of those things that needs to continue."[126]

Meyer brought the former prosecutor Lisa Jordan into the process. Lisa Jordan, who is a current advisory board member, also represents the continuum between Court Watch NOLA's traditions and its current work. It was her idea to approach Karen Herman, with whom she had worked in Harry Connick's District Attorney's Office.[127] Herman became the first executive director of Court Watch NOLA and served in the first half of 2007.[128] She was an extremely active executive director, speaking on the radio, going to community groups, and recruiting as many community volunteers as possible to go into criminal court and collect data.[129]

Karen Herman remembers training court watchers one-on-one[130] and Lisa Jordan remembers conducting trainings in the early days of Court Watch NOLA.[131] The first class of court watchers was made up of approximately a dozen volunteers.[132] Herman reports: "There was a real sense of community when the program started. Often it was senior citizens that had the time to sit in court during the week, and this group of early court watchers would often get breakfast in my home."[133] Early court watchers were diverse and Court Watch NOLA began working with some of the volunteers Councilmember Carter had brought together from the West Bank of the Mississippi River in the Algiers section of New Orleans. According to Nolan Marshal, "We were trying to be very conscious about diversity and we got diversity from that group- it was an important part of what we're trying to do."[134] These early court watchers would track individual felony cases, usually violent felony or sex offense cases.[135] The early court watchers would then go back to their community and recruit their fellow community members to be part of the courtwatching experience.[136] From the beginning, court watchers have been identified by the yellow clipboards they carry with them to court.[137] Herman spoke with the head of security for the courts in the Orleans Parish Sheriff's Office to ensure that court watchers, like court staff, attorneys, and jurors, would be allowed to bring their cell phones into court.[138] This privilege is not extended to members of the general public, witnesses, victims, and criminal defendants.[139]

Andrea St. Paul Bland was Court Watch NOLA's first board chair and served for two years.[140] In a recent interview, she admitted that the membership of that first board was not as diverse as its members would have liked. But, she said, "we stacked the first board of directors with former assistant district attorneys so we understood criminal court procedures."[141] At the time she became Court Watch NOLA's board chair, Bland was working at Trans-Oceanic with Greg Rusovich, who would go on to become chair of the New Orleans Business Council in 2010. Because of this relationship, Bland was able to secure funding from the Business Council in the early days of Court Watch NOLA. "The Business Council," she reports, "understood the importance of a safe city, they saw the big picture."[142]

Court Watch Nola's Data

With the data court watchers collected, Karen Herman, assisted by Rafael Goyeneche and the Metropolitan Crime Commission, created the first court-watcher reports.[143] Without that assistance, Herman admits, she would not have been able to create the graphs and put the first reports together.[144] Under its first three executive directors, Herman, Graham da Ponte, and Janet Ahern, Court Watch NOLA, like the Metropolitan Crime Commission, collected data that related exclusively to efficiency, with only a limited amount of transparency data. Court watchers collected data on whether criminal court judges arrived late to the bench and how many times and why a case was continued without disposition. Other data collected in the early days of the program included how often judges would have sidebars, the discussion between the judge and the parties conducted at the bench or in judicial chambers and outside of public earshot.

At the beginning of the program, Court Watch NOLA directed its court watchers to collect only efficiency data because of the difficulty and often the failure of the court system to function. Additionally, in its early days, Court Watch NOLA operated under the close guidance of the Metropolitan Crime Commission, which largely limited itself (and still does) to examining efficiency issues in the Orleans Parish Criminal Courts.

In the early days of the program, Karen Herman always asked court watchers what data they wanted to collect.[145] In recalling the early days of the program, Karen Herman remembered the large rallies and the outrage over the violent crime in the city.[146] I talked with Karen Herman and Court Watch NOLA's second board chair Kirk Gasperecz, who still serves on the board today, about the Central City massacre, the arrest of Michael Anderson, and the later reports that it was Telly Hankton and not Michael Anderson who was responsible for the Central City massacre.[147] In the early days of the program, the community was pushing for the violent crime problem to be fixed; the collective consciousness was not centered on ending the increasing number of wrongful convictions in Orleans Parish. In fact, at this juncture, the community had largely not yet been educated on the incidence of wrongful conviction. This was the environment that Court Watch NOLA was born into: a community that was so angry and disgusted that it gathered in the streets by the thousands to speak out against violent crime, a community so used to inaction that the community embraced the few elected officials who did act.

Until 2012, Court Watch NOLA remained committed to collecting only efficiency data and data relating to the occurrence of sidebars in court. Though Court Watch NOLA's first mission and objectives statement is lost to history, by 2009, executive director Graham daPonte had identified as Court Watch NOLA's core objective: "to promote efficiency within the Criminal Court system through monitoring cases involving violent crimes and other cases which are significant in indicating the efficiency of the system, and to bring accountability and transparency to proceedings within Orleans Parish Criminal District Court."[148]

While objectivity is not the focus of all court watcher programs, a court watching program that does prioritize objectivity should measure and compare court performance according to national best practices. Judicial think tanks now agree that remaining objective does not necessarily mean a court watcher group should examine only efficiency and case processing data. Back in 2007, best practices involved examining mainly this type of information. And while judicial think tanks were also talking about novel concepts, such as drug courts, and new problem-solving courts, such as domestic violence court, they were not offering many standards other than efficiency by which day-to-day court practices in felony court could be measured.

In 2003, the National Association for Court Management published its "Core Competency Curriculum Guidelines."[149] In 2005, the National Center for State Courts published "Court Tools."[150] These two best practices related to efficiency and state court caseflow management.[151] In 2011, Richard Van Duizend and colleagues published *Model Time Standards for State Trial Courts*,[152] which became a widely used tool for courts.[153] In 2009, David Steelman published "Model Continuance Policy," relating to when and how a case should be delayed.[154]

By 2012, this national best-practices trend started to change, with more diverse think tanks offering different standards and concepts by which courts could improve and by which the public could hold courts accountable. Some of the core standards that had already been developed around efficiency and caseflow management expanded to consider more diverse and layered perspectives.

The National Association for Court Management, for example, explains the expansion of its best practice standards as follows:

> Based on a field of court administration that has become increasingly professionalized and diverse, (the National Association of Court Management) NACM reviewed and revised the competencies over a three-year period from 2012 [to] 2015, through the financial support of the State Justice Institute (SJI). The end product, the Core, represents the multitude of changes that have occurred in the profession and is intended to be forward-looking to encourage not only competencies for professionals working in the field of court administration but also to promote excellence in the administration of justice.[155]

While the National Center for State Courts' "Court Tools" now includes standards that relate to access and fairness, ensuring fairness around financial obligations imposed by the court, these standards were adopted only later.[156] Back when "Court Tools" was first developed in 2005, the best practice standards offered to the courts and the public to assess the courts related primarily to efficiency: clearance rates, time to disposition, age of active pending caseload, trial date certainty, and reliability and integrity of case files.[157] These older best practice standards created by the National Center for State Courts are the concepts that most directly relate to the data to which Court Watch NOLA traditionally limited itself. These standards are still in use on the National Center for State Courts website, but unlike fifteen years ago, they are no longer the only standards in use.

David Steelman, vice president of the National Center for State Courts, is one of the most prolific writers of judicial efficiency and caseflow management literature in the country. In 2011, after working at the center for almost two decades,[158] he published the results of his study on the appropriateness of the Metropolitan Crime Commission's judicial efficiency reports in New Orleans.[159] In my interview with him by phone, he admitted that his views on court best practices have evolved:

> I have shifted my focus from efficiency to judicial accountability in other areas. When we look only at judicial efficiency, we miss the critical bottom line. An analysis of courts that only includes efficiency standards creates holes in the resources we collectively have available to us to determine judicial and court accountability. How do we know justice is being done? How do we ensure fair outcomes are reached with the resources we have? If you are a person of color, you often end up on the short end of the stick when it comes to outcomes, even when you measure cases apples to apples. How does an efficiency-only analysis cover any of these real questions?[160]

Like the national judicial think tanks in their reports of best practices, Court Watch NOLA also began to evolve in the data it collected. When its fourth executive director, Brad Cousins, took over the organization in 2012, he began studying the newest best practices lauded in the national think tanks and in 2014 introduced court watchers (and court stakeholders: the judges, prosecutors, defense, sheriff deputies, clerks of court and police) to the concepts of procedural fairness.[161]

Procedural fairness is an evidence-based practice that requires judges to pay attention to creating fair outcomes and tailor their actions, language, and responses to the public's expectations of providing a fair process. There are four basic expectations in procedural fairness: the ability of a party to participate in the case by expressing their viewpoint; neutrality of the judge; respectful treatment of a person's rights; and the care and sincerity that authorities show in trying to help the litigants.[162] In 2013, the year before Court Watch NOLA was implementing procedural fairness concepts into its data collection, the Conference of Chief Justices and the Conference of State Court Administrators jointly adopted a resolution encouraging state court leaders to promote the implementation of procedural fairness principles.[163] I asked former executive director Cousins what had changed at the time Court Watch NOLA began to collect data on procedural fairness, and he replied, "I think that nationally and locally the criminal justice system was starting to be seen differently at that point, starting to be seen more holistically."[164]

Court Watch NOLA'S Recent Progress and Remaining Challenges

In the summer of 2015, I became the fifth executive director of Court Watch NOLA. A lot had changed since the program was created. The first executive director, Karen Herman, had already been a sitting judge for seven years.[165] Hurricane Katrina's ten-year anniversary was around the corner. Vera New Orleans' Pretrial Services Program, which sought to objectively assess the risk of pretrial release for criminal defendants, was being widely debated, challenged, opposed, and changed. Later it would be adopted by the Orleans Parish Criminal District Court.[166] After a laudable amount of healthy public dialogue, the New Orleans Police Department had been placed under and largely benefited from the most extensive consent decree ever written in the United States.[167] Between 2011 and 2013, while the police department was under the consent decree, it was revealed that the department had routinely failed to investigate hundreds of reported sex crimes.[168] The Orleans Parish Sheriff's Office, after various deaths and suicides in its jail,[169] was also placed under a consent decree[170] but with significantly less progress to report. Orleans Parish became the parish or county with the highest recorded wrongful conviction rate per capita of any county or parish in the country with a population greater than three hundred thousand.[171] Louisiana became the highest state incarcerator per capita in the country,[172] and had the second highest female homicide rate in the country.[173] On a national level, President Barack Obama became the first sitting president to visit a federal prison.[174] President Obama commuted the sentences of more people than the previous ten presidents combined, allowed incarcerated people to once again receive Pell Grants to pursue college degrees, issued an executive order "banning the box" on federal job applications, released new Housing and Urban Development guidelines stating that denial of housing on the basis of a criminal record would be considered a violation of the Fair Housing Act, and banned solitary confinement of juveniles in federal prisons.[175] President Obama's White House issued a white paper that criticized the inequities and inefficiencies of fines, fees, and bail.[176] In 2011, the US Department of Education issued a letter to universities recommending various methods intended to reduce incidents of sexual assault on campuses, in response to charges that schools had poorly supported women who complained of sexual assault.[177] By 2015, five states had legalized recreational marijuana and twenty-four states had legalized medical marijuana;[178] by the time of writing this paper, many of these numbers have changed once again. The #Me Too movement emanating from the sexual abuse allegations against Harvey Weinstein demanded that the community regard sexual assault and sexual harassment with a degree of seriousness it had previously not.[179]

Why are all of these changes in our criminal justice system important and why do I list them? These changes are important not just because they have impacted those most affected by the criminal justice system. These changes are important because as a community both locally and nationally, we have fought for them. As we have made changes to the criminal justice system, we have evolved in our understanding. While we have debated and fought for these changes, we have also changed. We have pushed our public officials to embrace and make these changes to the criminal justice system. Public officials who had not heard the drumbeat of progress and did not understood the best practice standards created by learned experts in the field have been replaced or soon will be. Both Republican and Democratic public officials have made changes related to reducing incarceration and improving the treatment of crime victims. New Orleanians have engaged in this dialogue, and fewer now are willing to be kept in the dark on criminal justice issues. New Orleans is absolutely engaged in the criminal justice conversation and we have the right to be proud of that accomplishment.

Court Watch NOLA still collects data on efficiency in criminal district court, still seeing efficiency, case processing, and the time the public must wait to receive their day in court as important data on which to report. But, as the national best practice standards dictate, we collect other data that paints a larger picture of the practices seen in the New Orleans criminal courts. Thus, Court Watch NOLA has come full circle back to some of the original concepts Councilmember James Carter envisioned for the group.

In 2016, with funding from a grant awarded by a local foundation, Baptist Community Ministries, Court Watch NOLA began to monitor bail hearings in New Orleans Magistrate Court. In doing so, Court Watch NOLA became the first and only group recording data in magistrate court, such as the amount of bail set, the number of conditions required of the defendant before he or she is released pretrial, the demographics of the defendant, and whether the bail hearing was conducted without legal counsel (among other data collected). Again with the help of Baptist Community Ministries, Court Watch NOLA began to monitor New Orleans Municipal (misdemeanor) Court to ensure that criminal defendants had legal counsel during their court appearances. In New Orleans Municipal Court, court watchers also collect data on the number of fines and fees assessed by the court on criminal defendants. Having been informed by the Innocence Project of New Orleans that one of the consistent factors observed in wrongful conviction cases is the lack of scientific or hard evidence, Court Watch NOLA began collecting data on the frequency hard or scientific data is used to prosecute criminal cases. The group also collected data on victim rights and witness intimidation in all three courts, whether victims were present, how they were being treated by the stakeholders in Criminal District Court, and whether there were allegations of witness intimidation.

All of this data was supported by best practices on the national level. The National Center for State Courts had already featured the "Model Pre-Trial Services Implementation Kit" on its website, as well as various court best practice guides relating to creating bias-free environments.[180] President Donald Trump's Department of Justice was providing jurisdictions with grant money to ensure that the constitutional right to counsel was ensured, and where it was not ensured, that it was assessed and was implemented at the local and state levels.[181] Right-to-counsel standards were created and are listed on the American Bar Association website. Finally, the movement for victim rights had become a practical revolution. In November 2018, voters in five states decided on ballot-initiated victim-rights amendments.[182] The National Center for State Courts, the Center for Court Innovation, and the American Bar Association all list best practice standards relating to victim rights on their websites.[183]

On March 7, 2017, Court Watch NOLA founding board member and victim rights advocate Patti Lapeyre and I wrote a letter to the editor of the *New Orleans Advocate*, decrying the unequal treatment some crime victims receive in the New Orleans criminal courts if they do not know the right people or if their perpetrator happens to know the right people.[184] In its 2016 report, Court Watch NOLA had reported that 73 percent of crime victims in police reports were African American and 60 percent of crime victims were women.[185]

Also in 2016, Court Watch NOLA approached District Attorney Cannizzaro along with crime victim advocates Mary Claire Landry and Eva Lessinger to ask the District Attorney's Office to no longer request that sex crime and domestic violence survivors if they did not appear in court to testify against their perpetrators. Though for years crime survivors and their advocates had been begging District Attorney Cannizzaro behind closed doors to end the policy of incarcerating crime survivors for failure to testify,[186] he had continued to incarcerate crime survivors. When confronted with Court Watch NOLA's and victim advocates' opposition to this practice in 2016, Cannizzaro had politely but firmly refused to cease the practice. Several months later, after giving notice to Cannizzaro and his office, Court Watch NOLA published the (minimum) number of crime survivors Cannizzaro had pushed to incarcerate for failure to prosecute, including a rape crime survivor who had been incarcerated for nine days for failure to testify against the man who had raped her.[187] Also at this time, it was revealed that Cannizzaro had been signing documents that threatened jail time and fines for those victims and witnesses who did not cooperate with his office and calling such documents subpoenas,[188] when in reality, only judges (and certainly not prosecutors) can sign subpoenas in Louisiana.[189]

This news was first published in New Orleans by *The Lens*,[190] went international with the *BBC*,[191] and finally hit all major national print publications including the *New York Times*,[192] the *Washington Post*,[193] the *Miami Herald*,[194] and the *Full Frontal Show with Samantha Bee*.[195] As a result of Court Watch NOLA's releasing its data and the ensuing news coverage, four separate civil rights lawsuits[196] and two city council resolutions[197] have been brought against Cannizzaro. After the revelation of Cannizzaro's incarceration of crime survivors, 48 percent of white voters and 43 percent of black voters responded to a poll with an unfavorable opinion of Cannizzaro.[198]

Cannizzaro's treatment of crime victims has stubbornly remained in the news for over four years,[199] despite Cannizzaro's personal criticism of whomever raises the subject. Cannizzaro's endorsement of candidates running for election, often as judges, used to result in a win at the polls.[200] But since his public refusal to stop incarcerating crime victims, three out of four electoral candidates he has endorsed[201] have lost their election;[202] this group includes the front runner in the 2017 mayoral election and a talented and popular judge who lost once Cannizzaro endorsed her,[203] despite her having more money in her war chest than her opponents.[204] In one of the biggest demonstrations relating to criminal justice seen since 2007, approximately a hundred people gathered in front of the New Orleans Criminal District Court, led in song by the popular singer and New Orleans resident Ani DiFranco, to protest Cannizzarro's treatment of crime victims.[205] A few days later a smaller group, made up of crime victims, gathered to protest in front of the District Attorney's Office, only to be mocked on Twitter by the District Attorney Office's public information officer.[206] In 2019, the State of Louisiana passed legislation making it more difficult for a Louisiana district attorney to incarcerate sex crime and domestic violence survivors for failure to testify against their aggressors.[207] Throughout the Louisiana state legislative process, I was consistently told that Cannizzaro's office was the only District Attorney's Office in Louisiana that incarcerates sex crime survivors and domestic violence survivors. Finally, in a twist of irony, the director of Silence Is Violence became a plaintiff in one of the civil rights suits against Cannizzaro because of his persistent threat that he would incarcerate her for her work with crime survivors.[208] In 2007, Silence Is Violence had organized the biggest criminal justice rally New Orleans had seen in fifty years[209] that in many ways led to the election of Cannizzaro as district attorney. A year later the group promoted Cannizzaro at a rally on the steps of City Hall at their rally.[210]

For the work that Court Watch NOLA has done advocating for victims' rights standards, Cannizzaro has publicly attacked the organization and me, in my role as executive director, several times. For example, in a press conference Cannizzaro called, he said that I had "betrayed Court Watch NOLA's rich history as an objective and unbiased watchdog."[211] As a sign that times have changed and that the community will continue to demand change, the editorial board of the one media outlet that reported on the press conference responded swiftly and without solicitation from Court Watch NOLA, stating:

> In a press conference after the council meeting, Mr. Cannizzaro blasted Court Watch NOLA as an "anti-law enforcement, anti-prosecution, anti-public safety group." That isn't true. Court Watch NOLA, which was created shortly after Hurricane Katrina, is made up of volunteers who donate their time to watch court proceedings and make sure the justice system is ethical, transparent and professional. . . . He should just agree not to lock up another victim of sexual assault or domestic violence, rather than attempting to discredit the organization urging him to do the right thing.[212]

Since Court Watch NOLA released its report first identifying the problematic process of incarcerating crime survivors to compel them to testify, Court Watch NOLA has produced other reports that made national news. One such report reveals a criminal court judge who required criminal defendants to wear ankle monitors, sometimes for up to a year, steering them to use his campaign contributor's ankle-monitoring company, which charges criminal defendants ten dollars a day for the use of the monitors. Compounding the injustice, that same judge threatened defendants with jail if they did not pay his campaign contributor the money they could not afford to pay for the ankle monitors the judge required them to wear.[213] Court Watch NOLA has also reported that the Orleans Parish Sheriff's Office records confidential attorney-client phone calls, providing the recordings to the prosecution, which uses them in their case-in-chief against the defendants.[214] When Court Watch NOLA asked the Orleans Parish sheriff to stop recording confidential attorney-client phone calls, the sheriff replied that the his office had always made such recordings and he saw no reason to change this practice.[215]

While we still have a long way to go in changing the practices of some criminal justice stakeholders, Court Watch NOLA has made an immense amount of progress, most readily seen in the degree of public discourse and the community's level of education on criminal justice issues in New Orleans and outside of our city. Court Watch NOLA has worked with thirty-three different groups around the country that wanted to start programs, resulting in six successfully launched courtwatching programs. In New Orleans, Court Watch NOLA has educated thousands of court watchers. Court watchers are diverse in every sense of the word. They are black, white, Hispanic, Asian, old, young, rich, poor, angry, naive, optimistic, pessimistic, and previously impacted. Court Watch NOLA has taught students who will become our future prosecutors, police captains, sheriffs, defense attorneys, and judges about national best practice standards and the importance of public perception and public confidence in the criminal courts. The insiders to the system—the judges, prosecutors, defense attorneys, police, and deputy sheriffs—now read our reports in a way they never have done before. When these insiders, the institutional stakeholders, change their practices to comport with best practices, Court Watch NOLA commends them, as it has commended the chief of police and the chief judge of Criminal District Court, among others. Those who refuse to follow national best practices and those who believe that assessment of our courts should be based on efficiency and caseload management standards alone do not see the handwriting on the wall. The public continues to educate itself, and those who do not listen to the public will face defeat at the polls. History waits for no one. The community will continue to demand accountability and criminal justice reform from our public officials. Change will come on the community's time, history rolling over those who do not listen to the community's call for change.

Notes

1   Stephanos Bibas, "Transparency and Participation," *New York University Law Review* 81 (2006): 911, 916.

2   Emily Lane, "Public Corruption in Louisiana "Can't Get Much Worse," Says Outgoing FBI New Orleans Director," nola.com, November 3, 2017, https://www.nola.com/crime/2017/11/public_corruption_fbi_new_orle.html.

3   The only courtwatching group known to the author that is longer-lived than Court Watch NOLA, though it is run by an umbrella organization not initially affiliated with the court watching group, is WATCH. Founded in 1992, WATCH is a court-monitoring and judicial policy nonprofit located in Minneapolis, Minnesota. WATCH works to make the justice system more responsive to crimes of violence against women and children, focusing on greater safety for victims of violence and greater accountability for violent offenders. For more about WATCH, visit their website at http://watchmn.org/ (last visited June 30, 2019).

4   See the New Orleans Independent Police Monitor website at https://nolaipm.gov/ (last visited June 30, 2019).

5   See the New Orleans Office of the Inspector General website at http://www.nolaoig.gov/ (last visited June 30, 2019).

6   See Lilian Warner, "The Power of the Citizen Voice from Mourning to Rage . . . to Hope through Action Gambit," Citizens for 1 Greater New Orleans (video transcription), https://docplayer.net/40685480-The-power-of-the-citizen-voice-from-mourning-to-rage-to-hope-through-action.html (last visited June 30, 2019). (The New Orleans Crime Coalition was formed in 2007 by the Business Council of New Orleans; Citizens for 1 Greater New Orleans was a founding member and serves on the Executive Committee.)

7   "Justice System Struggles in New Orleans," NBCNews.com, June 24, 2006, http://www.nbcnews.com/id/13525692/ns/us_news-katrina_the_long_road_back/t/justice-system-struggles-new-orleans/#.XRA-WIjYpPY.

8   Joseph Paterson, Ira Sommers, Deborah Baskin, and Donald Johnson, "The Role and Impact of Forensic Evidence in the Criminal Justice Process," National Institute of Justice, report # 2006-DN-BX-0094, June 10, 2010, https://www.ncjrs.gov/pdffiles1/nij/grants/231977.pdf.

9   Calvin Johnson, telephone interview with the author, May 30, 2019; follow-up text messages, June 21, 2019.

10   Brandon Garrett and Tania Tetlow, "Criminal Justice Collapse: The Constitution after Hurricane Katrina," *Duke Law Journal* 56 (2006): 128, 136–138, https://scholarship.law.duke.edu/cgi/viewcontent.cgi?article=1296&context=dlj.

11   Ibid., 137.

12   Ibid.

13   Ibid.

14   Ibid., 138.

15   Ibid.

16   Ibid.

17   Ibid.

18   Ibid.

19   Ibid.

20   Ibid.

21   Ibid.

22   *The Katrina Impact on Crime and the Criminal Justice System in New Orleans: Hearing before the Subcommittee on Crime, Terrorism, and Homeland Security*, 110th Cong. (2007), https://www.govinfo.gov/content/pkg/CHRG-110hhrg34527/html/CHRG-110hhrg34527.htm.

23   Ibid.

24   Ibid.

25   Garrett and Tetlow, "Criminal Justice Collapse."

26   Ibid., 147.

27   Ibid., 148.

28   "Hurricane Katrina Coverage for Central Alabama," National Weather Service, August 29, 2005, https://www.weather.gov/bmx/event_katrina2005.

29   Garrett and Tetlow, "Criminal Justice Collapse."

30   Ibid.

31   Ibid.

32   Ibid.

33   Ibid.

34   Ibid.

35   Ibid.," 146.

36   See statement of Oliver Thomas in *Katrina Impact on Crime* ("Now, we've seen some disputes over the impact of crime statistics. We've heard that modeled one way or another, with generous population assumptions, our crime is relatively stable. We've heard that modeled other ways, assuming a smaller population, that crime has risen drastically. But none of that matters to people who live here. We are tired of hearing interpretations and assumptions. Whatever crime we have is too much, and whatever solutions we are putting in place can't be done fast enough"); Laura Maggi and Gwen Filosa, "Enough! Thousands March to Protest the City's Alarming Murder Rate Officials Reviled in Public Show of Mass Outrage," *New Orleans Times-Picayune,* January 12, 2007 ("Before this week, Riley had sought to downplay the rising murder rate as an exaggeration, arguing that the per capita rate of killings had been inflated by faulty population statistics. But in just the last six months of 2006, after much of the city's current population had returned, murderers killed 106 people. If the population is 230,000, an optimistic estimate, that means

the city has seen a rate of 90 killings per 100,000 people since July, a frighteningly high rate that clearly would make New Orleans the nation's murder capital").

37 "2007 Brings More Crime to New Orleans," *Los Angeles Times*, January 5, 2007, https://www.latimes.com/archives/la-xpm-2007-jan-05-na-briefs5.1-story.html.

38 Ibid.

39 See statement of the Honorable William J. Jefferson in *Katrina Impact on Crime.*

40 See Question and Answer with Jim Lettin in ibid.

41 See statement of the Honorable Robert C. Scott in ibid.

42 See statements of District Attorney Eddie Jordan and US attorney Jim Lettin in ibid. (Jordan: "And, finally, the most important item that we think that Congress can help us with is an expanded Victim Witness Assistance program. We need funding for this program because of the very real fear that many victims of violent crime have in the city of New Orleans; victims and of course, family members and witnesses of violent crime as well." Lettin: "The community won't cooperate because if I finger you as that violent felon I know in a few days you're back on the streets and I become the next victim, and I don't want that.")

43 Miguel Bustillo, "Violent Crime Engulfs New Orleans," *Seattle Times*," August 3, 2007, https://www.seattletimes.com/nation-world/violent-crime-engulfs-new-orleans/.

44 John Simerman, "Shrouded in Secrecy, New Orleans Man in 'Central City Massacre' Has Major Sentence Reduced," *Advocate*, July 21, 2018, https://braiservices.newscyclecloud.com/cmo_bra-c-cmdb-01/subscriber/web/startoffers.html.

45 Ibid.

46 Ibid.

47 Ibid.

48 Ibid.

49 Gwen Filosa, "Black Voters Boosted Cannizzaro into Office: Former Judge's 62 Percent Win Bested Capitelli in DA Runoff," *Times-Picayune*, November 6, 2008. ("Cannizzaro, a retired judge who has run successfully for office since 1986, was the runaway favorite in neighborhoods that have a 75 percent or higher percentage of registered black voters—beating Capitelli by a nearly 3-to-1 margin.")

50 Gwen Filosa, "Central City Massacre Verdict Challenged after Released of Contradictory Evidence," *Times-Picayune,* February 27, 2010, https://www.nola.com/news/crime_police/article_860d32c8-b5ef-5473-93c1-1e078d88c435.html.

51 Ibid.

52 Ibid.

53 Lauren Gill, "Notorious Jailhouse Informant Case Resurfaces as New Orleans D.A. Race Nears," *The Appeal,* May 24, 2019, https://theappeal.org/notorious-jailhouse-informant-case-resurfaces-as-new-orleans-da-race-nears/.

54 Jason Berry, "Hot 8 Fights for the Big Easy," *Los Angeles Times,* January 21, 2007, https://www.latimes.com/archives/la-xpm-2007-jan-21-op-berry21-story.html.

55 Maggi and Filosa, "Enough!"

56 Gordon Russell, e-mail message to the author, June 19, 2019.

57 See the Silence Is Violence website at http://silenceisviolence.org/ (last visited June 30, 2019).

58 Gill, "Notorious Jailhouse Informant."

59 Ibid.

60 Ibid.

61 Ibid.

62 Ibid.

63 Karen Dalton-Beninato, "Free at Last: Second Liners Released from Charges," HuffPost, February 21, 2008, https://www.huffpost.com/entry/free-at-last-second-liner_b_87912?guccounter=1&guce_referrer=aHR0cHM6Ly93d3cuZ29vZ2xlLmNvbS8&guce_referrer_sig=AQAAAFl8MB8knlnjtZEoyJKnrIIJgtER6zjKemINou-bqLNkkIfwsy-ucGx0JGwBM0o9c3J5_Q1hohAgJxhcGLoATnhzY8TJgLoC2QZ0yNY4XbOXXXlbvKXBNAcaUZMJOdg1S0Hs3-XsDDWv9e0dxcS0Xy7-SxmRq1eV55p2HK9bEOC.

64 Ibid.

65 Valerie Faciane, "Citizens Take to the Streets Today against New Orleans Crime," nola.com, January 9, 2009, https://www.nola.com/news/article_7dde93a9-3040-5166-9aca-fb921824addf.html.

66 Ibid.

67 Ibid.

68 Ibid.

69 For a biography of James Carter, see Carter & McKee, LLC https://cartermckeelawfirm.com/jamescarter.html.

70 Ibid.

71 James Carter, telephone interview with the author, June 3, 2019.

72 Ibid.

73 Ibid.

74 For a biography of Michael Cowan, see "Michael A. Cowan: Professor Emeritus," Loyola University, New Orleans, http://cnh.loyno.edu/lim/bios/michael-cowan.

75 James Carter, telephone interview with the author, June 26, 2019.

76 Michelle Krupa, "Mayor Mitch Landrieu Names Former Councilman James Carter 'Crime Commissioner,'" nola.com, April 28, 2011, https://braiservices.newscyclecloud.com/cmo_bra-c-cmdb-01/subscriber/web/startoffers.html.

77 New Orleans, La., Code §2-1121 (2017).

78 New Orleans, La., Code §2-1120 (2017).

79 Garrett and Tetlow, "Criminal Justice Collapse," 133.

80 Carter interview, June 3, 2019.

81 James Carter, e-mail message to the author, July 6, 2019.

82 Carter interview, June 26, 2019.

83 Michael Cowan, telephone interview with the author, June 3, 2019.

84 James Carter, telephone interview with the author, June 9, 2019

85 Carter to the author, July 6, 2019.

86 Carter interview, June 3, 2019.

87 Warner, *"Power of the Citizen Voice."*

88 Linda Roussel, telephone interview with the author, July 4, 2019.

89 Robert Tallant, *Murder in New Orleans: Seven Famous Trials* (London: W. Kimber, 1952); Richard Gambino, *Vendetta: A True Story of the Worst Lynching in America . . . and the Tragic Repercussions That Linger to This Day* (Garden City, NY: Doubleday, 1977).

90 Court Watch NOLA, *2013 Report*, http://www.courtwatchnola.org/wp-content/uploads/Final-2013-Court-Watch-NOLA-Report.pdf.

91 Hope Goldman Meyer, telephone interview with the author, May 29, 2019.

92 Ibid.

93 For a description of the Metropolitan Crime Commission, see their website at http://metrocrime.org/ (last visited June 30, 2019).

94 See "Judge Porteous Impeachment Trial, Rafael Goyeneche Testimony," CNN (video), September 14, 2010, https://www.c-span.org/video/?295450-6/judge-porteous-impeachment-trial-rafael-goyeneche-testimony.

95 Meyer interview.

96 Ibid.

97 Patti Lapeyre, telephone interview with the author, July 3, 2019.

98 The term "stakeholder" refers to "an individual, group, or organization, who may affect, be affected by, or perceive itself to be affected by a decision, activity, or outcome of a project." Seithikurippu R. Pandi-Perumal, et al., "Project Stakeholder Management in the Clinical Research Environment: How to Do It Right," *Frontiers in Psychiatry* 6 (May 28, 2015): 71, https://www.ncbi.nlm.nih.gov/pmc/articles/PMC4434843/.

99 Lapeyre interview, July 3, 2019.

100 Linda Roussel, telephone interview by the author, July 4, 2019.

101 Ibid.

102 Patti Lapeyre, telephone interview with the author, July 4, 2019.

103 Ibid.

104 Lapeyre interview, July 3, 2019.

105 Nolan Marshall, telephone interview with the author, July 4, 2019.

106 Ibid.

107 Greg Rusovich, telephone interview with the author, July 4, 2019.

108 Michael Cowan, telephone interview with the author, June 3, 2019.

109 Rusovich interview.

110 Cowan interview.

111 Carter interview.

112 Lapeyre interview, July 3, 2019.

113 Ibid.

114 Ibid.

115 Ibid.

116 Ibid. Initial seed money for Court Watch NOLA was provided by the Business Coalition ($12,000), Citizens for 1 New Orleans ($6,000) and Common Good ($6,000).

117 Cowan interview; Lisa Jordan, telephone interview with the author, June 10, 2019.

118 Cowan interview.

119 Metropolitan Crime Commission reports are posted at https://metrocrime.org/judicial-accountability-reports/.

120 See Metropolitan Crime Commission, *2016–2017 Orleans Parish Judicial Accountability Report,* September 17, 2018, available at https://metrocrime.org/judicial-accountability-reports/.

121 Cowan interview.

122 Andrea St. Paul Bland, telephone interview with the author, July 3, 2019; Ellen Yellin, telephone interview with the author, July 5, 2019.

123 Meyer interview.

124 Lapeyre interview, July 3, 2019.

125 Meyer interview.

126 Ibid.

127 Lisa Jordan, telephone interview with the author, June 10, 2019.

128 Karen Herman, text message to the author, June 21, 2019, and interview with the author, June 5, 2019; Kirk Gasperecz, interview with the author, June 5, 2019.

129 Herman interview; Gasperecz interview.

130 Herman interview; Gasperecz interview.

131 Lisa Jordan interview.

132 Herman text message.

133 Herman interview; Gasperecz interview.

134 Marshall interview.

135 Herman interview; Gasperecz interview.

136 Herman interview; Gasperecz interview.

137 Herman interview; Gasperecz interview.

138 Herman interview; Gasperecz interview.

139 Herman interview; Gasperecz interview.

140 Andrea St. Paul Bland, telephone interview with the author, July 3, 2019.

141 Bland interview, and e-mail to the author, July 7, 2019.

142 Bland interview.

143 Herman interview; Gasperecz interview.

144 Herman interview; Gasperecz interview.

145 Herman interview; Gasperecz interview.

146 Herman interview; Gasperecz interview.

147 Herman interview; Gasperecz interview.

148 Court Watch NOLA, "Semi-Annual Report," January–June 2009, 1, 7, http://www.courtwatchnola.org/wp-content/uploads/Semi-Annual-Report-Jan.-to-June-20091.pdf.

149 "Core Competency Curriculum Guidelines," National Association for Court Management, 2005, https://nacmnet.org/ (accessed June 20, 2019).

150 "Court Tools," National Center for State Courts, 2005, https://cdm16501.contentdm.oclc.org/digital/collection/ctadmin/id/1281.

151 David Steelman, "Caseflow Management," National Center for State Courts, 2008, https://cdm16501.contentdm.oclc.org/digital/collection/ctadmin/id/1281.

152 Richard Van Duizend, David Steelman, and Lee Suskin, *Model Time Standards for State Trial Courts* (Williamsburg, VA: National Center for State Courts, 2011), https://www.ncsc.org/Services-and-Experts/Technology-tools/~/media/Files/PDF/CourtMD/Model-Time-Standards-for-State-Trial-Courts.ashx.

153 Ibid.

154 David Steelman, "Model Continuance Policy," National Center for State Courts, June 23, 2009, https://ncsc.contentdm.oclc.org/digital/api/collection/ctadmin/id/1484/download.

155 "The Core® in Practice: A Guide to Strengthen Court Professionals through Application, Use, and Implementation," National Association for Court Management, 2015, 1, 2, https://nacmnet.org/sites/default/files/Resources/TheCoreGuide_Final.pdf.

156 Dan Hall, e-mail to the author, July 1, 2019.

157 Ibid.

158 David Steelman, telephone interview with the author, June 23, 2019.

159 David J. Hall, "Judicial Efficiency, Accountability, and Case Allotment in the Criminal District Court of Orleans Parish, Louisiana, National Center for State Courts, January 27, 2011.

160 Steelman interview.

161 "Fair, Functional, and Friendly: Citizen Suggestions for Making Orleans Parish Criminal District Court More user-Friendly and Procedurally Fair for Witnesses, Families, and the General Public," Court Watch NOLA, 2014, http://www.courtwatchnola.org/wp-content/uploads/Court-Watch-NOLA-1h2014-Report-FINAL-Optimized.pdf.

162 Kevin Burke and Steve Lebe, "Procedural Fairness: A Key Ingredient in Public Satisfaction," a white paper of the American Judges Association and the Voice of the Judiciary, (2007), 6,http://www.proceduralfairness.org/~/media/Microsites/Files/procedural-fairness/Burke_Leben.ashx.

163 Conference of Chief Justices and Conference of State Court Administrators, Resolution 12, July 31, 2013, https://ccj.ncsc.org/~/media/Microsites/Files/CCJ/Resolutions/07312013-Support-State-Supreme-Court-Leadership-Promote-Procedural-Fairness-CCJ-COSCA.ashx.

164 Brad Cousins, interview with the author, June 10, 2019.

165 See Louisiana Secretary of State, "Official Election Results: Orleans," October 4, 2008, https://voterportal.sos.la.gov/static/2008-10-04.

166 Heather Nolan, "Could New Orleans End Money Bail? Advocates Say Tools Are in Place to Do So," *Times-Picayune*, June 20, 2019, https://braiservices.newscyclecloud.com/cmo_bra-c-cmdb-01/subscriber/web/startoffers.html.

167 "Amended and Restated Consent Decree Regarding the New Orleans Police Department," Case 2:12-Cv-01924-Sm-Jcw Document 565, Filed 10/02/18, available at https://www.nola.gov/nopd/nopd-consent-decree/.

168 Campbell Robertson, "New Orleans Police Routinely Ignored Sex Crimes Report Finds," *New York Times,* November 12, 2014, https://www.nytimes.com/2014/11/13/us/new-orleans-police-special-crimes-unit-inquiry.html.

("A scathing examination of this city's Police Department has concluded that five detectives tasked with investigating sex crimes failed to pursue hundreds of reported cases, finding records of follow-up efforts in only 14 percent of such calls over three years. The report, released on Wednesday and prepared by the city's inspector general, Edouard R. Quatrevaux, found that of 1,290 sex crime "calls for service" assigned to five New Orleans police detectives from 2011 to 2013, 840 were designated as "miscellaneous," and nothing at all was done. Of the 450 calls that led to the creation of an initial investigative report, no further documentation was found for 271 of them.")

169 Ibid.

170 Ibid.

171 Paul Purpura, "New National Registry Details Wrongful Convictions, "*Times-Picayune*, May 21, 2012, https://braiservices.newscyclecloud.com/cmo_bra-c-cmdb-01/subscriber/web/startoffers.html.

172 Casey Leins, "10 States with the Highest Incarceration Rates," *U.S News. & World Report*, May 28, 2019, https://www.usnews.com/news/best-states/slideshows/10-states-with-the-highest-incarceration-rates?slide=11

173 Gabrielle Boykin, "New Report: Louisiana Ranked Second in Nation for Rate of Women Murdered by Men," "WDSU News, September 19, 2018, https://www.wdsu.com/article/new-report-louisiana-ranked-second-in-the-nation-for-rate-of-women-murdered-by-men/23310991.

174 Scott Horsley, "Obama Visits Federal Prison, a First for a Sitting President," NPR, July 16, 2015, https://www.npr.org/sections/itsallpolitics/2015/07/16/423612441/obama-visits-federal-prison-a-first-for-a-sitting-president.

175 Glenn E. Martin, *Six Ways President Obama Reformed America's Criminal Justice System*, NewsOne, November 15, 2016, https://newsone.com/3590472/president-obama-criminal-justice-reform/.

176 "Fines, Fees, and Bail," Council of Economic Advisers, issue brief, December 2015, https://obamawhitehouse.archives.gov/sites/default/files/page/files/1215_cea_fine_fee_bail_issue_brief.pdf.

177 Emily Yoffe, "The Uncomfortable Truth About Campus Rape Policy," *The Atlantic*, September 6, 2017, https://www.theatlantic.com/education/archive/2017/09/the-uncomfortable-truth-about-campus-rape-policy/538974/.

178 "Marijuana Laws by State," LawInfo, https://resources.lawinfo.com/criminal-defense/medical-marijuana/ (accessed June 20, 2019).

179 "From #MeToo to Trial: A Look at the Fall of Harvey Weinstein," Associated Press, January 22, 2020, https://apnews.com/b019b5ddda2c2b0a0980b270f9c49e1c.

180 See, for example, "Pretrial Services & Supervision," National Center for State Courts, https://www.ncsc.org/Microsites/PJCC/Home/Topics/Pretrial-Services.aspx (accessed June 20, 2019).

181 "President Donald J. Trump Is Taking Immediate Actions to Secure Our Schools," The White House, March 12, 2018, https://www.whitehouse.gov/briefings-statements/president-donald-j-trump-taking-immediate-actions-secure-schools/.

182 Jill Lepore, "The Rise of the Victims' Rights Movement," *New Yorker*, May 14, 2018, https://www.newyorker.com/magazine/2018/05/21/the-rise-of-the-victims-rights-movement.

183 See the National Center for State Courts website at https://www.ncsc.org/; the Center for Court Innovation website at https://www.courtinnovation.org/; the American Bar Association website at https://www.americanbar.org/ (all last visited June 20, 2019).

184 Patti Lapeyre and Simone Levine, "Letters: Stand Up for Victim's Rights," *Advocate*, March 7, 2017, https://www.theadvocate.com/baton_rouge/opinion/letters/article_b9929262-029c-11e7-89da-bbc8ebdd960d.html.

185 "Criminal District Court Annual Report," Court Watch NOLA, 2016, http://www.courtwatchnola.org/wp-content/uploads/2016-CDC-Report-3.pdf.

186 Alex Woodward, "New Orleans Sexual Assault Survivors Speak Out Against D.A.; Cannizzaro's Office Responds," *Advocate*, May 26, 2017, https://www.nola.com/gambit/news/the_latest/article_5189fc28-e21d-5b00-ba29-12f6f7cc38ae.html.

187 Ibid.

188 Ibid.

189 Ibid.

190 Charles Maldonado, "Prosecutor Tried to Jail Victim of Alleged Domestic Violence after She Didn't Obey Fake Subpoena," *The Lens*, June 14, 2017, https://thelensnola.org/2017/06/14/new-orleans-prosecutor-used-fake-subpoena-to-seek-arrest-warrant-for-victim-of-alleged-domestic-violence/.

191 Joel Gunter, "Why Are Crime Victims Being Jailed?," BBC News, May 6, 2017, https://www.bbc.com/news/world-us-canada-39662428.

192 "New Orleans Prosecutors Accused of Using Fake Subpoenas," *New York Times*, October 17, 2017, https://www.nytimes.com/2017/10/17/us/new-orleans-subpoenas.html.

193 Radley Balko, "Report: New Orleans Prosecutors Threatening Witnesses with Fake Subpoenas," *Washington Post*, April 26, 2017, https://www.washingtonpost.com/news/the-watch/wp/2017/04/26/report-new-orleans-prosecutors-threatening-witnesses-with-fake-subpoenas/.

194 Teresa Welsh, "The Women Were Sexually Assaulted—and Jailed to Make Sure They Cooperated in Court," *Miami Herald*, April 12, 2017, https://www.miamiherald.com/news/nation-world/national/article144257039.html.

195 "Elected Prosecutors: Doin' Whatever They Want," Full Frontal with Samantha Bee, March 14, 2018, Act 3, YouTube, https://www.youtube.com/watch?v=XC2jpKfgKko&list=PLBYB7BnFCWRvb-DfKk3H4DYJiN7VtNDLl&index=23&t=0s+min+2.25.

196 "Lawsuit Launches Organizations' Nationwide Efforts to Hold Abusive Prosecutors Accountable," ACLU, October 17, 2017, https://www.aclu.org/press-releases/civil-rights-corps-and-aclu-sue-district-attorney-leon-cannizzaro-end-coercion-and.

197 Kevin Litten, "New Orleans City Council Challenges DA on Jailing Crime Victims, Witnesses to Force Testimony," *Times-Picayune*, February 7, 2019, https://www.nola.com/sports/pelicans/article_e2ca610e-d58d-582c-be8e-af05520846bc.html.

198 Lamar White Jr., "Cannizzaro Popularity Craters Amid Widespread Claims of Abuse of Office," Bayou Brief, November 15, 2017, https://www.bayoubrief.com/2017/11/15/cannizzaro-popularity-craters-amid-widespread-claims-of-abuse-of-office/.

199 Ken Daley, "DA Cannizzaro Blasts New Orleans City Leaders for 'Ill-Conceived' Criminal Justice Policies," nola.com, January 25, 2017, https://www.nola.com/news/crime_police/article_3932a5c4-8c45-5c4e-b4f4-589bbad2c789.html; Matt Sledge, "New Orleans City Council, DA Trades Barbs over Budget; Cannizzaro Is 'Fearmongering,' Councilman Charges," *Advocate*, September 20, 2017, https://braiservices.newscyclecloud.com/cmo_bra-c-cmdb-01/subscriber/web/startoffers.html; Litten, "New Orleans City Council Challenges DA"; Jessica Pishko, "Are Prosecutors Above the Law?," *Slate,* February 6, 2020, https://slate.com/news-and-politics/2020/02/new-orleans-da-fake-subpoenas-absolute-immunity.html.

200 Andy Grimm, "Orleans DA Cannizzaro Signs Affidavit Supporting Marullo's Re-Election Bid Backing Comes Despite Their Past Differences," *Times-Picayune*, September 3, 2014.

201 "Judge Tracey Flemings-Davillier Receives Major Endorsement from the Independent Women's Organization," *New Orleans Agenda*, July 31, 2017, https://myemail.constantcontact.com/Judge-Tracey-Flemings-Davillier-receives-major-endorsement-from-the-Independent-Women-s-Organization--IWO--.html?soid=1011087220895&aid=KaZHK2ZNWFA; "Charbonnet Gets Endorsement of Local AFL-CIO, Leon Cannizzaro," WWLTV, July 21, 2017; https://www.wwltv.com/article/news/local/charbonnet-gets-endorsement-of-local-afl-cio-leon-cannizzaro/458629443. See also Heron Brylski @cheronbrylski, "DA Cannizzaro Endorses @SuzyMontero: I am urging the citizens of New Orleans to join me Vote Saturday! CDC-B," tweet, April 24, 2017.

202 See "Suzanne Montero," Ballotpedia, https://ballotpedia.org/Suzanne_Monter (accessed June 20, 2019); Matt Sledge, "Civil District Court Judge," *Times-Picayune*, October 14, 2017; "Desiree Charbonnet Concedes in New Orleans Mayor's Race," WDSU News, November 20, 2017, https://www.wdsu.com/article/desiree-charbonnet-concedes-in-new-orleans-mayor-s-race/13810426.

203 "Desiree Charbonnet Concedes"; "Charbonnet Gets Endorsement of Local AFL-CIO, Leon Cannizzaro," WWLTV, July 21, 2017, https://www.wwltv.com/article/news/local/charbonnet-gets-endorsement-of-local-afl-cio-leon-cannizzaro/458629443; Brentin Mock, "Will Criminal Justice Reform Survive Under New Orleans' New Mayor?," CitiLab, November 21, 2017, https://www.citylab.com/equity/2017/11/new-orleans-cah-money-mayoral-race/546269/. (Perhaps more controversial is Charbonnet's support from New Orleans District Attorney Leon Cannizzaro, who is the subject of several major lawsuits filed against him in the last

month alone. One lawsuit, filed by the national ACLU, charges Cannizzaro with using phony subpoenas to coerce witnesses.)

204 "Desiree Charbonnet Makes Last-Minute Campaign Push," WDSU News, October 14, 2017, https://www.wdsu.com/article/desiree-charbonnet-makes-last-minute-campaign-push/13022611. (Charbonnet has garnered the most support or endorsements and has raised the most money, more than $1.3 million.)

205 Ani DeFranco, tweet, May 14, 2017.

206 Chris Bowman, tweet, June 26, 2017.

207 Julia O'Donoghue, "DAs Oppose Bill to Stop Jailing Rape, Abuse Victims," *Times-Picayune*, April 16, 2019, https://www.nola.com/news/article_8ef63206-0a0a-5717-bf06-fb9868f07414.html.

208 *Singleton v. Cannizzaro*, US District Court for the Eastern District of Louisiana, Case No. 17-10721, filed January 25, 2018, 36, https://cdn.buttercms.com/ugtbsHPjT6KUVcdIkvRv.

209 Maggi and Filosa, "Enough!"

210 Faciane, "Citizens Take to the Streets."

211 Kevin Liten, "Leon Cannizzaro Accuses N.O. Council of 'Political Attack,'" *Times-Picayune*, February 8, 2019, https://www.nola.com/news/politics/article_143e693d-ffec-530f-8977-a29800d490e3.html.

212 "Domestic Abuse and Sexual Assault Victims Shouldn't Be Locked Up," *Times-Picayune*, editorial, February 10, 2019, https://www.nola.com/opinions/article_4be51880-2287-5f2b-90c8-3d159db2d783.html.

213 See *Orleans Criminal District Court, Magistrate Court & Municipal Court: 2018 Report,* Court Watch NOLA, http://www.courtwatchnola.org/wp-content/uploads/2018-Annual-Report.pdf.

214 Johanna Kalb, "Protect the Right to Counsel: Stop Recording Attorney-Client Calls," nola.com, June 23, 2018, https://braiservices.newscyclecloud.com/cmo_bra-c-cmdb-01/subscriber/web/startoffers.html.

215 Ibid.

Strategically Funded and Data-driven

Katrina and the Philanthropic Landscape in New Orleans

Ludovico Feoli

Ludovico Feoli has been active in philanthropy, serving on the board of the Greater New Orleans Foundation between 2003 and 2016, and as chairman between 2013 and 2015. He is executive director of the Center for Inter-American Policy and Research and a research associate professor in the Stone Center for Latin American Studies and the Department of Political Science at Tulane University.

This article explores the impact of Hurricane Katrina on the philanthropic landscape in New Orleans, drawing on the perspective of participants in the field—staff and board members of community, local, and national foundations and key nonprofits—who were surveyed or interviewed for this purpose. It does not offer a definitive statement about the disaster as it pertains to philanthropy; nor does it consider the crucial leadership role of the many individuals involved in the recovery process, even though that role often intercepted with the philanthropic sector. Instead, it seeks to identify general trends that emerge from a qualitative assessment of the collected data. Katrina was in many ways an unprecedented disaster: over a million people fled Louisiana, more than two hundred thousand dwellings in New Orleans were destroyed, 80 percent of the city was at some point under water, and two thousand lives were lost. Taking into account the scope of the impact of Katrina and the role typically played by philanthropy in such circumstances, this article inquires whether and how philanthropic activity was itself transformed by the storm, as interpreted by philanthropic participants.

The narrative that emerges from the analysis is one of significant transformation. Extraordinary circumstances called for extraordinary measures, and members of the philanthropic community responded, deeply transforming the philanthropic landscape in the process. These changes occurred at the local level but also percolated upward to national funders. The most salient examples the participants cited are presented here and are followed by a brief discussion of potentially missed opportunities and lessons learned.

The Philanthropic Field before Katrina

Before Katrina, the philanthropic field in New Orleans was significantly constrained. A very small group of committed donors were asked to support everything. Yet, grantors were not coordinated and, for the most part, not impact-driven. Much of the giving went to established institutions with traditional missions or was otherwise diffused in small amounts to many organizations. Grant making was not innovative or forward-thinking; it was mainly reactive.

176

Partly because of this limitation, and partly because of the deficiencies of local government, there was no single player capable of bringing together the vision, resources, and leadership necessary to significantly impact the central social and economic problems in the community. National funders were mostly disengaged from the city, citing its lack of capacity and legendary levels of public-sector corruption.

On the grantee side the field was fragmented, with many small organizations pursuing similar objectives but not communicating, much less collaborating, among themselves, and with their collective needs exceeding the existent giving capacity. The sector was disjointed. Critical areas such as public education were inaccessible because of the absence of viable conduits through which funders could reach them. On one hand, while well-meaning, nonprofits often had low capability levels in administrative, financial, and governance matters. On the other hand, innovative but unproven start-ups, such as the Youth Empowerment Project in juvenile justice, had limited access to funding.

A Changed Landscape

The plight generated by Katrina and the failure of the New Orleans levee system played out live on a twenty-four-hour news cycle. This continuous reporting greatly increased the national visibility of the city, casting it in an entirely new and terrible light. By showing the incongruity of widespread poverty and exclusion in a major American city known and beloved by millions of visitors, the reporting galvanized major national philanthropic actors into action. The city was catapulted from having barely any interaction with external philanthropists to facing hundreds of philanthropies wanting to play a role. New Orleans became a case study for impactful interventions in the areas of disaster recovery, rebuilding, urban renewal, education reform, and social services. The response from national funders was enormous as they engaged immediately and flocked to the city without prompting. So did thousands of volunteers who gave their time and labor for a variety of purposes, from gutting and building houses to teaching. Donations from multiple other sources also flowed to the state and led to the creation of the Louisiana Disaster Recovery Foundation, which is today the Foundation for Louisiana.

This influx of funding, directed to both established organizations and startups, changed the philanthropic landscape by increasing the number of nonprofits, encouraging competition and innovation but also collaboration, and driving institutional reform. The haphazard and uneven response by all levels of government—federal, state, and municipal—forced the nonprofit sector to assume much of the immediate responsibility for rebuilding and human services. In 2015, ten years after the storm, the Urban Institute reported that growth in the nonprofit sector in New Orleans had far outpaced national growth, in terms of revenue and the number of organizations.[1] In 2012, there were 950 registered nonprofits in New Orleans, not including religious congregations and other groups that did not submit tax documents to the IRS. This figure was 40 percent higher than what it was in 2000.[2]

This growth led to increased competition for funding, which itself focused the efforts of grantors and grantees on impact and outcomes. Many local foundations and individual donors started to target their philanthropy to specific priorities, particularly in those areas of greater need in the city, such as housing, public health, public education, and social and criminal justice.

Baptist Community Ministries, for example, turned to a renewed focus on invitation-only strategic grants. United Way of Southeast Louisiana became a single-issue organization focused on poverty and its root causes, the RosaMary Foundation decided that it would prioritize public charter schools and related entities over private schools and related entities, and the Booth Bricker Fund went from giving almost nothing to public education to making grants for nothing else. The Greater New Orleans Foundation (GNOF) rebranded its grant-making program as the Impact Grants, consolidating it into six key areas where it could channel larger grants.[3] It also engaged in advocacy to compound that impact, by developing the advocacy capacity of its grantees and exercising a more active voice itself. This refocusing on impact was also translated to the fundraising side. GNOF, for example, started emphasizing giving outcomes with donors rather than appealing to charitable impulse.

The increased focus on key sectors accompanied by the flow of funding spurred innovation in the nonprofit sector. This innovation took form in the emergence of new organizations but also in the provision of new services by existent organizations to confront the challenges created or aggravated by the storm. Among many examples of the first type of innovation are the emergence of new fundraising/grant-making organizations (Pro Bono Publico Foundation, Emerging Philanthropists of New Orleans); new advocacy organizations to assign responsibility for the levee failures (Levees.org), raise the salience of recovery issues (Women of the Storm), promote institutional reforms (Citizens for 1 Greater New Orleans), and build cross-sectoral consensus for reforms (Common Good); new organizations to provide funding, leadership, staff development, and other assistance to public schools (New Schools for New Orleans, Orleans Public Education Network); and new organizations to promote social innovation and entrepreneurship (Propeller, Tulane). The willingness of funders to take risks in supporting these (and many other) start-ups and in recognizing the need to endorse the changes they were advocating reflects the significant transformation that was occurring in the philanthropic sector.

An example of the second type of innovation—new services provided by existent organizations—is GNOF's introduction of capacity building for nonprofits in what it called Organizational Effectiveness, a program that leveraged national funding to help nonprofit organizations adopt best practices and develop leadership, management, and governance skills. The program enabled them to deal with the more stringent grant-making processes emerging in the city, while boosting their strength and resilience. In the aggregate, this process increased the effectiveness of the nonprofit sector and strengthened it as a whole. Other notable innovations at GNOF were its adoption of the promotion of philanthropy as one of its missions and the introduction of GiveNOLA Day. This initiative, a twenty-four-hour event focused on giving to nonprofits, introduced philanthropy to thousands of individual donors, increasing the number of people in the community who are involved with philanthropy. In its latest iteration (2019) more than fifty thousand donors made contributions to 752 nonprofits, reaching almost six million dollars in a single day. Paired with Organizational Effectiveness programs, GiveNOLA Day has also contributed to the development of fund-raising capabilities in the nonprofit sector.

In this context, philanthropic entities started to collaborate, coordinating funding and other efforts. For example, a small group of local funders, coordinated by GNOF, provided the original funding that seeded New Schools for New Orleans and Common Good. At a larger scale, the Community Revitalization Fund was a collaborative effort through which nine local foundations combined resources with eleven national foundations after Katrina to create a $25 million housing fund. The Greater New Orleans Funders Network emerged later to facilitate funder coordination and collaboration toward the advancement of lasting and comprehensive change in equity and justice goals. Its members are a collection of national and local foundations. More recently, but in the same vein, the Mobilization Fund has combined resources from national and local funders to promote the development of disadvantaged business enterprises through a network that also incorporates business and local government agencies.

A greater emphasis on partnering and collaboration also emerged among nonprofits with aligned missions. For example, the Greater New Orleans Housing Alliance organized after the storm as a collaborative of nonprofit housing builders and community development corporations advocating for the preservation and production of affordable housing. Under the auspices of GNOF's Organizational Effectiveness program and with the support of national funders, Communities of Practice emerged as a mechanism to increase partnerships among organizations and foster peer-to-peer learning in areas such as youth services, workforce development, and advocacy and civic action for children. Also important was the adoption of a service-learning requirement by Tulane University and its launching of the Center for Public Service. The Center highlighted the relevance of nonprofits in the recovery process and the importance of creating opportunities for engagement with the sector, placing it front and center in the minds and experiences of students and academics, while also providing a conduit for their own civic engagement.

This changed philanthropic landscape, where national funders had a stronger imprint, local funders became more purposeful, innovation flourished, and collaboration improved, contributed to the advancement of key institutional reforms in the city. Notable among them were the establishment of an Ethics Review Board and the Office of Inspector General to increase accountability and reduce waste and corruption in city government; the conversion and consolidation of levee boards to focus them on their key purpose and reduce their use as sources of patronage; the consolidation of city assessors into a single office to eliminate inconsistencies and favoritism in property valuations; the overhaul of a failing K–12 public education system into a charter system that, while controversial and still unproven, initiated a sustained trajectory of positive change in test scores, graduation rates, and college attendance; and more recently, a criminal justice reform to reduce incarceration rates. While many factors contributed to these reforms and a complete causal explanation is beyond the scope of this article, the evidence collected supports the counterfactual that they would not have occurred without the efforts of nonprofits backed by the philanthropic sector.

National Funders: Promoting Change and Changing Themselves

As has been noted, Katrina changed the perspective of national funders toward New Orleans. While they remained absent from the city before the storm, the opportunities Katrina created for impactful intervention drove them to engage, directly and in collaboration with local partners, often informed by local priorities, and sometimes not. Such engagement entailed innovation and, consequently, risk taking, but it contributed to the many transformations in the philanthropic field described earlier. National program officers brought best practices in addition to resources. They shared their networks and knowledge. All these actions were immensely valuable and transformational for local players. But the process also drove changes in the donors themselves and, in some ways, contributed to changing the views of the larger philanthropic community. A few examples may help illustrate these points.

Some of the country's largest foundations, including Ford, Broad, Walton, Surdna, Kresge, Kellogg, Rockefeller, and Bill and Melinda Gates, among many others, turned their attention to New Orleans after Katrina. To deal with the unprecedented scope of the disaster and its impacts, some of these foundations set aside their traditional policies and procedures. Their goal was to get money into the streets as quickly as possible. Lacking prior institutional relationships, they were at first limited to short-term disaster grant-making focused on food, shelter, clean-up, and initial planning. As relationships with local entities gradually developed, the funding started to become more programmatic and long-term, but the uniqueness of the circumstances still required considerable creativity.

A well-known example was the Rockefeller Foundation's partnership with GNOF and the Bush-Clinton Katrina Fund to develop the Unified New Orleans Plan (UNOP), an intense, five-month effort to create a citywide recovery plan that involved working with community stakeholders. A previous recovery plan issued by a mayoral commission had been broadly decried for proposing that certain sectors of the city remain as green spaces, essentially forfeiting their rebuilding. This was a key moment in the storm's aftermath. The ordinary citizens of New Orleans whose lives were most affected by the storm asserted their right to have a voice in the recovery process that until then had been largely ignored by planners and philanthropists. In that context, the UNOP venture took place amid widespread mistrust, and, because it included all stakeholders, it had the potential of becoming mired in the decision-making process. But, despite the risks, GNOF and Rockefeller moved forward and became key actors in the process, seeing it through to completion. The UNOP provided a conduit for citizen engagement and eventually became a base around which critical players and the city could align to direct the recovery process. The actions of philanthropy, not government, placed the recovery back on track after it had been derailed.

Other innovations involved capacity building in the nonprofit and public sectors. The Rockefeller Fellows program provided support to recruit and train mid-career development professionals from around the country to be placed in organizations working for the rebuilding of New Orleans. The Ford Foundation, in partnership with the Foundation for the Mid South, developed a "loaned executive program" to expand the pool of skilled professionals in city government. The Kellogg Foundation also worked to expand local capacity and leadership in multiple areas, including race relations. The foundation made a commitment to help New Orleans become a "child-focused" city, establishing a physical presence from which it continues to manage close partnerships with GNOF and other local actors.

In time, national funders invested in public, private, and philanthropic partnerships aimed at increasing the local community's capacity to drive social change through direct action and advocacy. These partnerships transformed the philanthropic field in New Orleans and established a link to the broader philanthropic world that did not exist before Katrina. As a result, New Orleans is now viewed as a source of innovation that is deserving of national resources and attention.

The changes in philanthropy promoted by Katrina also projected outwardly, to the national and even global levels. For example, as a result of its engagement in the city, the Rockefeller Foundation shifted its focus away from disaster management to resilience. It developed a program to improve the resilience of cities around the world—100 Resilient Cities—of which New Orleans was the first case. Another example is the Center for Disaster Philanthropy, which was created as a direct response to the realization, after Katrina, that conventional ways of responding to disasters are insufficient and unsustainable. It calls for a comprehensive approach to disaster-related philanthropy, which involves support for recovery needs before and after disasters. The emphasis is on the entire cycle of disasters and, as with Rockefeller, on building communities that are resilient to disaster. Katrina therefore contributed to a deep change in the philanthropic approach to disasters.

In a much broader sense, the exposure of incompetent public (FEMA) and private (Red Cross) responses to the storm spurred a reorganization of those entities for greater effectiveness. It also increased their accountability through public criticism and exposure by the press. The widespread impacts of the storm served as an incentive for municipal and state governments to improve their preparedness to deal with disasters. In short, New Orleans came to exemplify a modern disaster situation in a crowded urban space where pockets of poverty and inequality create uneven capacities to respond. It was a test case for what other cities would later experience (New York under Super Storm Sandy, Houston under Hurricane Harvey), contributing to their preparedness.

Missed Opportunities

While national foundations were quick to respond to the storm, local actors had to invest considerable efforts to convince them of the scope of the disaster. A large part of the early efforts by GNOF leaders and others consisted of giving "disaster tours" to foundation and government officials so they could internalize the extent of the devastation. The absence of a central focus point for the response meant that there was no shared vision to tackle the social and economic challenges the city faced. Some of the philanthropic participants interviewed for this article believe that, as a result, the sector was not bold enough in addressing the social and environmental injustices that were uncovered by the storm, and that this was a missed opportunity. Efforts did eventually coalesce around housing, schools, and employment, and considerable progress has been made in all sectors. Yet, some argue that the vision, resources, and infrastructure necessary to make a more significant mark on the region's social and economic indicators are still not available today.

Many philanthropies also naively invested in new organizations that emerged after the storm with good ideas but no experience or track record of success and that eventually failed to realize their ambitious promises. While innovation and risk-taking, as described earlier, were necessary and positive hallmarks of the sector's response to the disaster, such experiences are a reminder that they may be costly. Philanthropists should not be deterred from risk-taking as a result, but they can learn from these experiences. While there are others, two highly publicized examples can be cited here: the Pontchartrain Park Community Development project, and the Make It Right Foundation project in the Lower Ninth Ward. Both projects were high-profile philanthropic efforts boosted by celebrity power in key historic neighborhoods, so their failure had (and continues to have) a significant psychological impact on the community as a whole.

The Pontchartrain Park Community Development project was an initiative to build 125 affordable, energy-efficient houses in the namesake flood-ravaged neighborhood, led by the actor Wendell Pierce in partnership with the New Orleans Redevelopment Authority and an Ohio-based development company. After several years of very slow advancement, the partnership frayed, the Salvation Army and other supporters backed out of the project, and the Redevelopment Authority sued to regain control of its properties. Additional lawsuits for breach of contract and overdue loans followed from multiple parties, miring the project in legal troubles and leaving its goals unfulfilled. The Make it Right Foundation project was launched by the actor Brad Pitt with the goal of building 150 single-family, green, affordable houses in the Lower Ninth Ward, which had also been devastated by Katrina levee breaches. While more than 100 of the houses were built, complaints have emerged about collapsing structures, caving roofs, electrical fires, gas leaks, water leaks, and black mold. Many of the units are now vacant and home owners have sued the Make It Right Foundation, and the actor.

As was perhaps inevitable, some nonprofits that emerged during the heady early years of abundant funding disappeared and along with them, some talent. While these losses likely reflect a certain degree of healthy consolidation, some observe that smaller organizations have found it difficult to survive in the competitive environment that has resulted. At the same time, some redundancy persists, with different organizations seeking to provide the same services, and collaboration among nonprofits remains challenging.

Another missed opportunity for local philanthropy may have been not thinking more purposely about the long-term retention of external partners. While some prominent funders have remained engaged and have developed collaborative mechanisms, such as the Greater New Orleans Funders Network, many others have departed, and funding flows have waned. Though some loss of funding was expected, local partners could have done better at pairing the duration of funding to the time required for the complex social and economic transformations under way in the city. As noted, many of the programs created in the aftermath of the storm were about getting money out, not recapturing it. Local philanthropy did establish a link to philanthropy outside the region and gained the respect and confidence of national funders. The question, as raised by one of the participants interviewed for this article, is two-pronged: What can be done to increase the relevancy of national philanthropy in our region and ensure its continuing role in the city's recovery and transformation? And, who should lead in the development of this strategy and in maintaining an ongoing engagement with national philanthropies? In the absence of Katrina, compelling ideas must displace the storm as the key aggregating factor to garner interest from funders. The region's longstanding inequalities of class and race as well as the existential threats it faces from subsidence, rising seas, and strengthening storms are obvious sources.

Parting Thoughts

New Orleans has a limited corporate presence, which is still struggling to replace the former prominence of the oil and gas industries. The philanthropic sector will therefore continue to be vital, and its effectiveness will hinge on its ability to partner with national funders. Philanthropic participants in the city believe that the nonprofit sector is now stronger and more capable. They also believe that the overall philanthropic community is larger and the donor profile in the city more diverse than it was at any point in recent memory. At the same time, this philanthropic community has gained greater awareness of the city's problems and their potential solutions. Katrina and its aftermath fostered a new openness among locals to how things are done elsewhere and a desire to see New Orleans not just survive but thrive. The philanthropic community was forced to reimagine how the city could be better. Answering that call contributed to the development of a more sophisticated understanding of philanthropy.

The city has been transformed in many ways in the past fourteen years. It has become home to an entirely new generation of strivers and entrepreneurs, and it is a source of new investments, startups, and incubators. Bright young people have come to the city to volunteer or search for opportunity. Public education and public housing have undergone profound changes. The city has seen an increase in transparency and accountability in public administration accompanied by much lower tolerance for patronage and corruption. Nonprofits and foundations have been an integral part of these transformations. A strong sense exists that the recovery of New Orleans was led by its citizens and backed by philanthropy.

It is too early to claim success for many of these reforms, which, to be sure, have critics. Yet philanthropic participants believe that the best hope for solving the many challenges the city faces rests with an enduring commitment from nonprofits and foundations to continue building a just and resilient New Orleans.

Notes

1 Bruce McKeever and Thomas H. Pollak, "Ten Years after Katrina, Nonprofits Are Still Growing," *Urban Wire: Nonprofits and Philanthropy* (blog), Urban Institute, August 20, 2015, https://www.urban.org/urban-wire/ten-years-after-katrina-new-orleans-nonprofits-are-still-growing.

2 "New Orleans Charities Grew Fast in Decade After Katrina," *Chronicle of Philanthropy*, August 21, 2015.

3 The key areas for the Impact Grants are arts and culture, civic engagement, education, health, human services, and youth development.

How Data Became Part of New Orleans' DNA during the Katrina Recovery

Lamar Gardere[1]
Allison Plyer[2]
Denice Ross[3]

[1] *Lamar Gardere is executive director of The Data Center of Southeast Louisiana. He an expert in civic technology solutions and strategy.*

[2] *Allison Plyer is chief demographer at The Data Center of Southeast Louisiana. She is an expert in applied demography and user-centered communications.*

[3] *Denice Ross was co-director of The Data Center of Southeast Louisiana. She is an expert in designing data systems for the public good. She is now Fellow in Residence at the Beeck Center for Social Impact and Innovation in Georgetown University.*

Data intermediaries have a symbiotic relationship with government as the source of most of their information. The open-data movement in government and development of software-as-a-service technologies shaped the data landscape after Katrina. Through relationships and talent transfers with The Data Center, the City of New Orleans went from having its chief technology officer in federal prison and its data systems in shambles to being a nationally recognized leader in open and accountable government. To be effective during disasters, an intermediary should be (1) in place and widely respected before the event, (2) ready to respond immediately after the event and for the long recovery, and (3) continually scanning the horizon for changes in data and technology.

Data Capacity in New Orleans before Hurricane Katrina and the Levee Failures

Before the storm, decisions, program design, and funding in the nonprofit sector typically were based on anecdotes and preconceptions. The Data Center (originally named the Greater New Orleans Community Data Center) was founded in 1997 as a data intermediary. It had the dual goal of making statistics more relevant and accessible while building community willingness and the capacity to use numbers. To this end, we took a user-centered, demand-driven approach, starting with the statistics needed for grant writing and program design. We invested significant time attending meetings to find out what data the local nonprofit sector needed most. These observations, combined with interviews with nonprofit leaders, revealed that more than anything else, local nonprofits wanted basic demographic information about their neighborhoods to support grant writing and program planning.

In 2002, we created a highly usable website with Census 2000 data compiled for all seventy-three New Orleans neighborhoods. For each neighborhood, we published dozens of indicators, carefully curated and categorized to answer 80 percent of the questions that nonprofits had. This approach ensured that our audience did not have to plow through pages and pages of numbers to get to indicators of greatest interest. Surrounding the indicators were just-in-time explanations of what they represent and technical definitions of each indicator written in everyday language.

We also included a short narrative about each neighborhood called a "Neighborhood Snapshot" that described each neighborhood's distinctive features and history, with particular emphasis on the historic contributions of African Americans to each neighborhood. This emphasis was chosen with the knowledge that New Orleans, for much of its history, had been majority African American, and that the contributions of African Americans are too often overlooked in official history books. In addition, we created content that addressed common questions about data. We wrote one article about how to use a proxy when the statistics you want are not available, and a series about how famous African Americans throughout history used statistics to advance social justice aims.[1] These additional efforts were essential to ensuring that our audience would find the indicators on our website relevant and compelling.

To ensure that the data would be accessible, we conducted extensive usability testing of the website.[2] We knew from the literature that if our site was hard to use, the credibility of our content would be reduced.[3] Usability testing is a formal method of watching users interact with a system to complete a task. We conducted this testing in users' homes and offices, collecting and analyzing information about these real-world interactions to inform design improvements. Usability testing revealed specific ways to improve our categorization and labeling of indicators, as well as the location of links on the website.[4] After these improvements were made, the website was officially launched. It became widely popular with local nonprofits and yielded an average of five thousand unique visits a month—about five times more traffic than a similar website serving the even larger and wonkier market of Washington, DC.

While the website answered 80 percent of our audience's questions, the other 20 percent of their questions could be answered by a technical assistance feature we called "Ask Allison." To build trust, rather than generically labeling this feature "Technical Assistance," we featured a staffer well-known in the community for data presentations and grant-writing trainings. Through this feature, requesters could submit any data-related question they had and get a response within one business day. With the aim of building self-efficacy to access and use statistics, we crafted each answer as a step-by-step set of instructions about how to navigate the Census Bureau (or other) website. We wrote the instructions in an intentionally friendly tone with references to current events in the city (e.g., "Happy Mardi Gras") to ensure local credibility and a personal connection. We analyzed metrics created through the use of this feature to inform needed additions to the indicators on the website based on the most common requests. We received an average of one "Ask Allison" request every business day.

In the years before Hurricane Katrina, the nonprofit and civic sector was starting to make strides in their level of data sophistication.[5] For example, a spring 2005 internal evaluation of forty grant proposals to a local philanthropy indicated that 55 percent of applicants effectively used external metrics to make the case for their programming.[6] But data-driven decision-making was still the exception. Nonetheless, before Katrina, the Greater New Orleans Community Data Center had established a strong reputation as a credible, friendly, and reliable partner among New Orleans' grassroots nonprofit and community leaders.

In 2005, which predates the organized federal open-data movement codified by the federal Open Government Directive in 2009,[7] the City of New Orleans provided very little data to the public beyond that available through onerous public records requests. These were the days of e-gov, where costly front-end systems allowed users to look up one address at a time (for example, in the assessor or permitting databases) or to pay their property taxes online. Data-sharing between city departments or other government agencies (such as the Regional Planning Commission) tended to be ad hoc and quid pro quo. The city's website domain was, appropriately, cityofNO.com.[8]

It was easy to complain about the city's data management, but two real challenges prevented the city from realizing the value of metrics to improve efficiency, effectiveness, and equity of government services: civil service and procurement. Even in a fast-changing field like technology, civil service job descriptions had not been modernized in over a decade, and they included obsolete titles from the days of punch cards, such as "Lead Systems Programmer," with obsolete pay to match. As a result, contractors made up nearly half of the city's IT staff.[9] Crucial functions, such as enterprise geographic information systems (GIS), were outsourced, meaning that when Hurricane Katrina came, the city had little institutional knowledge and was unprepared from a data perspective. Because of the condition of the city's data management, The Data Center relied almost exclusively on federal statistics before the storm; but the rapid pace of change after Katrina made local metrics essential for paving the way for an informed and equitable recovery.

After the Storm

After the storm, federal statistics about New Orleans (including the Census 2000) became instantly obsolete. At the same time, old ways of making decisions—based on historical precedence, intuition, and personal relationships—no longer worked. The Data Center was inundated with requests from the media, nonprofits, businesses, national researchers, multiple federal agencies, community-based organizations, and federal, state, and local governments. Visits to the website went from 5,000 a month to 120,000 in the two months after Hurricane Katrina.

Despite the demand, numerical facts were hard to come by. Three months after the storm, a researcher with the Brookings Institution was quoted in the *New York Times* saying it had been easier gathering data for Iraq than for New Orleans.[10] At The Data Center, though our world had turned upside down, our user-centered approach meant that we knew where to start. What information do people need to accomplish what tasks? Our "Ask Allison" feature served as a funnel and a knowledge management system for the wave of increasing requests. Requests tripled from before Katrina and provided a treasure trove of evidence about the information people most needed. Population counts quickly emerged as the highest value data set. Neighborhood organizations needed information about which city blocks were at a tipping point of recovery so they could deploy their limited case management and volunteer rebuilding resources. Healthcare providers need to know where to place temporary and permanent clinics as neighborhoods slowly rebuilt. Funders needed to know which neighborhoods most needed childcare centers. Beyond the nonprofit sector, businesses needed to know neighborhood population density to consider opening or reopening stores. Federal, state, and local agencies needed population numbers to inform recovery efforts and continued program planning. Even evacuees needed facts on the repopulation of their neighborhoods to inform their own decisions to return.

The Census Bureau was unable to provide this data because between decennial census counts it produces only one annual population estimate at the county level with a nine-month lag time. These estimates were neither timely enough nor granular enough to capture the rapid changes as residents rebuilt and the city recovered. The Data Center researched a large number of administrative data sets that might be a good indicator of repopulation and publicly available with a short lag time. These sets included data from school enrollment, traffic volume, utility accounts, drivers' licenses, passenger car registrations, voter registration and participation, and United States Postal Service (USPS) National Change of Address records and residences actively receiving mail. USPS counts of active residences emerged as an indicator that best met criteria for a consistent relationship to population while being publicly available every month with only a two-week lag.[11] Although the numbers were publicly available, they were aggregated to ZIP codes and carrier routes. To measure recovery, The Data Center needed counts at a more granular level with consistent boundaries. We found that the direct marketing company Valassis had this information at the address level. In a move that foreshadowed today's movement to private-sector data philanthropy,[12] where the public benefits from privately held data, The Data Center partnered with Valassis to get monthly updates of households actively receiving mail at the address level.[13]

Additionally, technology was changing around us, as were the ways New Orleanians accessed information. Disruptive mapping technologies such as Open Street Map (launched in 2004) and Google Maps (2005) reduced barriers to producing interactive maps and fundamentally changed the user experience for navigating online maps.[14] The field of crisis mapping soon popped up,[15] and The Data Center began to think more about purpose-built maps and apps with a short life span customized to the needs of different phases of the recovery. In this new context we used Google Maps to build the "Repopulation Mapper" that displayed the Valassis counts on households receiving mail aggregated to the block level. More important, we posted metadata (explanation of what the data is and what it is not) in plain sight and in everyday language. We conducted usability testing in the field with tasks that replicated the frequent questions this mapper was designed to address. Usability testing yielded tweaks to titles, the location of the legend, and changes to the map display so that it was viewable even on the low-resolution screens still dominant among our local users.[16]

In addition to supplying high-demand information such as block-level repopulation, The Data Center found a pressing need to help community members, business investors, and policymakers at the local, state, and federal levels to better understand the pace of recovery. Katrina brought dramatic change and also flux for many years after the storm, which created chaos and confusion. Investors both public and private wondered about the strength of the economy and the housing market, the availability of needed infrastructure, and whether population was continuing to return to New Orleans. Rumors swirled about what happened to the billions of dollars of recovery funding allocated by Congress. Policymakers needed information about how to adapt and effectively deploy their resources. Operating under differing goals and priorities, decision makers found themselves in conflict with one another.[17]

To address these issues, The Data Center had to shift from disseminating raw indicators to analysis. We formed a partnership with the Brookings Institution to identify and analyze indicators of recovery in four domains: population, housing, economy, and infrastructure. To ensure that end users could make use of the statistical trends, we created a report entitled "The New Orleans Index," with graphics of each indicator and a one-page narrative summary of findings.[18] The report was published monthly for the first two and a half years (when change was most rapid), then quarterly, then biannually, and finally annually by the fifth anniversary of Hurricane Katrina. With the aim of creating a common understanding of the trends to help inform decision makers as well as the general public to move in a common direction, we extended our reach beyond our website. We began using local and national TV, radio, and newspaper as new avenues for disseminating our findings.

The New Orleans Index built on the reputations of The Data Center and Brookings for credibility, trust, and neutrality to develop a common understanding of the recovery that was expert (informed by Brookings's expertise in trend analysis) and locally relevant (informed by The Data Center's one-the-ground knowledge of post-Katrina New Orleans). In addition, The Data Center's expertise in human-centered design ensured that the publications responded to changing needs and questions and that the publications were easy to understand and use.[19] Through briefings and presentations, Brookings engaged federal stakeholders around the findings, while The Data Center engaged community groups and local officials. Media mentions averaged hundreds each year. An independent evaluation of this multi-year effort concluded that The New Orleans Index series of reports successfully:

- Built a shared understanding and common operating picture among diverse stakeholders
- Focused conversations on solutions and stopping debates about facts
- Communicated to officials and investors outside New Orleans, reducing uncertainty and spurring investment
- Helped decision makers identify needs and adapt priorities, policies, strategies, and programs
- Spurred innovation[20]

Another shift The Data Center had to make as the recovery progressed was to turn to the city for metrics on the recovery, since federal statistics were not timely enough or of sufficient geographic detail. The aforementioned data capacity challenges of the city became increasingly apparent. Months after the storm, Brookings alerted us that when they contacted the city's Department of Safety and Permits for the latest cumulative count of building permits, sometimes the numbers were inexplicably half the previous month's total. Years later we learned the cause: rather than adapting the existing permitting system to accommodate kiosk and online applications as demand for permits outpaced the ability of office staff to process them, IT contractors had built an entirely new permitting system (with a different data schema) to take in permits electronically. Thus, half of the permits were in-person using the pre-Katrina system and half used the new electronic interface. To compile a basic count of building permits issued post-Katrina, a city contractor had to combine these incompatible databases. This type of unnecessary complexity made any timely, meaningful analysis of city-held data nearly impossible and further entrenched the city's dependence on its ballooning force of contractors. Some of these IT contracting relationships would eventually land both the chief technology officer and the mayor in prison.[21]

With growing legal distractions among city leadership and increasingly pathological complexity in the city's IT systems, the role of The Data Center became even more important in the years following the storm. Interestingly, other data intermediaries (such as The Data Center's peers in the Urban Institute's National Neighborhood Indicators Partnership) have since played similar roles during crises in city government, notably Data Driven Detroit during the city's bankruptcy and Baltimore Neighborhood Indicators Alliance after the death of Freddie Gray in police custody.[22] When local government loses legitimacy, a trusted local data intermediary can help fill key gaps until local government gets back on its feet.

The New Role of Data in New Orleans

In the early days after the storm, data sharing was still largely bilateral between limited organizations, but an underground network emerged. For example, the city's emergency operation center distributed its "Daily Dashboard" to a list of select partner entities and these entities forwarded it to other peers in the nonprofit sector. The same thing happened with other data sets, such as the Rapid Population Estimates survey results and geographic information on the city's land ownership parcels.

Government's limited sharing resulted in a disparity of information access across neighborhoods. The Broadmoor neighborhood, which was inundated with high floodwaters, partnered with the Harvard Kennedy School of Government and was able to get special access to the city's building permit data, which helped inform that neighborhood's recovery.[23] Knowing how valuable such records were for all neighborhoods' recoveries, The Data Center maintained the drumbeat of equal access for all by obtaining and republishing data about the entire city, not just neighborhoods with the capacity to create their own numbers or connections to get special access to information. President Barack Obama's Open Government Directive came at a fortuitous time during the mayoral election, inspiring new possibilities of government transparency.

When Mitch Landrieu was elected mayor in 2010, he formed the Tech Transition Team to look into the city's data management and IT practices and make recommendations for his new administration. The Data Center's co-director Denice Ross was invited to be part of the team, and Allen Square, also on the team, ended up becoming the city's first chief information officer (CIO). As part of that work, the team reached out to some of the nation's premier municipal CIOs and chief technology officers in Boston, Washington, DC, San Francisco, and Tampa. This infusion of ideas allowed the incoming administration to rapidly modernize and open up. The new CIO focused for the first year on the uncelebrated work of creating updated civil service job descriptions (with competitive salaries), stabilizing IT systems, repairing the department's battered reputation, and modernizing procurement to accommodate new technologies, such as software-as-a-service that afforded more flexibility and agility and less risk. At the same time, the incoming CIO rediscovered the talent and experience already in place in City Hall. By listening to and empowering these seasoned voices in the city's IT department, along with hard work, tenacity, and steady management, the team was able to rebuild an old and failing infrastructure while nurturing skills that would be needed to maintain healthy systems. Healthy municipal technology systems are critical to government's ability to create, use, and share data for public benefit. With a renewed confidence and a fresh and determined focus on performance and innovation, the City of New Orleans began to attract the attention of the growing pool of tech talent developing in post-Katrina New Orleans. New Orleanians who had never before considered government service now found it a compelling career opportunity. The next CIO, Lamar Gardere, brought this effort to the next level with a citywide digital equity initiative, which included the active cultivation of high-potential New Orleanians from populations who are typically underrepresented in technology. This infusion of newly empowered voices, novel thinking, and data talent, combined with high-level commitment to open government, transformed the city into a legitimate competitor for participation in national innovation networks such as IBM Smarter Cities Challenge, the Code for America Fellowship, Rockefeller's 100 Resilient Cities, and Bloomberg's iTeams and What Works Cities.

Along the way, the city's increasingly sophisticated approach to data allowed for the same shift to analysis that The Data Center made after Katrina. Performance management was the driving force behind much of the city's data analysis. The city initiated public BlightStat[24] meetings (inspired by Baltimore mayor Martin O'Malley's CitiStat),[25] designed to bring together key staff and leaders from across city government to roll up their sleeves to meet Mayor Landrieu's audacious goal of eliminating ten thousand blighted properties in four years. Data management was a key topic of conversation for the first two years of these meetings (started in 2010). Data from multiple departments, including code enforcement and the city attorney's office, had to be compiled and verified to develop an accurate understanding of the status of each parcel. This initiative created an opportunity for the first compelling, easy-to-understand, use case for open data.

In 2012, Code for America fellows collaborated with city residents and staff to create an online tool called "BlightStatus," which—for the first time since the storm—gave residents, city staff, and leadership a single, shared view into the status of blighted properties.[26] Removing the asymmetry of information allowed the conversation to shift from arguing about the facts to discussing what the solutions might be. The city met their goal a year early, and by 2014 had reduced blight by thirteen thousand addresses.[27] Of note, The Data Center was a symbiotic partner in the reduction of blight, having set the baseline with their 2008 report called "Benchmarks for Blight," which took the innovative approach of using USPS records on addresses unable to receive mail (e.g., not active and not vacant) as a proxy for blight and then comparing that number across time and across cities.[28] The city and the public came to rely on The Data Center's independent analysis of progress against blight.

The success of meeting the blight reduction goal was a proof of concept that allowed the benefits of open data to permeate throughout city government. City workers who had previously feared negative repercussions from releasing data found that opening up the data, even with all its flaws, generated increasing trust among stakeholders, created a mechanism for improving the data, and most important, fueled community partnerships for accelerating progress. As fear of making city data freely available subsided, one by one, city departments began opening their data to the public. In particular, the successful BlightStat initiative inspired the New Orleans Police

Department to open their data, and once the police department was opening their data, it was hard for other departments to justify keeping their nonsensitive data in the dark.[29]

As the city got more tech savvy and created more data tools, they were able to more quickly spin out high-demand data visualizations, such as damage-assessment maps of tornadoes that struck the city in 2017 or the traffic-and-flood tracking app released in August 2017 to help residents navigate frequent street floods (http://streetwise.nola.gov/).[30] These tools and visualizations increased residents' confidence in city data. A virtuous cycle was created where data tools with relevant use cases created more awareness of the city's data and technology capacity. Potential data users shifted their approach from simply extracting city data and building their own tools to working in partnership with the city to build tools. This shift produced better results because the city could provide insights about internal business processes and how they affected the data and its interpretation, as well as point to additional city data that could be used in each partner's applications. For example, in 2016, after observing contractors in Detroit using proprietary methods to survey property conditions, the City of New Orleans's IT team partnered with a local firm to cheaply collect property-condition data automatically with city-designed sensor rigs. With help from ESRI, an interface design process informed by community input, and New Orleanians willing to volunteer their time to score property conditions, the city effectively leveraged the concept of "civic tech" to crowdsource data collection on blight and property conditions.[31]

Now, the City of New Orleans is recognized as a national leader in local government transparency, with more than two hundred data sets published and its work highlighted regularly in telling the story of how data can save lives.[32] The City of New Orleans was invited to talk about their data work at the launch of President Obama's Climate Data Initiative in 2014, and two years later, the city was on stage at the White House again talking about their leadership in the Police Data Initiative. The New Orleans Police Department (NOPD) was described as the "Queen of open data" in a 2015 FiveThirtyEight article, and the federal judge overseeing NOPD's consent decree described the city's new data capacity as "a miraculous transformation."[33] By 2016, Mayor Landrieu had signed the city's first ever Open Data Policy designed to facilitate and routinize the release of freely available, public data in New Orleans.[34] In 2018, the City of New Orleans became one of only thirteen cities nationwide to receive the prestigious What Works Cities Certification.[35]

Today, outside of attention garnered around major Katrina anniversaries (which increase the audience two-fold), the audience for The Data Center is once again primarily local, with about eight thousand visits a month to the website. The presence of this data infrastructure continues to give New Orleans a head start when changes come its way. For example, while other communities struggle to pull information together about Opportunity Zones for federal tax incentives, would-be investors in New Orleans are easily pulling numbers on those neighborhoods from The Data Center's website. Most important, those numbers are fortified with analysis from an equity perspective that increases the likelihood of their being used for good. People with financial resources and powerful social networks have always had access to the data they need to exploit neighborhoods; The Data Center levels the playing field so that agents for good also have access to that same information.

Lessons Learned

- Lead with the people and what information they need, not the technology. By starting with data the people needed and tying those data into a change process such as blight reduction, New Orleans created a narrative (the sky didn't fall when data were released and good things happened) that inspired other domains, such as public safety, to follow suit. Often the best course is to keep the complex technology behind the scenes, using it to create simple, easy-to-digest information for the public in media formats they already consume, such as radio and morning news shows or a simple address lookup like the BlightStatus tool.

1. Build data systems *with* not *for* stakeholders. Data needs to be not only technically credible but relevant and legitimate in the eyes of the community.[36] The only way to ensure relevance and legitimacy is to get feedback early and often from community stakeholders. One rule of thumb The Data Center has is that if you have to conduct a training to teach someone how to use your website, you have not designed it well.
   - The value of the data intermediary lies not just in its staff but also in its role in developing talent who, through working relationships and career moves, can then transfer their knowledge to other organizations. Intermediaries also create data-savvy social networks within cities that span local government and the nonprofit and private sectors, connecting them to state and federal government.[37]
   - Don't go it alone. New Orleans was able to accelerate its progress by partnering with respected national organizations such as Brookings, seeking out advice from municipal open-government leaders across the country, and participating in networks such as Bloomberg What Works Cities, Code for America, the National Neighborhood Indicators Partnership, and 100 Resilient Cities. A 2018 report by New America ranked New Orleans among the top 10 percent of networked metros.[38]

2. A data intermediary is crucial civic data infrastructure for navigating shocks and stressors, whether it be a hurricane, crime, or the emergence of smart cities technologies. An intermediary can also spur private and public investments by reducing uncertainty after a shock. It may be that community data capacity before a disaster serves as an amplifier of social capital that is well-recognized as a key element of resilience.[39] For example, Todd Richardson, who leads the research arm of the Department of Housing and Urban Development (HUD),[40] declared that he read The New Orleans Index every day after Hurricane Katrina to inform his decision making and that his highest recommendation for disaster-prone areas was that they replicate what The Data Center did for New Orleans.[41] His doing so is particularly important because a great deal of federal disaster funding is distributed through HUD. After years of advising communities who have undergone recent shocks, it has become clear to these authors that the time to build a data intermediary and build the necessary trust with the community is before disaster strikes.

Just as the previous decade has seen the advent of ubiquitous mapping, software-as-a-service, and open government, the next ten years will see similar uncharted territory emerge in smart-cities technology, private-sector data, and particularly in the ethical use of algorithms and artificial intelligence in local decision-making. The Data Center is positioned to develop the talent and social networks needed to leverage these emerging technologies to further improve data availability and use in New Orleans.

In addition, as The Data Center maintains its focus on the information needed most by residents of New Orleans and Southeast Louisiana, it is clear that our dissemination efforts must continue to track two existential threats to the region: disaster risk and increasing inequity. In the years since Hurricane Katrina, Southeast Louisiana has been struck by multiple hurricanes, including Ike, Gustav, and Isaac. In 2010 the massive BP oil spill damaged Southeast Louisiana's wetlands that provide the region's first line of defense against hurricane storm surge. And in recent years, frequent unprecedented rainstorms have flooded dozens of homes and businesses throughout the region.[42] In addition, income inequality is growing more rapidly in New Orleans than the national average. Growing inequity not only negatively impacts economic growth and the provision of essential city services but hampers social cohesion and trust in government, which are critical to the resilience of a community faced with shocks.[43]

A large share of the US population lives in areas at risk of natural disasters, such as earthquakes, hurricanes, flooding, and tornados, or even manmade disasters, such as industrial contamination or terrorist attacks.[44] Disasters compounded by inequity are growing nationwide; the challenges that New Orleans faces are not unique. Data intermediaries nationwide can play a critical role in disseminating statistics that help communities to be more resilient in the face of these current and future challenges.

Notes

1   Allison Plyer and Denice Ross, "You Can't Always Get What You Want," Greater New Orleans Community Data Center, August 2, 2005, http://www.datacenterresearch.org/pre-katrina/articles/corrdata.html; "Democratizing Data: Making Information a Tool of the People for the People," Greater New Orleans Community Data Center, February 21, 2003, http://www.datacenterresearch.org/pre-katrina/articles/democraticdata.html.

2   "Usability Testing for Community Data Sites," Greater New Orleans Community Data Center, accessed July 1, 2019, http://www.datacenterresearch.org/pre-katrina/usability/.

3   B. J. Fogg, Jonathan Marshall, Othman Laraki, Alex Osipovich, Chris Varma, Nicholas Fang, Jyoti Paul, Akshay Rangnekar, John Shon, Preeti Swani, and Marissa Treinen, "What Makes Web Sites Credible? A Report on a Large Quantitative Study," in *Proceedings of the SIGCHI Conference on Human Factors in Computing* Systems, 61–68 (New York: ACM, 2001), DOI: https://doi.org/10.1145/365024.365037.

4   "Usability Testing for Community Data Sites," Greater New Orleans Community Data Center, accessed July 1, 2019, http://www.datacenterresearch.org/pre-katrina/usability/.

5   "What Will a Cut in U.S. Census Bureau Funding Mean for America's Cities? Investigating the Importance of Supporting Federal Information Programs for Urban America," Brookings Institution, October 14, 2005.

6   Jane Arsenault, "Part II: Analysis of United Way Proposals for Technical Assistance Needs," July 2005, Nonprofit Knowledge Works archives.

7   "Open Government Directive," National Archives and Records Administration, December 8, 2009, accessed July 1, 2019, https://obamawhitehouse.archives.gov/open/documents/open-government-directive.

8   Dave Walker, "Rachel Maddow Wants New Orleans to Just Say 'Yes' on Its Official Website," nola.com, June 3, 2010, https://www.nola.com/entertainment_life/movies_tv/article_6228919f-7471-56c5-a5bf-bb7861d1293d.html.

9   "Transition New Orleans Tech Transition Team Report" (unpublished), April 29, 2010.

10 Clifford J. Levy, "After Katrina, a Trickle of Returnees, *New York Times*, November 13, 2005, https://www.nytimes.com/2005/11/13/weekinreview/after-katrina-a-trickle-of-returnees.html.

11 Allison Plyer, Joy Bonaguro, and Ken Hodges, "Using Administrative Data to Estimate Population Displacement and Resettlement following a Catastrophic U.S. Disaster," *Population and Environment* 31, no. 1–3 (November 29, 2009): 150–175, doi:https://doi.org/10.1007/s11111-009-0091-3.

12 Brice McKeever, Solomon Greene, Graham MacDonald, Peter A. Tatian, and Deondre' Jones, "Data Philanthropy: Unlocking the Power of Private Data for Public Good," Urban Institute, July 24, 2018, https://www.urban.org/research/publication/data-philanthropy-unlocking-power-private-data-public-good.

13 "Valassis Data Is at the Core of Community Rebuilding and Revitalization," Valassis, June 4, 2018, https://www.valassis.com/about-us/newsroom/item/180604/valassis-data-is-at-the-core-of-community-rebuilding-and-revitalization.

14 Christopher C. Miller, "A Beast in the Field: The Google Maps Mashup as GIS/2," *Cartographica: The International Journal for Geographic Information and Geovisualization* 41, no. 3 (October 10, 2006): 187–199, doi:10.3138/J0L0-5301-2262-N779.

15 Sophia B. Liu and Leysia Palen, "The New Cartographers: Crisis Map Mashups and the Emergence of Neogeographic Practice," *Cartography and Geographic Information Science* 37, no. 1 (January 1, 2010): 69–90, doi:10.1559/152304010790588098.

16 Denice Ross, "An App We Can Trust: Lessons from Katrina" (speech, Gov 2.0 Expo 2010, May 25, 2010).

17 Melissa A. Schigoda, "The Use and Impact of Disaster Recovery Indicators from the Perspective of Complex Adaptive Systems Theory: The Case of the New Orleans Index" (PhD diss., Tulane University Law School, 2016).

18 "The New Orleans Index," Brookings, July 29, 2011, https://www.brookings.edu/research/the-new-orleans-index/.

19 Schigoda, *Use and Impact of Disaster Recovery Indicators*.

20 Ibid.

21 Gordon Russell, "In Tell-all Book, Greg Meffert Reveals How He, Ray Nagin Launched Side Deal at Outset," *New Orleans Advocate,* August 28, 2009, https://www.theadvocate.com/new_orleans/news/article_2af4b36c-aa2c-11e8-95e2-d361d8ff2723.html.

22 Eric Burnstein, Eric, "Case Study: NNIP and Open Data in Detroit," National Neighborhood Indicators Partnership, July 2014, https://www.urban.org/sites/default/files/publication/22801/413188-Case-Study-NNIP-and-Open-Data-in-Detroit.PDF; Baltimore Neighborhood Indicators Alliance, "What Happened in Baltimore and What Can We Do? A Neighborhoods' Perspective," NNIP, January 7, 2016, https://www.neighborhoodindicators.org/library/catalog/what-happened-baltimore-and-what-can-we-do-neighborhoods-perspective.

23 *The Broadmoor Project: Progress Report*, Joint Project of the KSG/BCSIA Broadmoor Project and Bard College (Cambridge: Harvard University, March 2007).

24 Ann Carpenter, Emily Mitchell, and Shelley Price, "Blight Remediation in the Southeast: Local Approaches to Design and Implementation (2015-11-01)," FRB Atlanta Community and Economic Development Discussion Paper No. 2015-5), available at SSRN, https://papers.ssrn.com/sol3/papers.cfm?abstract_id=2774636.

25 Robert D. Behn, "The Varieties of CitiStat," *Public Administration Review* 66, no. 3 (2006): 332–340, http://www.jstor.org/stable/3843915.

26 Charles Chieppo, "New Orleans' Winning Strategy in the War on Blight," Governing, March 18, 2014, https://www.governing.com/blogs/bfc/col-new-orleans-blightstat-vacant-dilapidated-property.html.

27 Ibid.; William D. Eggers, "New Orleans' Fight with Blight Started with Data," Government Technology, October 25, 2017, https://www.govtech.com/fs/data/New-Orleans-Fight-with-Blight-Started-with-Data.html.

28 Allison Plyer and Elaine Ortiz, "Benchmarks for Blight: How Much Blight Does New Orleans Have?," The Data Center, August 21, 2012, https://www.datacenterresearch.org/reports_analysis/benchmarks-for-blight/.

29   Detroit noted a similar phenomenon, with police transparency inspiring other departments, such Code Enforcement and Public Works to follow suit. *Building and Restoring Civic Capacity: The Obama Administration's Federal-Local Partnership with Detroit (2011–2016)* (Washington, DC: Executive Office of the President, 2016), https://obamawhitehouse.archives.gov/sites/obamawhitehouse.archives.gov/files/documents/DFWG_Report_Final_120216.pdf.

30   Dan Swenson, "Animated Map: A Closer Look at Tornado Devastation in New Orleans East," nola.com, March 11, 2017, https://www.nola.com/news/article_6da09a0f-4740-5109-ae98-a98a67ad5b51.html; Kevin Litten, "New Orleans Launches Website Promising to Track Real-Time Flooding, Accidents," August 12, 2017, https://www.nola.com/news/weather/article_576c4127-bf47-5d8d-9052-b6474657f4e1.html.

31   "New Orleans Rapid Property Survey," nola.gov, 2013, nola.gov/rapid-property-survey/ (accessed February 24, 2020).

32   Erin Cunningham, "The New Orleans Fire Department Calls on Data to Save Lives," *StateTech*, August 6, 2018, https://statetechmagazine.com/article/2018/08/new-orleans-fire-department-calls-data-save-lives.

33   Jeff Asher, "Which Cities Share the Most Crime Data?" FiveThirtyEight, December 28, 2015, https://fivethirtyeight.com/features/which-cities-share-the-most-crime-data/; Matt Sledge, "Federal Judge Praises NOPD's Push for More Open Data but Says More Progress Needed," nola.com, November 17, 2016, https://www.nola.com/news/crime_police/article_cc910789-4351-5ab9-9620-4aaba577b24b.html.

34   City of New Orleans, "Mayor Landrieu Signs Executive Order to Make Data More Freely Available to Public," press release, September 1, 2016, https://nola.gov/mayor/news/archive/2016/20160801-pr-mayor-signs-executive-order-on-open-da/.

35   "What Works Cities Certification," What Works Cities, accessed July 1, 2019, https://whatworkscities.bloomberg.org/certification/.

36   Tischa Muñoz-Erickson, Clark Miller, and Thaddeus Miller, "How Cities Think: Knowledge Co-Production for Urban Sustainability and Resilience," *Forests* 8, no. 6 (2017): 203; Dave D White, Amber Wutich, Kelli L Larson, Patricia Gober, Timothy Lant, and Clea Senneville, "Credibility, Salience, and Legitimacy of Boundary Objects: Water Managers' Assessments of a Simulation Model," *Science and Public Policy* 37, no. 3 (2010): 219–232.

37   Allison Plyer has chaired the Census Bureau's Scientific Advisory Committee since 2001. Denice Ross (2001–2010) went from The Data Center to the Landrieu administration, where she launched the city's open-data initiative, and then to the Obama White House, where she co-founded the Police Data Initiative. Joy Bonaguro (2002–2009) went on to become the first chief data officer (CDO) for the City of San Francisco and set the gold standard nationwide for the emerging role of the municipal CDO. Melissa Schigoda (2008–2012) wrote her dissertation on the *New Orleans Index*, transitioned to the National Network of Public Health Institutes, and now serves as director of the Office of Performance Management and Accountability at the City of New Orleans. Ben Horowitz (2011–2014) moved on to create NOPD's now nationally recognized data-driven approach. The talent flow has also gone the other way into The Data Center, with Robby Habans, who provided GIS support for the post-Katrina Rapid Population Estimate Survey collection now serving as The Data Center's economist, and in 2017, Lamar Gardere moved from his role as the city's second chief information officer to executive director of The Data Center.

38   Tara McGuinness, Denice Ross, and Anne-Marie Slaughter, "Networks and American Renewal: Can Networks Supercharge American Ingenuity?," New America, December 13, 2018, https://www.newamerica.org/national-network/reports/networks-and-american-renewal/can-networks-supercharge-american-ingenuity/.

39   Virginia Gil-Rivas and Ryan Kilmer, "Building Community Capacity and Fostering Disaster Resilience," *Journal of Clinical Psychology* 72 (December 2016): 1318 –133; Fran H. Norris, Susan P. Stevens, Betty Pfefferbaum, Karen F. Wyche, and Rose L. Pfefferbaum, "Community Resilience as a Metaphor, Theory, Set of Capacities and Strategy for Disaster Readiness," *American Journal of Community Psychology* 41 (2008): 127–150.

40   "Todd M. Richardson," US Department of Housing and Urban Development, Office of Policy Development and Research, accessed July 29, 2019, https://www.huduser.gov/portal/about/bio-Todd-M-Richardson.html.

41 Roundtable discussion on disaster recovery metrics at the National Low-Income Housing Coalition on July 19, 2018.

42 "New Orleans Flooding Caused by Sudden Rain in What Might Be "a Taste of What Could Occur," nola. com, July 10, 2019, https://www.nola.com/news/article_e7cd222a-a329-11e9-8b2d-ab8749f9d28a.html; Danny Monteverde, "Mother's Day Flooding: Water in the Streets, but Not Like Summer 2017," *Eyewitness News*, May 13, 2019, https://www.wwltv.com/article/weather/severe-weather/mothers-day-flooding-water-in-the-streets-but-not-like-summer-2017/289-2f09a915-6fb1-4792-bbe2-b0f87b7bf449.

43 Edward L. Glaeser, Matt Resseger, and Kristina Tobio, "Inequality in Cities," *Journal of Regional Science* 49, no. 4 (2009): 615–646, http://scholar.harvard.edu/files/resseger/files/glaeserressegertobiojrs.pdf; Alan Berube, "All Cities Are Not Created Unequal," Brookings Institution, February 20, 2014, http://www.brookings.edu/research/papers/2014/02/cities-unequal-berube; Allison Plyer, Nihal Shrinath, and Vicki Mack, "The New Orleans Index at Ten," The Data Center, July 31, 2015, https://s3.amazonaws.com/gnocdc/reports/TheDataCenter_TheNewOrleansIndexatTen.pdf.

44 *Reducing Disaster Risk: A Challenge for Development* (New York: United Nations Development Programme, 2004), https://www.undp.org/content/dam/undp/library/crisis%20prevention/disaster/asia_pacific/Reducing%20Disaster%20risk%20a%20Challenge%20for%20development.pdf .

Closing Case Study:
Standing for the Whole

The Nutria That Roared: How Building Coalitions Can Empower the Small to Drive Great Change

Michael Hecht

Michael Hecht is president and CEO of Greater New Orleans, Inc., the economic development coordinating organization for the Greater New Orleans metropolitan area.

Hurricane Katrina saved the New Orleans economy. To be clear, Hurricane Katrina was not "good"—it was a devastating event, the most destructive storm in American history, costing thousands of lives and billions of dollars in damage. But when the books are written, and the story is told, the conclusion will be inescapable: Hurricane Katrina marked a profoundly positive inflection point in the New Orleans economy.

How Can This Paradox Be? How Can a Catastrophe Become Redemption?

It is first important to understand that Hurricane Katrina could not really have killed the New Orleans economy, because forty years of benign neglect and active malfeasance had taken care of that. While the "Big Easy" reveled in its history, ascendant cities like Houston, Atlanta, and Miami worked on their future: taking from New Orleans not just people and companies but entire generations and industries with impunity. New Orleans, once the Queen City of the South, grew jobs only 43 percent from 1969 to 2004, while places like Tampa and Raleigh grew by more than 250 percent; and, the population of New Orleans actually declined from more than 600,000 to 440,000 during those four decades. By the time Katrina hit on August 29, 2005, New Orleans was a place of the past.

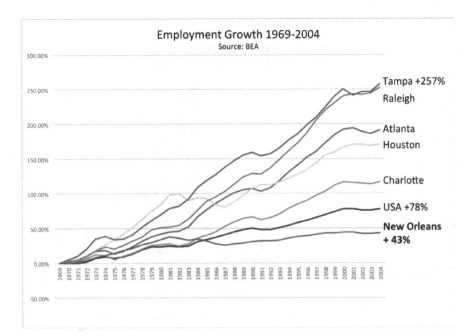

Employment growth in New Orleans and
select cities between 1960 and 2004 (US Department
of Commerce, Bureau of Economic Analysis)

No, it didn't kill the Crescent City, the opposite happened—Hurricane Katrina actually revived the New Orleans economy from its decades-long slumber. Like a heart attack to a morbidly unhealthy person—that deeply scares but doesn't actually kill—the storm has seemingly shocked New Orleans into a profoundly better way of life. And now, a decade past Katrina, New Orleans is becoming one of the best places to live and work in the United States—called by the publisher of *Forbes*, Richard Karlgaard, "the comeback story of our lifetime."

Consider these recent top rankings for New Orleans:

- #1 for economic development wins in the South (*Southern Business and Development*)
- #1 brainpower city in the United States (*Forbes*)
- #1 fastest growing tech sector in the United States *(Bureau of Labor Statistics)*
- #1 for foreign direct investment per capita (*State of Louisiana*)
- #1 place to visit in the world (*New York Times*)

The preponderance of evidence makes it clear: New Orleans is a region on the rise, and Katrina was the inflection point. From an economic development perspective, this point may be illustrated best by the fact that Greater New Orleans ranks a remarkable #2 in the South for major economic development wins over the past twenty years—but barely any economic development occurred before Katrina.

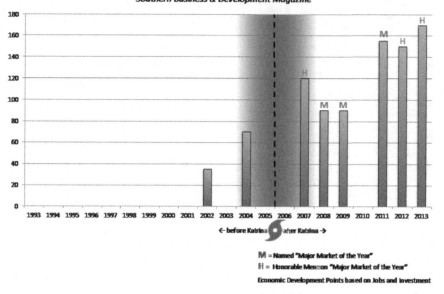

Greater New Orleans
Economic Development Points by Year
Southern Business & Development Magazine

Greater New Orleans economic development points by year (*Southern Business and Development*, July 3, 2019)

So, how did this happen? How did the unprecedented destruction of Hurricane Katrina, followed by the added blows of the Great Recession and the BP oil spill, become not the deathblows to a long-declining New Orleans but the opportunity for economic redemption?

What we will see is that there is a range of different tactics for turning crisis into opportunity, and this diversity of options makes up a "crisis tool-kit" that has served New Orleans very well. "Radical resilience"—the ability to not only survive but transcend—is generalizable: The crisis tool-kit employed in post-Katrina New Orleans can be exported to other cities, states, and nations in turmoil and under duress—and provide them with proven strategies for economically thriving after the disaster. The result can be transcendent performance that does not eliminate the facts of a tragedy but rather honors those who suffered by creating something better than was there before.

A number of tactics were successfully employed in New Orleans to revitalize the post-Katrina economy. These include:

- *The State of Louisiana Becoming the "Master of Disaster"—Solving Your Own Crisis Makes You Really Valuable to Everyone Else*
New Orleans is not only saving itself by stabilizing its coast and fixing its levees, it is also creating economic opportunity. Greater New Orleans has now established an "environmental management" industry that is helping others around the country and world address their own environmental challenges. The progenitor for this new industry is the Dutch, who drive about 4 percent of their GDP by selling their water management expertise.
- *Making Lemonade from Oily Water—Finding Counterintuitive Opportunity in Disaster*

The State of Louisiana was able to use the billions in damages from the 2010 BP oil spill to secure seed funding for the $50 million Coastal Master Plan. So, in the end, far from destroying the coast, the BP spill may catalyze its rescue with over $10 billion of funding, which is a fundamental imperative to the economy of Greater New Orleans.

- *United We Stand—The Triumph of Regionalism*
  Hurricane Katrina taught New Orleans that neither water nor people seeking jobs respect political boundaries. Thus, we had to work together if we were going to solve for both flood management and economic growth. This sense of the rationality of regionalism now extends to Baton Rouge, with whom New Orleans has created the unprecedented SoLA Super Region partnership—an active committee made up of business and civic leaders from both cities.

- *Focus, Fix, Repeat—Using a Common Approach to Fixing Problems in Order to Drive Transformational Change*
  Local leadership has done an excellent job identifying problems and then doggedly pursuing the path to fixing them. For example, the murder rate in New Orleans is now at a fifty-year low, and at the same time that incarceration is falling. This success has been achieved through the cumulative impact of years of refining police techniques, including introducing a "public health" approach to violence.

- *Breaking Bad—Out-of-the-Box Thinking, Combined with Opportunistic Action, Can Impact the Impossible*
  Before Katrina, New Orleans suffered with some of the worst public schools in the United States. An innovative local leader, Leslie Jacobs, thought to apply a bankruptcy model to public education. This move lead to the formation of the Recovery School District, which took over the failing schools, as a conservator would a bankrupt company. As a result of this innovative model, New Orleans schools have gone from over 65 percent failing to under 5 percent.

- *The Mother of Invention—Spurring Innovation through Policy and Parties*
  New Orleans is now one of the most diverse and fast-growing tech communities in the nation. This success was driven as much by policy (e.g., tax incentives) as by branding and celebration, such as New Orleans Entrepreneur Week—the "Mardi Gras of Ideas."

- *If Not / But For—How the Business Community Provides the Essential, and Often Missing, Element of Success*
  Despite being the United States' "most European" city, New Orleans had not benefited from a direct flight to Europe since 1982. A group of business leaders, including Gregory Rusovich and Stephen Perry, came together to pitch New Orleans to British Airways. As a result of this business leadership, New Orleans airport is international again, with near-daily service to Europe.

- *Relationships / Relevance / Results—How Finding Your Core Value Proposition is Essential to Success*
  Following Katrina, Greater New Orleans, Inc. (GNO, Inc.) was broken and bankrupt, along with the regional economy it was meant to support. In adopting the mantra "Relationships/ Relevance/ Results, GNO, Inc. established its value proposition and set out to prove it every day. Now, GNO, Inc. is regularly rated as one of the top economic development

organizations in the United States. But, the Relationships/Relevance/Results mantra remains the same.

All of these tactics have been critical to the economic revitalization of Greater New Orleans. And all of them are fungible and can be applied in other locations and contexts. Yet, perhaps the most important change, learning, and impact in the post-Katrina economy of New Orleans has been around coalition building. Greater New Orleans now considers its ability to build powerful, nimble, and effective coalitions to be one of its most important competitive advantages.

The power and importance of coalitions is perhaps best illustrated by the story of how Greater New Orleans fixed National Flood Insurance, thereby saving not only New Orleans but much of the nation.

National Flood Insurance

It started innocently enough; it always does. One of my former board chairs, Dale Benoit, sent me a text—"Check out this NFIP issue."

Now, I didn't know what "NFIP" stood for, but I knew that when Dale sent me a message, particularly a cryptic one, I should pay attention. Dale, the first chairman in GNO, Inc.'s history from Plaquemines Parish (the strip of land that funnels the last sixty miles of the Mississippi River), wasn't a big talker, but he was a savvy operator, and there was usually something important when he chose to speak. Like, if your hair were on fire, he might tap you on the shoulder and ask if your head was warm.

So, I pulled over, googled "NFIP" on my phone, and learned it stands for the "National Flood Insurance Program." NFIP was started in 1967 by Louisiana's own representative Hale Boggs to help insure homes and businesses in flood-prone areas. The program was conceived following Hurricane Betsy, when uninsured—but economically important—areas such as Galveston, Texas, where unable to afford to rebuild. Over the years, NFIP had actually done fairly well for a government program, taking in more than it paid out and quietly making living and working near water in the United States possible. This fact is important, because water is where commerce happens, and 55 percent of Americans live within fifty miles of it.

Hurricane Katrina changed all this, ripping a hole in NFIP as big as the one it tore in the roof of the Superdome. The largest storm in modern US history caused unprecedented human and material losses and ended up costing NFIP more than $24 billion. Coming out of Katrina, NFIP was deeply in debt; moreover, policymakers were suddenly concerned that NFIP might be creating perverse incentives for people to rebuild in flood-prone areas by not pricing "true risk" into policies.

To address the financial and policy concerns surrounding NFIP, Congress wrote the "Biggert-Waters Flood Insurance Reform Act of 2012." With unusually strong bi-partisan, bi-cameral support, Biggert-Waters was meant to help stabilize the program, reduce moral hazard, and address suspected abuses.

Clearly, Biggert-Waters was authored with good intentions. But when it was implemented, a raft of unintended consequences began to flow from the legislation. These consequences first manifested in southeast Louisiana, where new Federal Emergency Management Agency (FEMA) flood maps, which triggered the legislation, were first to be rolled out. The fundamental problem was that Biggert-Waters relied on these maps—and the maps were wrong. For example, large levees, if they were not federally certified, were deemed nonexistent (even if they were paid for with federal funds). In one remarkable instance, NFIP director David Miller stood on top of a levee in Lafourche Parish that had successfully protected the capital city of Thibodaux during Hurricane Isaac—and was told that, according to his maps, it didn't exist.

The other major issue was that Biggert-Waters removed "grandfathering." This meant that even if you had built your house exactly where FEMA told you to, at the right height, had always maintained insurance, had paid your taxes, and *had never flooded*, you could still see your insurance rates skyrocket if new maps said you were situated too low. That is, you could have done everything right—and suddenly be told you were badly out of compliance.

The result of bad maps and loss of grandfathering is that homeowners and business owners in the New Orleans region—even ones that didn't take a drop of water during Katrina—were getting notices that their insurance was going up as much as 5,000 percent or more. A typical example was a local insurance broker (who we can assume was a smart consumer of insurance), with a house that never flooded, was going to see his annual premium skyrocket from $630 to over $17,000.

It is not hard to image what the impact would be on homeowners of flood insurance going from a few hundred to many thousands of dollars. It would be unaffordable—homeowners would lose their insurance. As a result, their mortgages (federally required to have flood insurance) would go into default. Owners would lose their homes, banks would lose their portfolios, business would lose their workers, cities would lose their tax base. It was possible to foresee Biggert-Waters taking out entire communities as the dominos of unaffordable insurance fell. The great irony was that, in the end, these losses would destroy the NFIP itself, because it would go into a "death spiral" from loss of policyholders.

So, in a nutshell, the new law designed to protect property owners and ensure the sustainability of flood insurance . . . would destroy both.

To add insult to injury, we then made a startling discovery. A 2006 report from the National Academy of Science revealed that up to 40 percent of the homeowners in the United States who should be paying for flood insurance, were not. In other words, NFIP was claiming insolvency, while failing to collect nearly half of its revenue. When we presented this fact to FEMA, their response was that they were "indifferent" to collecting this money and replied that if the 40 percent participated in the program as required, there would simply be 40 percent more claims, and thus no financial benefit to NFIP. (This thinking goes against both insurance practice of spreading risk—and common sense.)

Back in Greater New Orleans, the first place in the country to get the new, incomplete maps, a policy disaster was unfolding. What Dale's text should have said is: "Legislative bomb dropped on Greater New Orleans—please defuse before economy destroyed."

At GNO, Inc. we began to go through the typical stages of grieving:

- *Denial*—This can't possibly be true. Who would create a law that would destroy the very people it was meant to protect? We looked at a few insurance statements from local homeowners and business owners: apparently the federal government, that's who.

- *Anger*—Why is this happening to us? Wasn't Katrina enough? Why do we now have to face a man-made storm of bad policy?
- *Rationalization*—If we just talk to the nice people in Washington, D.C., they will have sympathy and change the law. But we had a problem: Washington was tired of us; everyone outside of our delegation was suffering from "Katrina Fatigue." Frankly, they were exhausted with Louisiana and the Gulf Coast, and felt they had helped enough. (To be fair, we had sometimes acted in ways that contributed to this exhaustion.) To compound this problem, Washington was profoundly gridlocked. The government couldn't pass a law saying the sky is blue. How were they going to reform major national legislation, and particularly a law that had just passed with rare bi-partisan support and fanfare?
- *Depression*—We are sunk. After seven years of intense—and largely successful—effort, Biggert-Waters was going to pull the rug from under the recovery, rendering large parts of Greater New Orleans uninhabitable. The bureaucrats were going to do what Mother Nature could not—destroy southern Louisiana.

But then something began to happen. Thankfully, we never made it to the final, "Acceptance" stage of grieving. A conference call with our regional parish presidents made it clear that people wanted to fight. The resilient spirit of the "new" New Orleans came through.

So, we planned a trip with fourteen of our parish chief executives to Washington, D.C., to go meet with the staffers who had written Biggert-Waters. Surely, they would be aware of the unintended consequences of their own legislation and would be interested in finding a fix? We retained legal counsel with two locally based firms, Adams & Reese and Jones Walker, and went to Washington.

The first meeting didn't go very well. Sitting across from the legislative aide who had personally written Biggert-Waters, we explained the problems with the legislation. "Oh, I understand," he said, looking serious, if not slightly annoyed. "For some homeowners, their rates may go up 200 or 300 percent. That will be hard."

"No," I responded. "For some homeowners, who have never flooded, their rates will go up 5,000 or 6,000 percent." Then I showed him the insurance statement as proof.

His look said it all: deer in the headlights. This was news to him. And, therefore, probably to everyone else in Washington. At that moment, we realized that before we could even begin to lobby for a solution, we would have to convince Washington there was a problem.

And, in retrospect, this is where we began to pivot. The moment that we—a motley group from southeastern Louisiana—realized that we were probably the most knowledgeable in the nation on flood insurance (more knowledgeable, in fact, than the bill's authors), we realized we were going to have to lead. Tiny and not really wanted though we were, our knowledge and personal stake with flood insurance compelled us to get in front.

As a former management consultant, I tend to think in PowerPoint and express myself in bullet points, so my first impulse was to create a presentation. We read the byzantine legislation. We talked with experts, like Dwayne Bourgeois from Lafourche; Dwayne was fascinated with Biggert-Waters the way normal boys are with baseball cards. We collected evidence in the form of actual insurance statements from local residents and businesses. Working with Caitlin Berni from GNO, Inc., who would unexpectedly become the point-person for a national effort, we drew from this Kafkaesque morass three key principles for the National Flood Insurance Program.

1. Be sustainable long term
2. Be actuarially responsible
3. Protect home and business owners who have "played by the rules" by building to code, maintaining insurance, and not having repetitive losses

Then, we started educating elected officials, the public, and the media. The reaction was immediate. People were shocked at the fact that hard-working Americans, through no fault of their own, were going to lose their homes. They were angry that up to 40 percent of properties that were supposed to carry flood insurance were simply ignoring the law (Maybe this is why NFIP was broke?). And they were incredulous that FEMA was "indifferent."

We started holding periodic conference calls to update our local constituents. As our presentation circulated, the media picked up the story, and the call to action grew. Then, on August 12, 2013, the *Wall Street Journal* picked up our story, with the headline "Flood Insurance Prices Surge," and suddenly our conference call was a national affair.

Jim Cantwell, a state representative from Massachusetts, became a regular; he was concerned about Cape Cod. Nancy Willis, from the North Dakota Realtor's Association, joined up; she was worried about the way Biggert-Waters treated tornado shelters. Pat O'Neil, a councilman from lovely Sullivan's Island, South Carolina, came on the call, led by concerned homeowners on the barrier island. The country was beginning to see that Biggert-Waters was not the light at the end of the tunnel, but rather an out-of-control policy train coming right at them.

Caitlin and I realized we were on to something: GNO, Inc. was becoming the pied piper of flood insurance. We decided on a name for our growing group: the Coalition for Sustainable Flood Insurance (CSFI) and designed a simple logo. Next, of course, was a website—csfi.info—and suddenly, in today's world of electronic virtual reality, CSFI was legitimate.

Key takeaway: Although it may seem peripheral, it is actually very important to choose a good name and logo for an initiative. And, if possible, make sure the name shortens into a decent acronym. The right look and feel helps establish the brand of an effort and at the same time consigns legitimacy. Our staff makes fun of my obsession with logos, but I am convinced that in today's "blink" world of instant impressions, the right name and logo can be a competitive advantage.

In the beginning, CSFI mostly included organizations from New Orleans and the Gulf South, where the new FEMA maps had been introduced and were triggering Biggert-Waters. Our numbers were growing, but despite the occasional success in New England or the Dakotas, we were still having trouble getting our message across to a national audience.

Many in Washington were still skeptical. They thought the wild Cajuns of Louisiana needed tough love so they wouldn't go and rebuild in harm's way ("Who would build down by a river?"). Truth be told, even some in the South were against us—Senator Richard Shelby from Alabama railed against "beach home bailouts" (a real, but small minority of the cases), though many of his own constituents in Mobile where threatened.

Washington leaders were against us. Most critically, Representative Jeb Hensarling from Texas, chairman of the powerful House Financial Services Committee, was a longtime opponent of public flood insurance, calling it "ineffective, inefficient and indisputably costly." This was a major problem, since any reform to Biggert-Waters would have to be approved by his financial services committee. Representative Randy Neugebauer, chair of the insurance subcommittee, was also against us. And in New York City, though I had worked in the Bloomberg administration and our COO, Robin Barnes, had deep philanthropic and foundation connections, we were getting very little support. Simply put, most people didn't see flood insurance as their issue.

Hurricane Sandy changed all of this. Sandy's storm surge hit New York City on October 29, 2012, flooding streets, tunnels, and subway lines and cutting power in and around the city. Damage in the New York and New Jersey area amounted to $65 billion. As New Yorkers began to assess a flooded Wall Street, attitudes toward the plight of Louisiana softened considerably.

Suddenly, former colleagues in New York City wanted to talk to us. How do you support flooded businesses? How do you access and spend federal dollars? What is Davis-Bacon (long story)? Robin's knowledge was suddenly in such demand that she was asked to join the White House's Hurricane Sandy Rebuilding Taskforce. And for some reason, people stopped asking why New Orleanians had been so foolish as to build near the water.

Politically, Sandy was a watershed moment for our effort. Leaders from the Northeast now joined our federal delegation, which thus far had been led by the Louisiana team of Senators Mary Landrieu and David Vitter and Representatives Steve Scalise, Cedric Richmond, and Bill Cassidy. Senator Charles Schumer, from New York, and Senator Robert Menendez, from New Jersey, became new friends of New Orleans. Others, like feisty Representative Michael Grimm, whose Staten Island district was devastated by Sandy, came on board. Sandy instantly changed the scope of our constituency and broadened our power base. Our New Orleans island was suddenly the experienced end of a NY-NOLA axis.

Now that we had a small but powerful group of federal legislators in our camp, the coalition began to grow organically. Using our PowerPoints and talking points, they began to recruit other colleagues from across the country. Senator Johnny Isakson, a Republican from Georgia and former real estate broker, brought us additional bi-partisan heft from outside of Louisiana. Representative Maxine Waters, the Democrat from Los Angeles, went on record to say that Biggert-Waters "was a big mistake" and that she "never imagined" the types of increases we were seeing.

Key take-away: Find connections to build coalitions. Sandy was obviously our connection to New York City. Real estate was our connection to Isakson from Georgia—as a former real estate broker, he understood how Biggert-Waters would devastate the property-selling industry, and so he wanted to stop it. We brought on large national groups, such as the American Banking Association, because we connected with them on an issue important to their members—protecting their mortgage portfolios.

To maintain momentum—as well as our leadership—we began to hold our update conference call weekly and to give it the rather aspirational name of "CSFI National Update." Every Friday we would spend an hour reviewing progress and challenges from the past week and plans for the coming week and hearing from members of the coalition from around the country. It was a remarkable and sometimes surreal thing to behold: Caitlin and I, often sitting in a car or a coffee shop, running a conference call with up to two hundred attendees—ranging from senators to homeowners—from around the country. Since we didn't possess the technology or funding for sophisticated call monitoring, we never truly knew who was on the call and always had to begin with a "off-the-record" warning to the media who had undoubtedly dialed in.

It was an awkward, highly imperfect mode of communication—with regular interruptions of honking horns, blowing noses, and occasional urinals flushing—but it worked: the calls established GNO, Inc., our small organization, with no previous subject matter expertise—as the national leader. We were perceived as knowledgeable, proactive, and honest. We provided information and leadership, and the country followed.

We doubled-down with the press, working the national media and placing articles and editorials in major journals such as the *Wall Street Journal*, the *New York Times* and *USA Today*. Seeing CSFI in print further legitimated the coalition and amplified our numbers and influence.

Soon, CSFI had grown to nearly 250 organizations, across thirty-five states. More important, some large national organizations joined our effort. The National Association of Homebuilders, the National Association of Realtors, and the American Banking Association all joined CSFI. All of these organizations were clearly aligned with our interests, but without GNO, Inc., they would have been acting separately. Our coalition brought all of these powerful national organizations together, ensured they had the same talking points, and effectively made the whole greater than the sum of the parts.

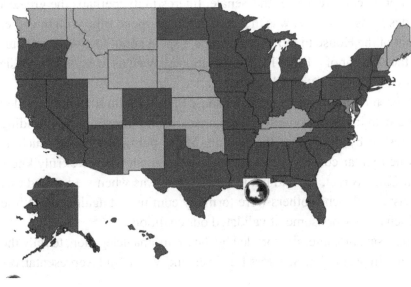

- GNO, Inc.
- Parish Presidents
- American Bankers Assoc.
- Independent Comm. Bankers Assoc.
- Mortgage Bankers Assoc.
- Nat'l Assoc. of Counties
- Nat'l Assoc. of Home Builders
- Nat'l Assoc. of Realtors
- **35 states**
- **200+ organizations from across USA**

States that belong to the Coalition for Sustainable Flood Insurance

In hindsight, it was probably not only our proactiveness but, ironically, our powerlessness that allowed us to lead. That is, we posed no threat to large groups like the American Banking Association, so they were happy to let us set direction.

Key take-away: Powerlessness can be a strength in coalition building. Being a threat to no one allowed us to lead everybody. The key is to establish relevance, or usefulness. Then, like a tiny pilot fish that cleans the scales of a shark, a symbiotic relationship can be established that allows the little guy to not only survive but thrive. In national flood insurance, our powerlessness made us acceptable, while our knowledge made us useful.

Back in Washington D.C., people were beginning to take notice. The media was writing stories. Constituents were beginning to call their representatives. And complementary advocacy groups were cropping up around the country. In New Jersey, a real estate agent named George Cosimos started "Stop FEMA Now," a grassroots effort that put unrelenting pressure on elected officials.

The political stakes were swiftly rising. Back in May, no one in Washington even understood there was a problem. For a while, we were met with indifference. Now, Representative Jeb Hensarling, chairman of the crucial House Finance Committee, told us that this had become a "top" issue for him to address. This statement from Representative Hensarling was all the more remarkable because he clearly felt he had no choice.

While the coalition continued to grow nationally, we were careful not to neglect the original core group from southeast Louisiana. In addition to our national call, we also held a weekly "core group" call with the fourteen parish presidents who had made the original trip to D.C. with us. These weekly calls kept us grounded and continually reminded us that our first job was to protect the communities of Louisiana. The local presidents also reinforced the urgency to act, since they were the ones hearing from scared constituents every day. For example, St. Charles Parish president V. J. St. Pierre was moved to tears when his constituents came to a press conference with their house keys and proceeded to turn them in, since they would never be able to go home if we didn't stop Biggert-Waters.

With CSFI now the accepted lead for flood insurance reform, we were asked to testify in front of the House and then lead a press conference for the Senate. Interestingly, perhaps the greatest benefit of these events, besides press exposure, was the opportunity to spend time with the other side. Waiting to speak in front of the House Finance Committee, I spent about forty-five minutes chatting with David Miller, the director of NFIP. This conversation allowed us to establish a basic level of communication that would prove extremely valuable.

By this point, NFIP had become a hot issue on the Hill. House Speaker John Boehner included flood insurance reform along with immigration reform, Obamacare, and transportation funding as the key issues to be addressed by the end of the session. Major political journals, such as *Politico*, were giving our issue regular coverage. But perhaps the moment when we truly knew that from our little office on Canal Street, we had made the big time was when we learned that the billionaire political activists the Koch brothers were formally coming out against us. While the financial might of the Kochs was worrisome, it validated our coalition.

What followed was a bi-partisan, bi-cameral effort, led by the Louisiana delegation, to rally the country to stop Biggert-Waters. In particular, Senators Landrieu and Vitter, and Representatives

Scalise, Richmond, and Cassidy, using CSFI as a platform, rallied their friends and members to our side.

In January, led by Landrieu and Vitter, the Senate passed a bill by a 67-to-32 supermajority to delay Biggert-Waters by one year. While this bill did not completely solve the problem, it was a milestone—the tide of bad flood insurance legislation was turning.

On the House side, prospects were more complicated. A major problem was Representative Hensarling. Despite our entreaties, and even the efforts of his fellow Texans (Houston stood to be devastated by Biggert-Waters; Hensarling was from Dallas), Hensarling was unmoved: For whatever philosophical or political reasons, he hated flood insurance and wanted it attenuated by any means necessary. Any legislation to fix flood insurance would have to go through Hensarling's committee; he was a choke point on the solution.

And then something remarkable happened, which told us that our coalition had grown stronger than even we knew. House majority leader Eric Cantor, the second most powerful official in Congress, took leadership of the issue in the House, effectively superseding Representative Hensarling. Apparently, Cantor had counted the votes and realized that enough bi-partisan support for reform existed in the House that if leadership opposed it, they risked getting rolled over. And so Cantor got out in front and started engineering a solution on the House side.

In March, the House did something in a bi-partisan fashion similar to that in the Senate but even more far-reaching: By a 306-to-91 vote, they essentially rolled back Biggert-Waters. The flood insurance reform effort, still sustained by GNO, Inc.'s weekly "National Update" conference calls, had sparked a legislative war in D.C.: Which house could go further in fixing flood insurance?

From that point, resolution came quickly. With a few important modifications, the Senate accepted the House's further reaching bill, and the National Flood Insurance Homeowners Affordability Act was sent to the president. Obama, though his own Office of Management and Budget had previously come out against the reform, signed the bill on March 14, 2014.

Southeast Louisiana, and All of Coastal America, Were Saved

At an appreciation dinner to celebrate our unlikely victory, our group of parish presidents, lawyers, and friends reflected on the past year, during which we managed to pivot from insignificance and helplessness against our fate, to national effectiveness and prominence, including shaping the rewriting of federal law. "The signing of this bill marks the end of a long journey," Terrebonne Parish president Michel Claudet said. "Had this bill not been passed and signed into law it would have been the end of our way of life in south Louisiana as we know it."

We built a large coalition not from wealth and political clout but from organizational and subject-matter leadership. As a result, our power was multiplied exponentially, and we were able to pivot from derailing the impending disaster of Bigger-Waters to reforming flood insurance not just for New Orleans but the nation. As of this writing, CSFI has been formalized into a national 501C3 and is playing a leading role in the newest effort to reauthorize and reform National Flood insurance in 2020.

Coalition-building is a powerful public policy and economic development tool; it can confer great soft-power and allow small economies—from New Orleans to Singapore to Switzerland—to prosper.

Printed in the United States
By Bookmasters